THE TEXAS
Native Plant Primer

THE TEXAS
Native Plant Primer

225 Plants for an Earth-Friendly Garden

ANDREA DELONG-AMAYA
LADY BIRD JOHNSON WILDFLOWER CENTER

Timber Press
Portland, Oregon

Frontispiece: Purple coneflower with mealy blue sage and brown-eyed Susan

Page 5: Large Buttercup and friends

Page 6: (clockwise from top left): Sensitive briar (*Mimosa roemeriana*), drummond phlox (*Phlox drummondii*), lace cactus (*Echinocereus reichenbachii*), Spanish dagger (*Yucca treculeana*), yellow passionflower (*Passiflora lutea*), cenizo (*Leucophyllum frutescens*)

Photography credits are available on page 241

Timber Press
Workman Publishing
Hachette Book Group, Inc.
1290 Avenue of the Americas
New York, New York 10104
timberpress.com

Timber Press is an imprint of Workman Publishing, a division of Hachette Book Group, Inc.
The Timber Press name and logo are registered trademarks of Hachette Book Group, Inc.

Second printing 2025
Printed in Dongguan, China (TLF), on responsibly sourced paper

Text design by Mary Velgos based on a series design by Debbie Berne
Cover design by Leigh Thomas based on a series design by Amy Sly

The publisher is not responsible for websites (or their content) that are not owned by the publisher.
The Hachette Speakers Bureau provides a wide range of authors for speaking events. To find out more, go to hachettespeakersbureau.com or email hachettespeakers@hbgusa.com.

ISBN 978-1-64326-110-2
A catalog record for this book is available from the Library of Congress.

Contents

9   **Preface**

13   **What Is a Native Plant?**

19   **Why Grow Native Plants?**

29   **Using Native Plants in the Garden**

57   **Using This Book**

61   **Groundcovers and Turf**

75   **Perennials and Annuals**

143   **Grasses and Grasslike Plants**

161   **Cacti and Succulents**

173   **Shrubs and Small Trees**

209   **Large and Shade-Producing Trees**

229   **Vines**

238   Bibliography

240   Acknowledgments

241   Photography Credits

242   Index

Preface

My hope for what lies ahead in the field of landscape design . . . is not a revolution against the use of non-natives, but a resolution to educate ourselves about what has worked for Mother Nature through the ebb and flow of time and to put that knowledge to work in the planned landscapes that are everywhere a part of our lives.

—*Lady Bird Johnson*

Like so many of us who were lucky enough to be nannied by the great outdoors, I felt a deep belonging and centeredness in the rural Michigan woods surrounding the trailer park where I spent the summers of my early years. Here began my connection with the natural world, observing a walkingstick insect surveying a maple tree trunk, collecting a rainbow of leaves from those same maples come fall, pushing a finger into the earth-scented, spongy moist moss that our neighbors complained about invading their lawn, and eating huckleberry pie baked by my dad from fruits the neighborhood kids and I so proudly and competitively foraged. My father introduced me to my first wildflower guide. I was astonished that there were such things as wild onions and that you could *eat* them (even though I didn't particularly like the endless aftertaste!).

◄ Gayfeather and Iconic tower at the Wildflower Center

Wildflower Center founders Helen Hayes and Lady Bird Johnson

Moving to Austin shifted my seven-year-old understanding of nature from the soft and gentle Michigan summers (let's ignore the winters for now) to the staggering brutality of Texas heat. It is understandable how newcomers find themselves flummoxed facing a nightmare of writhing bugs, uncooperative soils, and capricious weather. Coddling plants from far-flung lands often results in disappointment and wasted resources. Gardening here can seem hopeless.

But, just as plunges into Austin's bracing Barton Springs pool, glorious summer thunderstorms, and winter days often balmy enough to be enjoyed in shorts adjusted my attitude with time, gardeners, too, may find rich rewards by embracing the embodied wisdom that native plants have accumulated through millennia, sculpted by the victories

Wetland Pond at the Wildflower Center

Lady Bird Johnson

of rolled-up-sleeve evolutionary rumbles. Our home team flora are best equipped to endure the extremes they face. After all, they grow and thrive here naturally without our assistance.

The deep respect, appreciation, and awe for the natural world that consumed me as a child continues to grow with me. It is what led me to the important work and mission of the Lady Bird Johnson Wildflower Center where I first became a member, then shortly thereafter fortuitously joined the staff ranks as a gardener in 1998 (I don't understand the math here . . . I guess I must have been twelve years old when I started!).

The organization, a signature piece of Lady Bird Johnson's environmental legacy, was founded by Mrs. Johnson and Helen Hayes. Dedicated on December 22, 1982, on Mrs. Johnson's seventieth birthday as the National Wildflower Research Center, it was renamed as the Lady Bird Johnson Wildflower Center in 1997 in her honor. From the beginning, Mrs. Johnson was ahead of her time in understanding and promoting native plants as an important effort in support of the natural environment as well as for human welfare.

Having matured from our humble east Austin site to the 284 acres we currently steward in south Austin, we are now an Organized Research Unit of the University of Texas at Austin, where our values of ecological resiliency drive our mission of inspiring the conservation of native plants. We practice this through internationally recognized Texas native-plant gardens, regenerative landscape stewardship, plant conservation, education and outreach programs, and research.

What Is a Native Plant?

Periodically the question arises regarding how long a plant needs to be in a location before it is considered native or indigenous. "I have 100-year-old roses from my great-grandfather, do they count?" Bluntly: no. Even though we freely throw around the phrase "native plants," the concept is complex and often muddied. In shorthand, we could claim them to be plants that occur naturally where they evolved without human introduction.

Your great-grandfather's roses may be well adapted and flourishing, but they were brought in by human hands, and their relatively short tenure here pales compared to the hundreds or thousands of years it takes for significant (observable) evolution to occur. However, given that genetics change with every generation, imprecision plagues our definition. Stating a minimal duration for a plant to be legitimately native to a place feels arbitrary, but prior to European colonization—beginning in earnest around the early 1600s—marks a commonly cited timeframe for the United States, after which begins a period of previously unmatched speed and volume of new plant introductions from across the Atlantic.

◀ Skeletonized prickly pear with aster

Even within that framework, a gray area exists because early Indigenous peoples are known to have moved plants back and forth throughout Mexico, the US Southwest, and beyond.

The semicultivated devil's claw was used for textiles and food by practically every tribe in these areas, *Agave americana* has been the raw base for mezcal making, and chile pequin has been widely used as seasoning. The products from these plants were so important that people brought propagules along when they traveled from one community to the next. Most of us broadly embrace these species as native where they occur, even though these earliest settlers are likely responsible for their placement.

People have been tinkering with plant genetics for millennia. Through generations of discerning collection and planting, the devil's claw mentioned above was selected for longer claws best suited for basketry. Most of the peppers enjoyed in our modern diets derive from our native *Capsicum annuum*, including jalapeños, serranos, and bell peppers. These are known as cultigens or cultivars, deliberately bred by cross-pollinating parents with desirable traits to create offspring with enhanced features based on the interest of the hybridizer. Other variations originate as naturally occurring mutations, referred to as sports (a rare flower color, for example), and some breeders induce mutations with radiation or chemical treatments. Vegetative propagation ensures clones with persistent desirable traits, while seeds, by nature of cross-pollination, embody genetic diversity. Cultigens and cultivars grown from seed usually revert to parental traits eventually, though sometimes completely new expressions arise.

Controversy swirls around the idea of using cultigens and cultivars of native plants. Should they be considered native? Do they provide enriched or degraded habitat value compared to pure natives? Perhaps it's better to use a native cultivar (nativar) instead of a common exotic plant to take advantage of drought resistance and other benefits of natives. Or maybe the altered genetics of a nativar presents a contamination risk to nearby native plant populations. Genetic diversity makes populations more resilient, but would a few cultivated nativars in residential-scaled gardens make a significant negative impact?

I certainly don't have all of the answers, and studies indicate that results vary from species to species or cultigen to cultigen. More research is needed. Decision-making parallels that of natives versus non-natives, and depends on your objectives. A restoration project most certainly calls for the use of pure natives, avoiding manipulated traits and ideally opting for a local genetic source. On the other hand, simply propagating from an unusual but naturally found white-flowered spiderwort would likely have vanishingly negligible detrimental effects, if any.

Geography

Another critical aspect of the definition relates to geography. Native to where? Texas? North America? The planet Earth? You get to decide how narrowly to define the parameters for your gardening project. Your motivations will help you conclude if you want to use natives exclusively, predominantly, or as supplements in your landscape.

An ecological restoration calls for local provenance and represents the purest interpretation of the idea. On the other hand, if conserving water drives your plant selection, you might decide to broaden your choices and use water-thrifty plants from outside of your local region. However, Texas's vastness and varied weather, hydrology, and soil extremes create environments influencing plant ranges. Maximize your chances of success by taking extra care when selecting species from other parts of the state. You wouldn't plant a southern magnolia from east Texas in Big Bend, would you? A Mexican olive smiles at guests touring the San Antonio Botanical Garden, but in Waxahachie, it quickly succumbs to Jack Frost's sharp bite. Just because a plant hails from Texas doesn't mean it lives happily anywhere in the state. Generally speaking, the closer to its home range, the better.

Adapted, Naturalized, and Invasive Plants

As we contemplate the question of what is a native plant, an examination of what isn't native facilitates the conversation. Common ornamentals mistaken for Texas natives—such as pink skullcap (*Scutellaria suffrutescens*), 'Indigo Spires' sage (*Salvia longispicata ×farinacea* 'Indigo Spires'), and 'New Gold' lantana (*Lantana camara* 'New Gold')—actually originate in Mexico and other countries, or may be new to nature as human-invented cultivars. Although from outside of the United States, plants from nearby Mexico, of course, likely fit more appropriately in a Texas garden than a variety from distant Maine but nonetheless are not native to Texas. Frequently found in water-thrifty landscapes, these introduced examples include plants that are well adapted to our climate and soils. As long as they remain well-behaved and not invasive—defined as proliferating excessively outside of cultivation—they add options.

Early in my studies as a naturalist, I erroneously assumed that, because they sprouted in wild areas, plants such as heavenly bamboo (*Nandina domestica*) and Chinese tallow trees (*Sapium sebiferum*) were indigenous. Only later would I recognize their introduced and invasive status. Synonyms describing species not native to a location where they are found include non-native, exotic, introduced, or alien. Plants from Asia are introduced to North America. Plants from North America are exotic in Australia. Although the term *alien* is generally accepted, I prefer to avoid it due to its association with human noncitizen residents or little green people from galaxies far, far away.

Non-native escapees can be minimally problematic or very harmful. For example, annual henbit (*Lamium amplexicaule*) invades crop fields and other disturbed land but is too weak to displace established vegetation. Exotic garden plants or crops that remain after their caretakers have departed but fail to increase noxiously fall into the persistent or naturalized category. These remnants generally pose little to no harm, but if they thrive beyond our control we consider them invasive.

Gardeners curse plants as invasive when the plants betray their trust by heavily seeding out or running amok in their beds. Put into perspective, invasive under cultivation (i.e., with altered soils, supplemental water, and other protections from the elements) means something fairly different from invasive on an ecological scale. One poses a nuisance (albeit not insignificant), the other results in potential species extinctions. According to the Presidential Executive Order 13112, issued in February 1999, invasive species cause "economic or environmental harm or harm to human health." Of course, not all introduced plants become overly aggressive or even naturalized. And regardless of how long it has been here, a naturalized plant, by definition, does not become native.

Indigenous peoples historically moved plants around intermittently over long periods of time. Settlers from east of the Atlantic, on the other hand, brought their familiar ornamental and food crops to the New World at historically unprecedented rates and quantities, too fast for many indigenous species to effectively adapt and literally hold their ground. What's more, these imports arrived at their new digs without their associated predators and pathogens from their homelands to keep them in check. These novel colonizing plants displaced, and continue to displace, the original species, inflicting havoc on interdependent native organisms. We think of invasive plants as thugs, but it's not their fault. They merely take advantage of the opportunities we give to them.

Horticulturists sometimes discount the negative effects of non-native invasives, claiming that because they are additive, they actually increase biodiversity. While this may hold true in the short term, over time as the colony increases, they outcompete natives and diminish habitat for fauna from thrashers to thrushes. A cautionary tale from watching escaped pampas grass (*Cortaderia selloana*) over many years along a local highway in Austin demonstrates that a few plants here and there may seem benign, lying latent for many years, even decades, before the population explodes under favorable conditions, hogging territory away from beloved bluebonnets, little bluestem, and other natives.

Prickly pear backed by the Wildflower Center's Great Hall

Sadly, botanical gardens, designers, home gardeners, and the horticulture profession in general have contributed a good percentage of pesky plants to our environment.

Some discussions contend that non-invasive exotic species can and do play a beneficial role in landscapes and that their evaluation should emphasize ecological performance over place of origin. In theory this seems reasonable. However, we must put our hubris in check: We cannot sufficiently understand all of the complex and intertwining secrets of nature to fully determine a plant's role in its community. For example, kudzu (*Pueraria* spp.) from Japan, initially featured at the 1876 Centennial Exposition in Philadelphia, was later used by land managers to halt soil erosion. It seemed like a good idea at the time, but eventually the plant earned the infamous reputation as "the plant that ate the South."

If invasive plants don't seem like that big of a deal, consider the impact of other invasive species such as imported fire ants that not only sting humans but existentially threaten Texas horned lizards, ground-nesting birds such as bobwhite quail, and other wildlife. Within fifty years after the arrival of the imported chestnut blight, the American chestnut was all but eliminated, resulting in a crash of the squirrel population and the extinction of seven moth species. The cascading impacts cut deeply. Invasive plants destroy living communities as effectively as other invasive organisms, even if we don't recognize the damage as readily. We may not suffer the impact directly, but other living beings fundamentally feel the effects.

To be fair, we must acknowledge that even some natives can misbehave in disturbed environments or under unfortunate land management (such as excessive fire suppression or overgrazing). Since most livestock find prickly pears and mesquite unpalatable, those plants increase under intense grazing or browsing. In the postsettlement era, with the goal of protecting our homes and businesses, we've unintentionally quashed the fires that once limited the spread of Ashe juniper (*Juniperus ashei*), allowing it to become one of our most consequential native aggressors. Unlike introducing exotic invasives, planting aggressive or opportunistic natives in your managed landscape won't contribute to

their invasive nature since they've always been in the area. Whether or not they morph into bullies depends on how land is managed.

Climate Uncertainty

Huge question marks loom in our future regarding climate. As we witness milder winters and overall warming trends, our weather simultaneously dishes out more extreme and erratic events. Intense cold, heat, wind, drought, and floods shape natural distributions more than average weather patterns. Over the last several decades, plants including huisache, retama, Mexican olive, and others have slowly pushed their upper boundaries farther north, into higher and cooler elevations, or have been planted outside their normal ranges only to succumb to punishing and prolonged freezes such as those experienced in 2021 and 2023. As these climate events continue, we expect ranges to get pinched.

In response to climate change, ecologists contemplate plans for assisted migration. Since plants move too slowly on their own to find new potentially safe grounds, this somewhat untested strategy involves speeding up relocations by deliberately planting species into new projected ranges— assuming appropriate habitats still exist, and they may not.

Opposing views, often held by the very same supporters of assisted migration (demonstrating our lack of confidence on the topic), point out that relying on predicted average weather isn't sufficient. We need to plan for the extremes, but is that even possible? Our best guesses may be wrong, leading to adverse genetic mixing of disparate populations, wasted valuable plant propagules, and diverted time better spent on more certain endeavors. And, of course, this prompts a philosophical discussion about the essential definition of "native."

We can only touch on the topic here, and there is still so much we don't know. Ecologists currently recommend selecting plants already exhibiting wide-ranging adaptability, while sadly recognizing that specialists will eventually be left behind.

Texas redbud
Cercis canadensis var. texensis
Legume Family
(Fabaceae)

Blooms: February – April
Range: Central TX to OK
Habitat: Wooded hillsides on calcareous soils

Why Grow Native Plants?

> We abuse land because we regard it as a commodity belonging to us. When we see land as a community to which we belong, we may begin to use it with love and respect.
>
> *—Aldo Leopold*

North American plants are disappearing at an alarming rate due to human activity such as invasive species introduction, urban development, large-scale agriculture, and chemical application. Over decades, loss of native plants has led to wildlife habitat loss, erosion, reduced genetic diversity necessary for balanced ecosystems, and a disconnection of people from the land.

These problems compound when non-native species displace natives in cultivated landscapes. The persistent use across the United States of a short list of readily available exotic plants—such as red tip photinia (*Photinia ×fraseri*) or heavenly bamboo, made popular by landscape architects and designers who are familiar with a limited number of plants, along with easy propagation and distribution—is responsible for a homogenized landscape susceptible to pests and diseases. Cultivated non-native species typically consume large amounts of water and fertilizer, provide degraded habitat for wildlife, and those that escape sometimes aggressively outcompete natives for resources.

◀ West Texas Mountain Garden at the Wildflower Center

The garden, its caretaker, and the greater natural community all benefit when native plants are thoughtfully chosen for the garden. The closer their cultivated settings resemble their wild habitats, the more likely they will thrive indefinitely with minimal attention. In this way, native plants truly promote the most sustainable gardens.

While preserving natural stands of native plants is paramount, you can reestablish natives by choosing them for your landscape. Regardless of the scale of the project, carefully selected plants conserve water and other natural resources while preserving and celebrating your region's personality and charm. Native plantings encourage the presence of native insects, the animals that eat them, and other macro- and microorganisms, all while connecting us with our natural world. Establishing natives requires nearly as much work as installing and caring for non-natives; however, once your plantings acclimate, you will save time, energy, and money while supporting a local character only regionally native plants provide.

Since you are reading this, I bet you are already convinced that gardening with native plants is a great idea. The following points might reinforce your commitment or provide a rationale to share with others who haven't yet joined us.

Great Horned owlet coveting its sibling's lunch

Water Conservation

Water conservation motivates gardeners to plant natives more than any other single reason, not only to see smaller water bills but also to be responsible citizens in light of an ever-shrinking water supply. Even the wealthiest fool willing to pay a premium for water cannot create more of it. Each of us is obligated to not waste this critical and finite resource. Native plants adapted to local conditions survive average rainfall years with minimal to no supplemental water. A little extra water during summer drought prevents dormancy and keeps plants fresh and flowering more generally. Regardless, conventional landscapes inevitably use more water for comparable results.

Texas spiny lizard

Soil Amendments, Fertilizers, and Mulch

Standard horticultural practices teach us to add compost, top with mulch, and fertilize everything. Study up and save yourself time and money. Native plants, adapted to their native soils, need no amendments provided you have made an appropriate match. (Note that builders often use inferior fill such as sandy loam, also known as "red death," that would benefit from amending or replacing with new soil.) Although many wild plants respond favorably to fertilizers, and Wildflower Center gardeners might push a little with organic plant food now and then to enhance floral displays or nurture a plant suffering from some form of abuse, native plants flower and gardens beam largely on their own without added nitrogen, phosphorus, and potassium. Fertilizers are optional. After all, Mother Nature isn't casting Makit-Gro onto the prairie while we sleep. Mulches provide a slew of benefits, particularly for new plantings, but mature groundcovers and any vegetation with foliage that blankets and protects the earth also act as living mulch.

Disease and Pest Resistance

Pathogens and animal pests can and do predate upon natives; however, indigenous plants benefit from the millennia-long evolutionary arms race. A diverse array of plant types provides more resilience than a monoculture, while discouraging the buildup of pests. These gained protections increase resistance and survivability against such assaults.

Stymie Invasive Species

By selecting natives over exotics, we eliminate the risk of unleashing a new invader into the landscape. Invasive species displace natives, both plants and animals, and degrade habitat overall.

Regional Identity

Lady Bird Johnson declared, "Native plants give us a sense of where we are in this great land of ours. I want Texas to look like Texas and Vermont to look like Vermont." With the expansion of the built environment, we experience the homogenization of the American landscape. Can we tell where we are by looking out the window? With ubiquitous red tip photinia hedges and monkeygrass (*Liriope muscari*) borders, we lose the character of a place and its vibrancy appears diluted. Through natives, we achieve a deep harmony of authenticity while honoring our natural heritage.

Connect with the Natural World

Human nature instills within us the tendency to collect that which we admire. Never is this truer than while gardening. The simple act of cultivating a plant expresses a reverence for it. It becomes a gesture of regard. Native plants provide us a connection with the natural world. What a thrill it is to witness a sphinx moth with its extended proboscis as it narrows in on a *Datura* trumpet, or ponder why leafcutter ants target mistletoe (*Phoradendron* spp.) flowers. What does a *Sedum* tell us when it grows here but not a foot away? With each plant we get to know in the garden, we gain a new friend. Some of my best friends are plants! When we see them growing wild, we garner a richer understanding and appreciation for them.

Native Plants are "New"

Gardeners yearn for novel additions to their yard. For better or worse, there remains a profusion of garden-worthy natives that horticulture has not yet adequately explored. Their relative unfamiliarity allows for exciting discoveries! Learning the quirks of each plant makes us overall more successful gardeners. Texas harbors over 5,000 plant taxa. How many can we weave into our created landscapes?

Native Plants are Cool!

Decades ago, while working at a retail nursery, I assisted a customer who emphatically shunned native plants. "Too bad," I thought, and proceeded to show him a variety of options, including several natives, without revealing their status. They were lovely choices and he scooped them up with great interest. Score! Gardening with native plants shouldn't feel like an obligation to eat your broccoli. Enjoy them for the gems that they are.

Wildlife Resources

Natives provide superior food and shelter for wildlife. Endangered golden-cheeked warblers, for example, are specialists who depend exclusively on fully mature (and often maligned) Ashe junipers for nesting material. Even though our most at-risk animals rely on specific locally native plants, other wildlife, namely the abundant urban generalists (such as grackles, famed for dumpster diving and called "trash species" by the mean-spirited) take advantage of indigenous and exotic plants and will eat just about anything.

Entire books address best methods and resources for converting your yard into a menagerie and cover the topic more thoroughly than we can here. But let's indulge it just a bit before moving on. With declining habitat negatively affecting all but the most generalist species, this is a deeply worthy cause. And patiently watching critters of all sorts

American Robin

can be more entertaining than TV (even if that's a low bar!). The discussion here highlights specifically how native plants invite wildlife into your garden.

Wildlife need access to water, shelter, food, and space to carry out the business of their lives. We cannot know all relationships between and among organisms, but we can assume there is much more going on than we are aware of. Provide for a diversity of animals with a variety of habitats by using vegetational layers (groundcovers, forbs, grasses, shrubs, trees, and transitions in between). Note that not all species need each of these layers, so offering a mosaic of conditions helps cover the bases. Finally, be conscientious when using pesticides (synthetic or organic), as they can be toxic, even lethal, to nontarget species. Birds, frogs, caterpillars, and other critters, as well as kids and pets are particularly vulnerable to pesticides.

Seed-eating birds, including cardinals, buntings, grosbeaks, and finches, seek plants in the sunflower family (Asteraceae) due to high fat content in the seeds. Sunflowers (*Helianthus* spp.), Engelmann daisies, and zexmenia offer such fodder, as do a number of other groups including native grasses, *Croton*, *Oenothera*, and others. Acorns supply crucial sustenance for woodpeckers, turkeys, and jays. Conifers such as pines (*Pinus* spp.) and junipers (*Juniperus* spp.) nourish cedar waxwings and nuthatches. Doves, titmice, chickadees, and juncos consume more generally, noshing on many different dry seeds.

Fleshy fruits attract ringtail cats, mockingbirds, cedar waxwings, robins, tanagers, buntings, cardinals, and other species. Choice Texas native fruit-bearing plants include sumacs, American beautyberry, yaupon holly, possumhaw holly, persimmons, chile pequin, prickly pears, and many more. Wildlife appreciate a selection of fruits that ripen throughout the seasons. It is ill-advised to plant berry-producing exotics like Hall's honeysuckle (*Lonicera japonica*), *Nandina*, and *Pyracantha* in order to attract birds, as the birds then deliver seeds to locations far and wide, contributing to the problem of invasive species. These tenacious non-native invaders squeeze out native vegetation, including less common plants that specific wildlife rely

Cope's treefrog on dwarf palmetto

American Robin juggling a yaupon berry

Cottontail rabbit inspecting a prickly pear tuna

on for sustenance, thus leaving them hungry and further degrading the ecosystem.

Regardless of what the calendar says, spring for me arrives on the wings of hummingbirds. Over my lifetime I've enjoyed scores of hours observing these airborne acrobats, and to this day I am never bored. Devoutly territorial, bold, liquidly lissome, and forever ravenous, these flying jewels endlessly entertain. Hummingbirds have a weak sense of smell and are cued largely by vision. Hummers prefer orange or red flowers with long throats such as flame acanthus, coral honeysuckle, and many salvias and penstemons. But their tastes reach beyond those, and echinaceas, sunflowers, and mealy blue sage also appeal to the birds. Especially when with young, hummingbirds supplement their diet with protein from small spiders and insects that are also, in turn, supported by native plants. A feeder is unnecessary if a good selection of nutrient-packed flowers are available consistently throughout the season, but it can lure the birds to a convenient viewing site such as a window or outdoor seating area. Keep diseases in check with daily feeder cleaning.

Entice adult butterflies to your garden with plant families such as Verbenaceae (verbenas and lantanas), Apocynaceae (milkweeds and kin), Lamiaceae (salvias, skullcaps, and horsemints), and Asteraceae (sunflowers, daisies, thistles, asters, and mistflowers). These plants produce flowers in close clusters, allowing the insects to conserve energy by not having to fly from one flower to another. Even better, flat-topped heads such as those of lantanas or sunflowers offer perches during nectaring.

I know no gardener who frowns upon butterflies in the garden, but I know plenty who detest the "worms" responsible for the shredded leaves on their prized ornamentals. Before you go pinching caterpillars, see if you can identify what you have. Often your pest is, well, just a pest (from a gardener's perspective), but you may find you have a butterfly in the making and you'll have to decide how much chewing you can tolerate. Sometimes caterpillars feed on what we consider "weeds." Giant ragweed (*Ambrosia trifida*), for instance, may not have any obvious beneficial qualities

Hummmingbird chicks receiving a protein meal

Male Black-chinned hummingbird transporting pollen

for humans, but young bordered patch butterflies thrive on it. Nettles nourish red admirals. Allowing a few select weeds in strategic garden locations will make a future butterfly quite happy.

If you've come to the limits of your tolerance, you can eliminate a particularly pesky species of Lepidoptera (moths and butterflies), such as webworms or oak leafrollers. The biological control Bt (*Bacillus thuringiensis*) is an effective bacterium that is nontoxic to other organisms, but can negatively impact nearby desirable butterflies and moths, so use it judiciously. When deciding whether to save, spray, or squish, don't categorically disregard moths. Some flaunt bold colors and patterns and, as in the case of sphinx moths with up to a 4-inch wingspan, they can grow quite large and handsome too. But beauty isn't everything, right? Even drab insects provide pollination services for flowers or food for birds.

Most flowers need pollination to reproduce. Pollination occurs when pollen from one plant is transferred to the receptive female structures of another plant, allowing fertilization to occur. A fertilized flower yields seeds, which grow into new plants. Since flowers can't get up and walk over to the cutie at the neighboring barstool, they rely on animals (or rain, wind, or water) to deliver pollen for them. As nature lovers, we are lucky to find beauty in flowers and the butterflies, hummingbirds, and other creatures that assist in pollen transfer. The center of their universe, of course, is not us. And their appeal is not merely for our benefit. Rather, they must be attractive to each other. For many native plants, the presence or dearth of appropriate pollinators means life or extinction. Nectar is the sweet reward for this vital service.

Flower shape, color, and pattern drive which pollinators visit. This combination of features is called a pollinator syndrome. Bees, for example, typically seek fresh-scented white, blue, or yellow flowers with nectar guides (patterned colors largely invisible to us that lead to the nectar source within the flower). Barbara's buttons, mealy blue sage, prickly

Black Swallowtail nectaring on prairie verbena

Tufted Titmouse with a juicy haul

White-lined sphinx moth honing in on mealy blue sage

pears, and partridge pea are popular examples. Most folks aren't particularly interested in attracting flies or beetles, however, they are also commendable pollinators. Flies aim for shallow, brown or dark purple flowers, while beetles opt for open flowers of white or green containing ample pollen. Even some wasps snack on flowers.

We often think of bats as pollinators, but nearly all Texas bats are insect hunters that don't seek flowers for nectar. With the exception of an accidental pollination that might occur when seeking insects in flowers, most bats do not transfer pollen from flower to flower. Our only true pollinating bat is the Mexican long-nosed bat, which migrates through the Trans-Pecos. Night-blooming flowers endowed with pollen and nectar, strong scent, and white or light colors serve to guide these nocturnal pollinators to the goods.

Oh, Deer!

Our native flora evolved alongside deer. It wasn't until recently that the deer population surged after people started hunting mountain lions, coyotes, and other shared predators of livestock and deer. In addition, in 1982, the screwworm parasite that once helped keep the deer population in check was effectively eradicated in the United States in order to protect livestock. We now have problematically high numbers of hungry deer.

Here's the brutal truth: The only deer-proof plants are made of silk or plastic. Realistically, by necessity we downgrade the term to deer resistant. Fortunately, we have a number of native plants that hold their own against the deer . . . usually . . . sometimes . . . maybe . . .

Generally, pungently aromatic plants (damianita or horsemint) or those with white, silver, or fuzzy foliage (cenizo and velvet mallow), evade total destruction from deer. Many tough succulents such as cacti, and "woody lilies" like agaves, yuccas, and sotols, also show resistance. But flowers within reach might get chomped. And don't get your hopes up, because thorns won't necessarily deter deer, either. Roses for example, receive nonstop harassment by these notorious garden menaces. Deer mostly browse rather than graze, meaning they eat flowers, shrubs, and trees, but normally not grasses, so hope shines a little brighter for grasses in the garden.

Perhaps you've witnessed relentlessly nibbled new plantings, or plants simply ripped from the ground and left to shrivel. Deer curiously sample recent arrivals only to spit them out if they aren't to their liking. One theory overheard at a party surmises that plants fed salty fertilizers are particularly delicious and should be protected until the plants metabolize the fertilizer.

Rock rose pavonia in one neighborhood may be consumed by deer, yet ignored by a herd in another area. It

White-tailed deer

confounds when someone announces that deer don't eat such-and-such in their yard, only to face contradiction by a friend who retorts, "Well, they sure eat it in mine!" A decent strategy is to observe what is spared on your block and do more of that. Effective when applied regularly, you might try topical repellents such as carnivore urine (I know, I don't want to think about it either!), or surround susceptible plants with strongly resistant species.

For spacious gardens, an effective approach involves covering an area with 8-foot-wide mesh fencing rolled out and lifted 6 to 12 inches above the ground with cinder blocks or the like. This creates an unstable walking surface that deer hesitate to traverse. Grow vines such as Virginia creeper, snapdragon vine, or dewberry through the mesh for camouflage. An 8-foot-tall deer fence gives the best protection, allowing a garden to include delectable species too.

Using Native Plants in the Garden

To help clear up confusion and ensure you get the correct plants, let's explore what we call them. Common names vary from region to region and from person to person. And many unrelated plants share the same common names. Tricky. What would you expect from a specimen labeled "primrose"? Would you have a member of the genus *Primula* or *Oenothera*? Or wait . . . maybe it's *Ludwigia*? These very different plants demonstrate assorted flower colors, mature sizes, bloom periods, growing requirements, and other qualities. Substituting one for another based on common names predictably leads to trouble.

Botanical names on the other hand, follow accepted international convention, albeit the taxonomy may be outdated or occasionally debated. However, scientific nomenclature proves more reliable than common names and is recognizable to those who pay attention, making it more universally useful regardless of the language spoken. Some folks understandably find scientific names intimidating, but you don't have to pronounce them if you present them in writing to a reputable garden center that sells natives.

◀ Texas natives populate an English-style mixed border

Gardening in Texas spans the entire calendar. We plant regionally adapted natives throughout winter, and there is a chance of blossoms any time of year during a warm spell. Responsible planting halts in summer to conserve water, but flowering continues with heat-loving rock rose pavonia, flame acanthus, and the like. Given this, Texas flora lack the urgency to complete all of their business in a condensed season like their northern counterparts, who have only a few months to conduct their "florgy." In Michigan, for example, summers are a rave of flowers, but the trade-off is months and months of winter downtime. The expanded Texas growing season offers opportunities to choreograph a succession of seasonal interest.

Overall, native plants outlast and outperform their non-native counterparts. But importantly, a few are not well suited to traditional gardening. Some specialists require certain minerals or a particular soil structure. Tomatoes prefer rich, highly composted soils, but try growing bluebonnets in the same bed and you will end up with large, floppy plants frosted with mildew and only a smidgen of flowers. Black-foot daisy easily rots under irrigation, and more vigorous neighbors easily outcompete a small lace cactus in a rich bed. This book leaves out the most finicky natives while offering tips to fortify native plant gardeners for successes.

Another category of indigenous plants not recommended for ornamental landscapes are rare plants, sometimes described as species of greatest conservation need (SGCN). Examples of rare plants that find themselves on the tables of Texas garden centers include Hinckley's golden columbine (*Aquilegia chrysantha* var. *hinckleyana*) and big red sage (*Salvia pentstemonoides*). This issue is complicated, but here are a few considerations for protecting our most vulnerable plants based on the expertise of Texas Parks and Wildlife's rare plant botanist and Wildflower Center plant conservationists.

Depending on the species, it may be important to keep genetics from disparate populations separate. From the perspective of retailers and customers, it would be virtually impossible to match cultivated plants with appropriate planting locations.

Big red sage

Propagation over generations changes underlying genetics. When these altered plants grow in residential or commercial landscapes (in contrast to conservation-minded public gardens) near wild populations, cross-pollination could influence the wild population's survivability. Conversely, these garden-cultivated plants potentially lose their ability to return to unpampered wild areas.

Promoting plants for horticultural use has, and does, make rare plants, such as many cactus species in west Texas, targets for poaching from natural areas.

Ultimately, it is far better to protect rare plants in their wild settings. Cultivating them for ornamental purposes wouldn't benefit wild populations unless they are nearly extinct. In those cases, it is best to cultivate these plants professionally in consultation with plant conservationists.

Understanding Garden Ecology

The foundation of a successful native garden begins with understanding plants in their home context. Visit them in their native habitats that resemble your garden and plagiarize nature. Gardeners can extend a plant's normal range by pampering it with extra water, protecting it from frost, or tinkering with soils, but the simplest approach matches plants to their most comfortable settings.

Ecoregions of Texas

Texas is vast. Very different circumstances confronting plants in one part of the state to another determine plant distributions. These areas are defined by environmental conditions including climate, underlying geology, hydrology, and soil type and are called ecological regions, or ecoregions, which translate into vegetational areas. Following Texas Parks and Wildlife, we recognize the following ten ecoregions.

Pineywoods: Tall pine-hardwood forests, rich bottomlands, rolling landforms, and occasional pastures characterize the region. Humidity is typically high, with 36 to 50 inches of rain annually. Soils are acidic sandy or sandy loam and elevations are just 200 to 500 feet above sea level.

Gulf Prairies and Marshes: Remnant tallgrass prairies, oak mottes, and oak woodlands on acidic sands and sandy loams intersperse the region, with salt-adapted grass marshes lining estuaries and bays. Clay-based bottomlands support tall woods, and barrier islands protect the mainland coast. Humidity remains high throughout the year and annual rainfall averages 30 to 50 inches. Flat topography, less than 150 feet above sea level, results in slow-draining landscapes with rivers and creeks braiding throughout.

Post Oak Savanna: Grasslands punctuated by post oak and pockets of woodlands characterize this southwest-to-northeast running strip of savanna. Gently rolling landscapes range from 300 to 800 feet above sea level. Soils

Cypress swamp at Shangri La Botanic Garden in Orange, Texas

Vegetational Areas of Texas

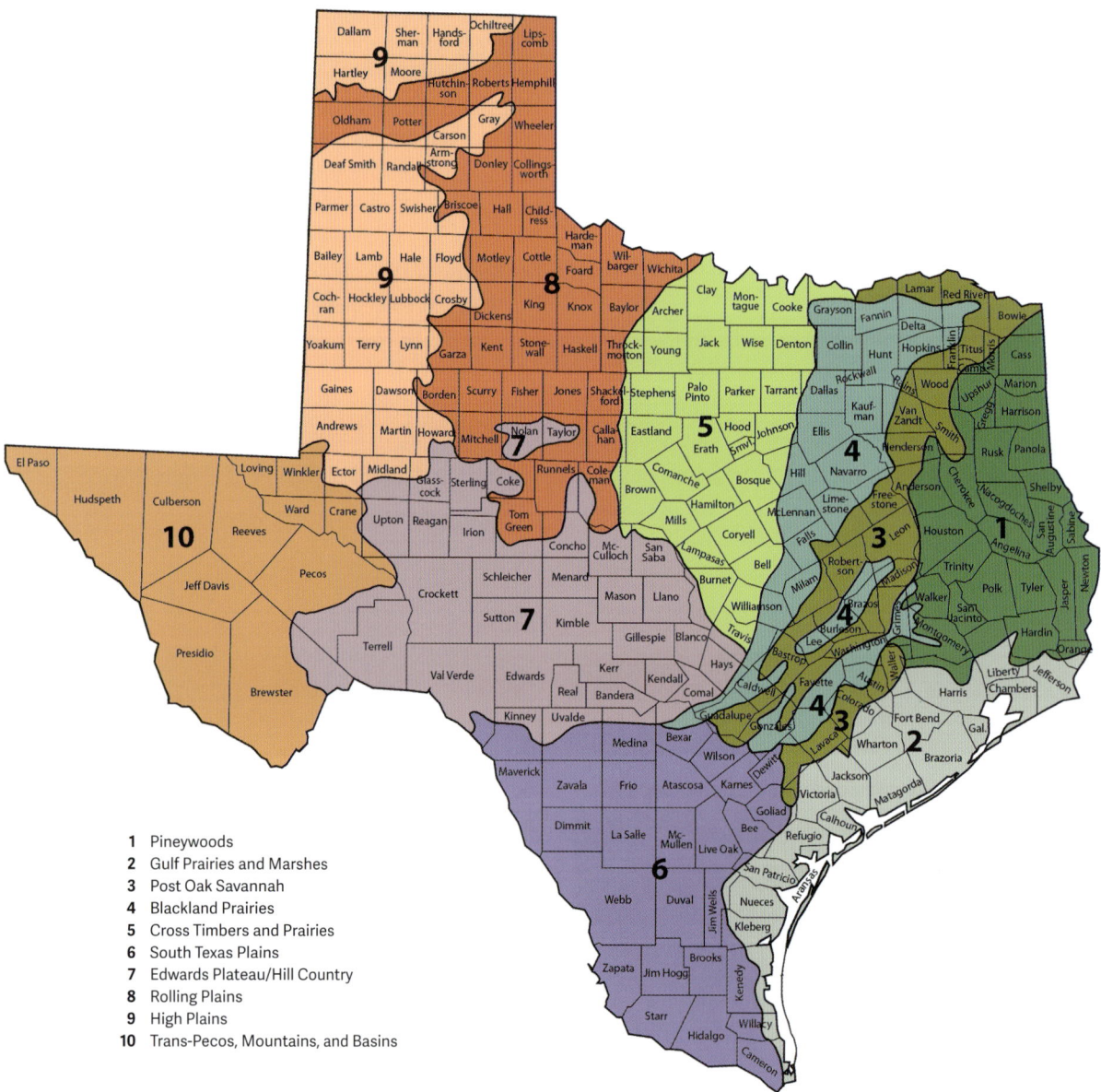

1   Pineywoods
2   Gulf Prairies and Marshes
3   Post Oak Savannah
4   Blackland Prairies
5   Cross Timbers and Prairies
6   South Texas Plains
7   Edwards Plateau/Hill Country
8   Rolling Plains
9   High Plains
10   Trans-Pecos, Mountains, and Basins

Modified from *Checklist of the Vascular Plants of Texas* (Hatch et al. 1990).
Nearly identical maps have been used in numerous works on Texas, including Gould (1962) and
Correll and Johnston (1970).

consist of acidic sandy loams and sands in uplands and sandy loams and clays in the bottomlands. The region receives 28 to 40 inches of rain per year, with highest amounts in May and June.

Blackland Prairies: Switchgrass, Indiangrass, big bluestem, and little bluestem defined the tallgrass prairies that historically dominated this region. The alkaline, deep, rich "black gumbo" clays, with pockets of sandy loams, have now all but completely been converted to croplands due to their high fertility. Level to gently rolling lands range from 300 to 800 feet above sea level, receiving 28 to 40 inches of rain annually.

Cross Timbers: Dense woodlands and irregular plains and prairies on sandy to loamy soils characterize the region.

Vegetation ranges from tallgrass and woodlands in the eastern sections to shortgrass moving westward. The erratic nature of rainfall often leads to drought during part of the growing season.

South Texas Plains: Thorny scrub, open grasslands, and small trees (including palms and other tropical species along the Rio Grande Valley) grow on alkaline to slightly acidic clays and clay loams. Annual average precipitation is between 20 to 32 inches a year, decreasing heading west. Less rain falls in winter and the area welcomes higher rainfall in late spring, and again in fall. Where soils are deepest, taller plants including mesquite dominate. Shallow soils (often caliche) support shorter brush. The region hosts a rich diversity of plants and animals, counting many rare species.

Big Bend bluebonnets and other wildflowers at Big Bend National Park

Edwards Plateau/Hill Country: Vegetation here consists of grasslands, juniper-oak woodlands, and savannas peppered by mesquite and escarpment live oak. Alkaline, limestone-based clays, caliche, and gravel lie atop a parent rock of water-soluble limestone, which leaves the subsurface riddled with caves and extensive river systems forming a number of major aquifers. Annual precipitation is 15 to 34 inches on average, but "average" obscures the pattern of storms delivering multiple inches within a mere few hours. Heavy rainfall combined with impervious rock leads to regular flash flooding between periodic drought. The varied topography rises from 100 to over 3,000 feet above sea level. A large number of rare and endemic species find their home in the region.

Rolling Plains: Historic tall and midgrass prairies have given way to mesquite-shortgrass savanna due to decades of heavy cattle grazing. Hardwoods populate floodplains, while junipers grow on slopes, cliffs, and river-cut canyons.

Wildflowers at Big Bend National Park

Prairie fleabane thrives on limestone

Four-nerve daisy loves limestone, too

Landscapes from 800 to 3,000 feet above sea level receive 20 to 28 inches of rain annually, largely in May and September, sandwiching arid summers. Soil pH spans from neutral to slightly alkaline, and vary from arroyos and streambeds of coarse sands to tight clays and shales.

High Plains: Over decades, shortgrass prairies of buffalograss and blue grama have largely succumbed to irrigated crops and mesquite and yucca invasions due to overgrazing. Shin oak and sand sage now dominate sandy landscapes, and juniper encroaches onto the plains. The high-elevation plateau ranges from 3,000 to 4,500 feet above sea level, with 15 to 22 inches of rain each year, seeing the best chances of showers in spring and fall, with drought common. Clays

in the north and sand farther south are underpinned by caliche throughout.

Trans-Pecos, Mountains, and Basins: Complicated geology and the corresponding variety of soil types, along with extreme ranges in elevation beget a lavish diversity of plant life. Communities of creosote-tarbush desert scrub, desert grassland, yucca-juniper savannas, and mountainous piñon-oak forests typify the region. The assortment of soil textures include sands, loams, and clays, and may be igneous (generally neutral pH) or limestone (alkaline) based; some contain high concentrations of salt and gypsum. Elevations range from around 1,500 feet above sea level in the low deserts to Guadalupe Peak, the highest point in Texas at 8,750 feet. Rainfall quantities vary by elevation and year, but average a scant 12 inches, mostly during summer.

Habitats

Within these ecoregions exist more granular layers of microclimates and habitats where life happens on an organismal level and encompasses all of the elements in a territory needed for an organism to thrive including food, water, space to exist, and shelter. Grasslands, deserts, woodlands, wetlands, cliffs, roadcuts, canyons, and backyards are all habitats that can occur within an ecoregion. If a plant struggles in your landscape, seek the wisdom of nature. What conditions normally nurture this species? Some seemingly persnickety natives would be just fine if grown in the right situations. Plant to your soil rather than changing your soil.

For example, four-nerve daisy, damianita, blackfoot daisy, and most cacti happily grow in nothing more than a lean layer of dry caliche on top of a limestone shelf—something a typical gardener would not consider soil. Most of us don't recognize the value of this "crappy" caliche cache, or how lucky we are if we have it. With even just a few inches of soil or a crack for roots to anchor into, there are species that will thrive in a rock or crevice garden.

Shallow soils found in areas such as rocky outcrops, uplands, ledges, and slopes inhibit root penetration, so larger plants cannot support themselves. Due to soil depth and slope, these landscapes drain and dry out more quickly than lower-lying areas. Thin and dry substrates support fewer and smaller plants, resulting in less biomass. This results in less organic matter nourishing the soil as plants and associated organisms decompose.

These leaner soils foster particular kinds of plants, like those mentioned above, that would not necessarily thrive in conventionally well-composted and thoroughly irrigated conditions. Plants adapted to lean soils may grow lush and floriferous for a while when planted in a traditionally prepared garden only to sour in overly wet conditions, especially during rainy spells in seasons when plants are semidormant, namely summer and winter. If you see these plants wilting, it's possible they might need a drink, but too much moisture in rich cultivated soils often induces rot with similar drooping symptoms.

Conversely, woodland plants such as golden groundsel, pecan, or baby blue-eyes often grow in decomposed leaf litter on deeper soils supporting denser vegetation, which in turn contribute more organic matter to the soils. Generally speaking, woodlands have richer soils. Rivers and creeks stand out from a distance by the presence of trees, and the same concept of biomass converting to compost applies here, too—just add more moisture. Woodland plants appreciate organic matter and may prefer extra dampness or dry shade depending on the species.

Members of the pea/legume family (Fabaceae) "fix," or capture, nitrogen from the air to produce their own food (combined with photosynthesis) and often prefer poor substrates. For instance, bluebonnets respond to rich and fertile soils by overproducing leggy foliage, underproducing flowers, and succumbing to powdery mildew. We find healthier bluebonnets growing in crushed granite paths than in prepared flower beds!

Putting these ideas into practice, you would be wise to offer more compost to shade-loving plants, and do a little research when planting hard-core caliche lovers that might prefer leaner conditions. Most native species appreciate—or at least tolerate—medium or high levels of organic matter/compost, but in the case of those that prefer minimal organic matter, you will save labor and expense by not adding unnecessary soil additives.

Ecological Succession

The process by which a community of all of the species in an area changes over time is referred to as ecological succession. In the early stages of succession, we see disturbed sites becoming colonized with fast-growing plants, typically annuals. The plants themselves change the conditions, making a more hospitable environment for later successional species. Over time, slower species such as perennials and woody plants establish themselves until a relatively stable climax community settles in. A prairie or forest can express a climax community, and can be reset to an earlier successional state by fire, flood, or other disturbance.

We can start with our beloved state flower as an example of an early successional, or early colonizing, species. *Bluebonnets are weeds.* Wait . . . what?! Ecologically speaking, a weed is described as a plant whose lifestyle pattern involves rapid growth and reproduction, often living for only a short while; an annual, for example, or even a relatively short-lived, aggressively spreading woody plant such as retama or box elder (*Acer negundo*). Their motto could be "live fast, die young!" Their biologically programmed competitive strategy is to swiftly colonize exposed ground disturbed by overgrazing, mowing, fire, flood, erosion, construction, or . . . gardening. Gardens are indeed disturbed ground, because we cultivate soil precisely to deter weeds or tuck in new transplants. Common garden invaders are overly enthusiastic annuals whose role is to quickly stabilize the soil while slower perennials establish themselves. Over time, the wimpier annuals fizzle out as the pushier perennials get stronger. This is one reason why annual weeds generally pose less of a concern than perennial weeds, and why folks find it difficult to maintain a wildflower patch comprised largely of annuals.

The most successful human-created wildflower meadows (gardens, really), involve a selection of annuals and

Blanketflower amidst grasses

perennials, including grasses, and the recognition that a weed with pretty blossoms gets named a wildflower. An all-annual garden would require constant disturbance and editing out of undesirable early successional weeds. That's a lot of work. Of course, a number of wildflowers live long lives as perennials too. Be sure to add them to the mix as seeds or transplants. Often discounted, grasses provide an essential matrix in which the roots of other species grow. They reduce erosion, benefit wildlife, and are attractive in their own right. True meadows lean toward approximately 50 to 80 percent grasses, but can be thinned periodically to open up space for showier species as desired.

Imagine a "Howdy from Texas!" postcard illustrating an ocean of bluebonnets so dense you can smell them right off the paper. April blows a balmy breeze. Luminous honey mesquite leaves frame the scene on one side, a fully armed prickly pear cactus unnecessarily guards a barbed-wire fence in the foreground, and a studly longhorn fills the remaining view.

Interestingly, this iconic Texas scene tells a story of succession continuously being reset by the disturbance of heavy cattle pressure. Cattle are grazers, meaning they consume more grass than forbs (herbaceous, nongrass, flowering plants). That said, they do eat a certain amount of palatable forbs and bear responsibility for significant decline of those species. Other plants such as bluebonnets, mesquite, and prickly pears increase as livestock eat away the competing grasses and edible flowers. If you've ever chewed and chawed with a rancher, you'll know that bluebonnets don't fatten cattle. In their eyes, they are most certainly weeds!

Seasonal Succession

Ecological succession lies in the realm of years, decades, and even centuries. On a residential scale, gardeners generally concern themselves with seasonal succession (i.e., the transition from one season to the next). Most gardeners face a real challenge keeping their gardens looking great during "off" times of year. Where some folks opt for bedding plants to supply seasonal color, gardens at the Wildflower Center consist exclusively of Texas natives, so bedding with pansies or coleus isn't in the cards. Instead, this design puzzle is solved by integrating the concept of timesharing.

In his book *Sunbelt Gardening: Success in Hot-Weather Climates*, Tom Peace proposes a strategy of timesharing that takes advantage of the tendency for herbaceous plants to lie inactive (if only on the surface) in winter while growing during the warm season, or actively grow in cooler months with a summer dormancy. By selecting a combination of perennials and reseeding annuals with matching cultural requirements and alternating growing seasons, we maximize the function of spaces under cultivation while saving the effort and cost of seasonal bedding installations. Pollinators appreciate a more continuous source of nectar and pollen, and otherwise naked soils get dressed with vegetation over the span of seasons, making them lovelier to look at and permitting fewer weed incursions. And by reducing the amount of plants used for switchouts, we waste less plastic pots and trays, cut the greater carbon footprint needed for transportation, and consume fewer production-related resources including water, synthetic fertilizers and pesticides, and potting mixes (often containing peat moss with highly environmentally damaging harvesting processes).

Say you have a lush stand of Turk's cap going all summer and into the fall, then the first freeze of winter renders it a sad bank of black mush. You cut it back to nubs and stare glumly at the bare ground all winter. Great news, y'all! This scene is avoidable. Plants grow, and Texans can garden, all year! Finding winning seasonal combinations is all about experimentation. Mix and match to see what works best for you. Here are a few solutions:

Turk's Cap/Giant Spiderwort

To complement the winter-latent Turk's cap, couple it with giant spiderwort, which features winter-evergreen daylily-like foliage. Giant spiderwort awakens in fall, grows actively through winter, and flaunts copious blue, purple, magenta, or white flowers throughout the spring. Plants completely disappear around May, handing the show back to scarlet-blossomed Turk's cap just emerging from dormancy as temperatures rise. For a bonus of all-year greenery, overlay a matrix of creek or meadow sedges.

Partridge Pea/Winecup

A fast-growing summer annual, partridge pea sports cheerful yellow blossoms all season, and its open and airy greenery allows enough sunlight to filter down to the scaled-back summer foliage of winecup. During winter months, winecup's deeply lobed dark green leaves add beauty at ground level before rich magenta flowers push out to bless the spring.

Texas Lantana/Bluebonnets or Pink Evening Primrose

Texas lantana sprouts late in spring but carries off the warm seasons with sunny yellow and orange flowers. Cold weather knocks it into dormancy for the winter, leaving room for bluebonnets to sprout. To get this combination to work best, cut back the lantana by November to allow bluebonnet seedlings to absorb as much sunlight as possible over the winter in preparation for the spring show. If the underplanting is the pink evening primrose, let the two wrestle for the space as they will. The primrose covers the winter ground with red-dotted leaves, blooming as early as March before shutting down as summer heat settles in and rain dwindles.

Growing Native Plants

Wise plant choices and siting are critical. Simply being native to the state does not guarantee a plant is suited to your location. Conditions in Kingsville and Kingsland differ much more than their names. Gardens brimming with healthy vegetation are regarded as beautiful. For a resilient garden requiring minimal pampering, your best bet is to use plants from your neck of the woods. Inform your plant selections to ensure long-term viability by matching your site with the plants' region and habitat, including an examination of moisture, light patterns, and soil type.

Available Water

Supplemental irrigation isn't necessary to keep well-sited species alive. But while a well-planned nonirrigated garden might endure, it may produce fewer flowers and dormant vegetation during drought. We like seeing flowers, and wilted plants make us sad. With irrigation we can temper a drought situation to resemble an average rainfall season.

Of course, not all indigenous plants appreciate parched sites. Ponds, dry creeks, rain gardens, and swales call for species that specialize in these and other wet

Virginia blue flag and zigzag irises like wet feet

Waterlilies and maidenhair fern adorn this native-planted pond

situations. Consider slough-loving yellow water lilies, irises, or ditch-dwelling bushy bluestem. Fortunately, a rich assortment of plants have evolved from wide-ranging habitats. Whatever site conditions you have, appropriately selected natives, once established, will endure with less attention than non-natives.

Light and Shade

Plants need light to grow. They have the unique talent of translating energy from the sun into sugars they need to sustain themselves. Humans eat them. Animals either consume plants directly or take in other creatures nourished by plants, and that is pretty much where all food comes from. For this, we venerate photosynthesis as the magical foundation of life.

Texas suffers seasonally from too much of this life-giving light. In contrast, say, in Michigan, full sun has a decidedly different meaning than full sun here. Our summer rays are withering. Separating the impacts from sun versus heat is impossible, and in combination they make a formidable duo! Our sun-loving (or at least sun-tolerant) native plants have developed work-arounds for dealing with such extremes. Sometimes lending a silvery appearance, fine hairs and waxy coatings help shield plants from intense UV radiation and reduce heat absorption and moisture loss. Many heliophiles grow tight and compact, with fine or small leaves to minimize exposed surface area. Cacti, cenizo, black dalea, woolly stemodia, and others demonstrate these protective strategies.

Adaptations to punishing sunlight often overlap or are influenced by compounded heat and soil extremes. For example, most plants better withstand harsh heat and drought when they are situated in soil with more organic content. Being located in a zone with cooler temperatures might also allow a plant to endure all-day sun.

As people, we welcome a tree-shaded yard and home, but that same canopy limits choices for colorful flower displays. In building a shady oasis, seek plants having large leaves adapted to capture scarce light. Shade-thriving plants likely lack protective wax or hairs and they might even demonstrate a glossy surface that readily sheds rain, reducing fungal inflictions. Woodland residents such as Carolina buckthorn, American beautyberry, and Turk's cap highlight some of these qualities.

Morning sun with afternoon shade suits most plants ideally, with strong light hitting while temperatures remain relatively mild most of the year. Conversely, west-facing woodland edges with cool morning shade followed by a gut punch of afternoon sun describe some of the most difficult growing conditions. Plants preferring full shade scorch, while sun lovers become malnourished by the scarce sun energy, resulting in leaning, mildewed, or overall puny growth. What kind of godforsaken plant will tolerate such brutal extremes? Try Texas lantana, Turk's cap, velvet mallow, chile pequin, or shrubby boneset.

Be aware not only of how light plays during the course of a day, but also how it travels throughout the year. Northern exposures become dark in winter, whereas in summer, brightness prevails when the sun is higher in the sky. A winter garden may suffer a scarcity of light due to the lower angle of the sun, while areas situated under a deciduous canopy enjoy ample golden rays during the cool season. Pecan trees leaf out relatively late, allowing plenty of rippling sunshine through for early spring bloomers such as golden groundsel or baby blue-eyes. And keep in mind that as trees grow, a sunny garden will yield to shade over the years, likely requiring plant adjustments.

Soil

Dirt is dead. Lacking living organisms, it is essentially moderate to fine mineral particles. Soil is alive. Decomposed parent minerals, moisture, air, and the living community of macro- and microorganisms consisting of worms, insects, fungi, and bacteria, along with the organic matter and humus they leave behind as waste or from death, foster conditions for plants to prosper. Roots themselves penetrate and loosen soil, while promoting habitat for subterranean creatures.

The foundation of soil is, in fact, dirt. Mineral particles sorted by size range from sand on the coarse end (2 to 0.05 millimeters), to silt in the middle (0.05 to 0.002 millimeters), to clay, which has the finest particles (less than 0.002 millimeters). Igneous rocks such as granite derive from volcanic activity, whereas sedimentary limestone was formed by ancient seas once covering much of Texas. Both serve as parent materials that break down into soils, which are identified by the combination and percentage of each material (silty clay, sandy clay, sandy loam, etc.).

The tight, waxy, compacted structure of clays leave little space for air between particles. This characterizes many prairie soils that support grasses and perennials with fibrous roots reaching deep into the clay. Clays hold water for long periods, causing unsuited species to rot. Yet once desiccated, clays resist rehydration and form deep fissures up to several feet down that often break roots apart, causing serious stress or mortality to maladapted plants. Nutrients necessary for plant vigor such as iron bind to clay, leading to chlorosis, a yellowing of foliage due to iron deficiency, and other maladies.

The relatively large pores between bits of sand, on the other hand, allow for water to move quickly through, leaching away nutrients over time, keeping plants dry overall, and promoting acidic conditions. Long taprooted plants, such as butterfly milkweed, find pushing through sand much easier than clay.

As previously discussed, a little compost benefits most plants. Some require more, some less than others. Rich soils refer to those with high amounts of organic matter, whereas lean soils have moderate to low levels of organics.

There is a kind of sandy loam in Texas that is known as "red death." This low-quality fill with high sand content and low organic matter leads to exceptionally fast drainage and hard compaction when dry. It is cheap and easy to work with, so builders blanket it around new construction. But unless your plan relies on plants specifically adapted to sandy stream banks, you will need better soil.

Crushed or decomposed granite incorporates various particle sizes including gravel. It works well for pathway

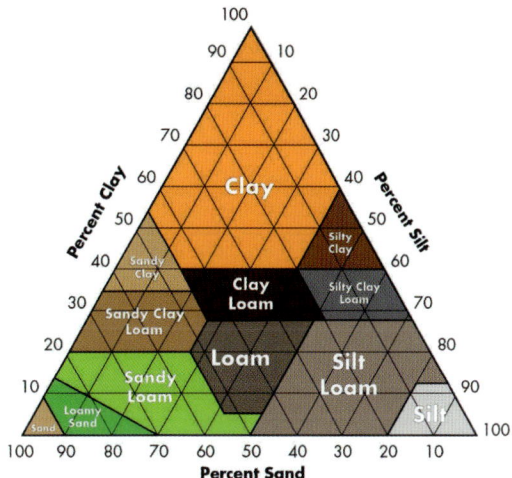

surfaces, and added to gardens, helps plants from granite regions feel more at home. Caliche also incorporates variously sized pieces, commonly cemented together with calcite, and is considered a limestone-based medium, often with high pH values. Chalk soils specifically derive from limestone and also have a high pH (7.1 to 8). Limestone-based soils trend alkaline, or basic, whereas sandy soils lean neutral to acidic depending on other conditions.

Gardeners transplanted from the eastern United States occasionally overlook the importance of pH. They might as well water their azaleas and camellias with tears if they attempt cultivating these acid lovers in the alkaline soils common throughout our state. Better-suited natives would put a smile back on their faces.

It's understandable that struggling plants would inspire their caregiver to test the soil. Readily available kits make basic home testing easy, and Texas A&M AgriLife Extension Service and other labs offer more comprehensive reports. I confess that I have never tested soil. Certainly there is no harm in testing, but matching plants to their preferred conditions takes care of all of that. Following a similar rationale, aside from compost, most other soil amendments seem pointless. The word "amend" naively implies the earth is lacking in some way. Natives by claim flourish in their home environments. However, working with imported soils (such as builder's fill) begs exception.

How to Grow a Wildflower Meadow

Adapted from a "How To" article on the Wildflower Center website: wildflower.org.

Mother Nature makes it look easy. But for most of us, growing a wildflower meadow is harder than it looks. Natural meadows evolve over many years as plants, animals, and all other organisms develop intricate associations with each other and their environmental conditions to create an interactive community, not just a collection of individuals. Refer to the previous section on ecological succession to establish a framework to understand how this different type of garden works. Note that most meadows represent a transitional stage, and without intervention, grasses, shrubs, and trees typically replace the herbaceous flowers over time. Long-term management is critical to reset or suspend this succession if you want to maintain a high percentage of wildflowers. The following is a general guideline for a successful wildflower planting.

Preparation:

- Identify or create an appropriate site with sun or part sun and good drainage.
- Eliminate robust weeds such as Bermuda grass and Johnsongrass (note that these are difficult to spot when they are dormant) that will outcompete desirable species. This may be the single most important step for a successful project!
- Tilling is optional and will likely encourage early successional weeds. It can also create conditions for wanted early successional plants like bluebonnets, partridge pea, or horsemint.
- For sites with existing desirable vegetation, mow short and rake before seeding.
- Soil additives are not necessary for healthy soils. Seek expert advice if you are uncertain.
- Select native species appropriate to your site, considering soil type, moisture, and climate. Include:
  - a variety of annuals and perennials that will sort themselves out over time (some will thrive and others will decline)
  - species with overlapping blooming seasons
  - mostly warm-season grasses and flowering forbs
- Ensure none of the plants you are considering are invasive or on the state's noxious weed list.

Planting Tips:

- Prepare your site in time for autumn planting, which is generally the best planting season in Texas.
- Warm-season native grasses germinate in spring when soil temperatures reach above 65°F, or late summer/fall until approximately ninety days before average frost.
- Containerized or dug perennial transplants typically fill in faster than seeds and allow for more controlled placement, but may cost more.
- Seeds provide a great option to cover larger areas inexpensively, but seedling distribution is less predictable than transplants.
- Many people opt for a combination of seeds and transplants. To avoid disturbing fragile seedlings, plant rooted plants before laying seeds.

Seeding Methods:

- Mix seeds in a container according to recommended seeding rates.

- Add sawdust, sand, or other carrier to aid even distribution.

- Broadcast by hand like you're feeding chickens or with a handheld or broadcast spreader, depending on the area size.

- Use a rake to encourage good seed to soil contact. Lightly covering the seeds is fine, but avoid burying them deeper than twice their diameter. Small seeds should not be buried at all.

- Absent adequate rains, water the seedbed enough to prevent the surface from drying out. As roots extend deeper into the soil, water less frequently but soak more thoroughly.

Into the future:

- Learn to identify weeds and remove them quickly. The most effective methods depend on the target species.

- Most weeds are fast-seeding annuals, so remove the seed source before they drop.

- If seed-setting wildflowers look unsightly, tolerate them long enough for seeds to ripen before mowing or cutting them back. Mow at a high setting and allow clippings to fall back onto the ground.

- Best mowing times are typically early to midsummer, and late winter.

- Annual and biennial wildflowers will dominate the first few years, giving way to perennial flowers and grasses. Over several years, grasses will likely dominate. If your goal is to keep some annuals such as bluebonnets going, reset the successional clock by occasionally removing some grasses, or even burning, which effectively inhibits woody growth. Of course, burning requires consulting the expertise of professionals.

- Continue adding new species over time to intensify diversity.

- Observe and be rewarded with joy!

Site Preparation

For new plant installations, begin with weed elimination. Most weeds readily surrender to pulling, smothering, or solarizing (the practice of covering the area with plastic sheeting in summer to kill weeds with heat). A few exceedingly stubborn exceptions that might require herbicide include Johnsongrass (*Sorghum halepense*), Bermuda grass (*Cynodon dactylon*), and nutsedge (*Cyperus esculentus* and others). I'm not typically an herbicide proponent, but sometimes it is the lesser of the evils. Replacing invasive weeds with habitat-supporting natives might be worth the one-time eradication of these plant pests. Repeated applications might be necessary, but once these bullies disappear, so does the existential threat to your garden. Dealing with these more stubborn weeds gets much harder after planting.

As explained above, soil additives are often needless. If builder's fill plagues your site, consider removing and replacing it with weed-free native topsoil if available, or work with a soil vendor to approximate a medium that best suits your needs. If replacement is not an option, amendments can help.

Planting

It's true that the best antidote for spring fever is gardening. But if the glory of bluebonnets and paintbrushes in April inspires you to grab your hat and shovel, add sowing those seeds to your fall calendar. After late spring and summer daytime highs lingering persistently in the upper nineties Fahrenheit and above, we put our trust in the promised cooler temperatures of autumn. This is the best time to plant! Setting out transplants as early as September lessens plant stress and allows for root growth and establishment before summer's inferno. Cold-hardy plants acclimated to living outside, versus tender from a greenhouse, can go into the ground all winter.

Preference for fall planting holds true for most native seeds and plant starts. However, those plants at the coldest boundary of their range, such as chile pequin or Texas lantana outside of the southern parts of our state, survive better if set out in spring, giving them the longest possible time to get situated in warm weather before the winter. And though seeding for most wildflowers occurs in autumn, March or April is not too late to sow for summer- and fall-blooming wildflowers such as partridge pea, devil's claw, clammy weed, wild poinsettia, common sunflower, and tropical sage. As weather warms, seeds germinate and grow, gracing us with cheerful color later in the season.

The term *wildflower* sometimes tricks people into assuming the plants in question are indigenous, but wildflower seed mixes often include species from Eurasia or elsewhere that struggle in their new environs or establish too well, such as ox-eye daisy (*Leucanthemum vulgare*), becoming noxious agricultural pests or outcompeting native species for habitat. A wise consumer reads label ingredients on seed mixes. You may even curate your own custom blend for peace of mind. Creating your own seed mix, although requiring more time and thought, allows you to select the species best suited to your site and that bloom at different times of the year.

Colorful blossoms capture the most attention, but grasses function in many important ways and should not be overlooked. Grasses provide food and cover for wildlife (including microorganisms), reduce soil erosion, promote soil tilth, structurally support neighboring plants, and add attractive color, form, and texture in their own right.

Availability might decide what to plant for you. If finding a particular species for purchase proves difficult, try harvesting your own seeds for direct sowing, or plant into pots to set out later. Small local nurseries and plant sales at the Wildflower Center are possible sources of hard-to-find plants. Local chapters of the Texas Native Plant Society conduct plant and seed swaps and sales, and organize rescues from doomed sites. When collecting from private

◄ Drummond phlox mingling with squarebud primrose and prairie brazoria (*Warnockia scutellarioides*)

property, be sure to get written permission—some Texans carry guns!

Tip: Water transplants immediately upon planting, even if the ground is already moist. It is ideal to "mud them in" by making a slurry of water and soil as you plant. This eliminates large air pockets and settles soil particles around roots, helping plants adjust quickly. Plants need regular watering until they become established, and younger plants settle in more quickly than older ones. Initially, ensure new plants receive frequent moisture, tapering off with longer intervals and deeper soakings. Eventually, you might be able to hold off entirely, except during drought.

Mulch

Plants are not able to move to a shady spot when the sun gets too hot. But you can offer aid by protecting their roots with some kind of mulch. In addition to keeping soil and roots cooler, mulches:

- Inhibit seed germination (of weeds as well as desirable species)
- Reduce water evaporation from the soil
- Moderate soil temperature extremes
- Add organic matter (organic mulches) and minerals (mineral mulches) with decomposition
- Diminish erosion during heavy rains
- Lessen compaction on areas with heavy foot traffic (organic mulches)
- Help hide irrigation pipes
- Give a more finished look and contribute to a desired aesthetic

Mulches fall into three categories: organic, mineral, and living.

Organic mulches derive from plant parts such as pine bark or needles, pecan shells, or shredded hardwood and cedar. Leave fallen leaves for a free and effective cover, but take care not to let a deep layer smother herbaceous plants. Organic mulches build soil by contributing organic material as they decompose. Plants adapted to rich prairies or woodlands where leaves and other decomposing biomass fall especially appreciate the added compost.

Mineral mulches include decomposed granite, crushed limestone, pea gravel, or crushed recycled glass. Typically, they allow moisture to drain away from the bases of plants, lowering humidity and inhibiting fungal infections. Desert dwellers and succulents prefer mineral mulches.

Living (or green) mulches grow as low dense groundcovers and taller plants that blanket the ground (zexmenia, Gregg's dalea, muhlys, and the like), vigorously pushing out most weeds and shading the soil from blistering sunlight.

Mulches left to right: fallen leaves; pecan shells (a by-product of the pecan industry); native shredded hardwood; crushed and tumbled recycled glass

Gregg's dalea grows as a living mulch, thick enough to suppress other vegetation

Once filled in, living mulches function essentially like other mulches. Select plants like frogfruit or horseherb even allow for pedestrian traffic. Living plants eliminate the need for purchased mulch, while also enhancing wildlife habitat. Plants play this role in most natural settings.

Match the mulch with site conditions and plant requirements. Organic mulches may hold too much moisture during wet spells, causing fungal problems for plants that prefer dry conditions, and may contribute excess organic matter as they break down. A mineral mulch would better accommodate cacti or plants like blackfoot daisy or damianita, which are adapted to leaner soils.

How much mulch is too much mulch? Thick layers absorb moisture from light rains, limiting percolation through to roots, and some mulches form a hard crust or tight mat that sheds surface water altogether. Soaker hoses or drip irrigation under the mulch layer mitigate these concerns, but you'll still miss out on nourishing natural rain. Pull mulch 2 or 3 inches away from plants to avoid the common error of burying stems and trunks, which encourages rot.

A couple of noteworthy exceptions where mulched soil would not be advised: Wildflower and other desirable seeds require solid soil contact and may not grow if lying on top of mulch; and buried seeds get smothered, so leave them uncovered. Mulches inhibit all seed growth and cannot discern wanted species from weeds! Ground-nesting bees and wasps also require open soil, so welcome them with a small bare plot here and there.

Design Considerations

Lots of ink has flowed regarding garden design, but indigenous plants bring particular topics to the fore. Notably, the uncanny bias against them. Shunned as common, native plants are often discredited. Many of us don't even see our most common green neighbors—a condition called plant blindness. However, familiarity can offer a sense of well-being and belonging.

Many assume native gardens will inevitably look messy and unmanaged. Where did the idea originate that native gardens must look wild? Perhaps it's because native plant enthusiasts have a fervor for nature that regularly translates into gardens resembling those venerated wild spaces. Historically, native plants have almost exclusively been confined to naturalistic designs, appealing to those of us who enjoy less formal settings. However, our broader culture recognizes gardens that look intentional. Formal or stylized gardens are all about being deliberate, and naturalistic gardens are often not perceived as cultivated landscapes. But whether a planting is viewed as a garden might be less important than having it simply appreciated for its beauty and function.

The best constructed landscapes stem from a marriage of ecology and horticulture. Without doubt, gardens are a cultural construct. In their book *Planting in a Post-Wild World: Designing Plant Communities for Resilient Landscapes*, Thomas Rainer and Claudia West are spot on when they declare, "A designed plant community is a translation of a wild plant community into a cultural language." Mother Nature's measured design processes determine over decades or millennia which plants settle halfway up the swale and which colonize the bottom; which inhabit this prairie and which end up in that one. She has literally eons more experience than we do! Each of our design decisions is an inevitable interpretation of nature, since conditions in the created landscape invariably differ from a mature wild plant community, especially given the concessions made for functional and aesthetic preferences. A garden, or even a restoration, at best paraphrases nature, as evolution is driven by the practitioner as much as by ecological processes.

A cedar elm exquisitely coached into a bonsai

Although not typically associated with them, native plants can promote a formal design. The actual species used may be the same regardless of the type of garden. Formal spaces tend to be less busy and more soothing, and by incorporating symmetry and geometric shapes, such as turf centered on a front door or a bed curved to a perfect circle, a project nudges toward formality. Clean lines and well-defined borders implemented with hardscape materials such as brick or steel edging also contribute to a controlled aesthetic, as do reserved and disciplined color choices and simple or massed plantings of single species. Formal spaces are generally less concerned with displaying plant collections than with overall beauty, and various natives lend themselves just as well as exotics to the tortures and contortions of bonsai, pollarding, espalier, and topiary.

Many experience comfort in the organization and predictability of a formal layout while others enjoy the variation and freedom of a naturalistic landscape. Of course, you don't need to commit to one or the other. Styles fall on a continuum or matrix and gardens can have elements of

Native plants dress up Italian terra cotta

Container Gardens

Apartment dwellers and those whose shovel obstinately resists their few millimeters of so-called soil may find potted plants to be their best choice for gardening. Many folks tend bedding annuals or delicate non-natives in pots, but many Texas natives tolerate captivity too.

Container gardens in groupings or as individual specimens enhance wildlife habitat, dress up balconies or patios, and add flair to existing gardens. Potted plants are mobile, making it simple to change a plant's position as often as you like without disturbing delicate roots. And as arrangements transition into their offseason, you can cart the whole thing away and replace it with a fresh container. Transportability also allows gardeners to protect plants from weather extremes including strong sun, wind, and freezing temperatures.

For specialized plants, pots can help maintain specific growing requirements such as soil type, pH, and moisture levels. Perhaps your landscape is designed to thrive without supplemental water but you are willing to pamper a few pots of river fern, horsetail, or columbine. Or instead of digging out and building a full-scale water garden, experiment with aquatic plants in a large sealed pot or small stock tank. After all, a pond is essentially a container without drainage holes.

In gardens with lush, billowing vegetation, small, delicate plants such as lace cactus, spice lily, and prairie fleabane may be overwhelmed. A dish or shallow pot garden is often just the right solution, and vessels mounted at eye level make for easy viewing.

Case Studies from the Lady Bird Johnson Wildflower Center

Formal Home Inspiration Garden

To connect with a larger audience, the Wildflower Center explores innovative ways to use natives, arranging them in unique patterns not necessarily found in nature. To define formality in the space, the Formal Home Inspiration Garden incorporates mirrored symmetry, limestone pathways, a limited number of plant species, and a circular lawn fitted with crisp metal edging enveloped by a square border. "We don't have so many examples of how to use native plants to look like a more conventional landscape," says Jill Nokes, who designed this garden.

A formal design carried out with Texas native plants

An ornamental water source in the Texas Mixed Border Inspiration Garden

Texas Mixed Border Home Inspiration Garden

In the Texas Mixed Border Home Inspiration Garden, English style meets Texas flora. A sun-soaked twin border of colors and shapes works as a unit through repetition of trees, shrubs, grasses, vines, and herbaceous species. Tightly clipped dwarf yaupon hollies amble loosely along the length of the main axis walkway. Seating areas offer comfortable viewing of a birdbath and places to visit with friends. Interplay is balanced between formal elements and the softened, relaxed, and engaging drift planting, all of which is framed by an arbor laden with native wisteria and tucked inside a French Gothic–style picket fence.

Naturalistic Home Inspiration Garden

Plant geeks yearn for one of everything. Diversity results in complex, seasonally dynamic, and ultimately more fascinating gardens. Organic forms and asymmetry, or no symmetry, support a casual vibe in unrestrained spaces like the Naturalistic Home Inspiration Garden. Intention may be subtle, but don't let anyone get away with categorically describing informal or naturalistic gardens as having less structure than formal gardens. Any well-designed planting presents discernable structure and clarity in composition. Developing patterns of recurring color, form, and foliage texture work toward achieving visual unity and cohesion. Garden elements like this site-collected stone bench demonstrate appropriate proportions, mass, and scale fitting to the space, and well-thought-out views from important vantage points leave no doubt of the designer's intention, even if the effect is nuanced.

Hill Country flowers frame a rotting log, home for invertibrates, lizards, and fungi

both. I remain agnostic, preferring not to judge style preferences; any well-designed garden should be celebrated. Native plants, with all of their benefits, can provide the basis for any style. It's your garden, so make it something that inspires you. It is possible to make gripping, artistic, and conservation-friendly gardens with native plants—regardless of the style of garden you prefer.

With the many compelling reasons to cultivate natives instead of, or along with, non-native species, it would be a shame for gardeners to reject native plants under a false assumption that they are inappropriate for a home landscape, or that they only work in naturalistic designs. The desire for a formal garden should never provide an excuse to pass over indigenous plants.

Fortunately, it is not destiny for a native plant garden to be mistaken for a weedy lot. Gardening still must happen. And thoughtful garden makers can conjure just about any style, from informal to formal, to naturalistic or stylized. How a garden is designed and maintained dictates its style, not whether the plants used are native or not.

Stewardship

When an overgrown garden of familiar exotics gets out of control, we fault the caretaker: "Oh, what a shame they've let their garden go." When a native garden goes rogue, "those native weeds" get the blame. While unfair, this double standard presents a reality. Honestly, any neglected garden will present as messy regardless of whether or not natives or non-natives predominately populate it. Native plants often endure a reputation of looking unkempt. We admire their need for fewer resources to thrive, but they still need care to look good according to cultural norms. To flip the bad rap native plants get, the onus is on us to do some grooming. This, friends, is gardening.

From a maintenance perspective, the gardener's hand striving for control in a formal space reaches for a rake and a pair of shears. Strategic intervention is also critical to keeping a naturalistic garden attractive. To avoid a

neighbor's ungracious judgement, you may not need to box your hedges, but you'll still want to trim wayward branches and weed, shape, and deadhead select perennials for a tidy presentation, even if more loosely executed. The number of hours spent cultivating a naturalistic garden may be fewer than in a formal one, but a talent for plant identification and subtle artistic decision-making lead to best outcomes. Garden historian Mac Griswold famously recognizes that "gardening is the slowest of the performing arts."

Both experienced horticulturists and designers will posit that a significant portion of a design gets carried out through management over time. If designer and gardener are not the same, strong communication is critical for successful execution of a vision. Removing random strays, for example, preserves the original design intent. Allowing free-seeding flame acanthus to overtake your mealy blue sage ultimately leads to a very different garden.

Basic tasks such as weeding, raking, sweeping, shaping, trimming, or mowing along pathways signal intentionality. A naturalistic landscape with a mowed edge or interpretive signage indicates that despite its possibly perceived messiness, the space is actually intentional and cared for. Most of these "maintenance" tasks are to please us people, otherwise the native plants do just fine on their own, thank you!

We have discussed the ecological meaning of *weed*, but in common usage the term often refers to a plant growing where it is not wanted. Otherwise desirable plants growing out of place—say a bluebonnet in a crack in the sidewalk, or a towering frostweed along a walkway—are considered weeds. While birds are often responsible for these seed misplacements, they are not the only couriers of unwelcome vegetation. Some plants travel by wind, or thumb a lift on the hides of beasts. Some even sneak over undetected as seeds on shoelaces or mud-caked loafers.

How do you know what is or isn't a weed? Other plant people are often eager to help, and studying seedling identification is empowering. You may want to allow unfamiliar plants to grow under close supervision. Once in flower—and some may be quite minute—you can more easily identify them. Warning: Don't let weed seeds drop and overrun your garden! Pull young weeds before their roots get a strong grip—moist ground makes removal easier. A good layer of mulch smothers young annuals and helps control germination of weed seeds, but also inhibits desirable wildflowers. Plants with dense ground-surface foliage such as big muhly, zexmenia, or Texas lantana make impenetrable living mulch to outcompete wimpier neighbors.

Taming the Wild

Shaping, trimming, and grooming represent some of the most daunting tasks in the garden. Perhaps you're terrified of trimming Turk's cap, or shaky about shearing switchgrass? Maybe you're worried that the Garden Police will slap you a ticket for deadheading your purple coneflowers before the goldfinches finish their seedy feast? Most people lack horticultural confidence when tending herbaceous ornamentals, particularly natives.

Every garden needs direction to read as a "garden" and not some errant patch of weeds. Aside from removing damaged or diseased plants (or parts of plants) to sustain a healthy garden, it may be comforting to know there is no single right way to manage plant growth (although there are plenty of wrong ways!). Untrimmed wild plants survive just fine without a gardener's hand, but may not support a preferred garden aesthetic. What looks good to you and how much time and patience you have are important factors to consider.

Deadheading is a good place to start. This term describes the removal of old flowers and stems before seeds form. It cleans things up and encourages new blossoms to please your eyes and nourish pollinators. But you may want to hold back on cutting purple coneflower, zexmenia, or the like until wildlife polish off the seeds—or until seeds meet the soil if you're aiming to encourage a new generation of plants.

Some spent flowers can also look appealing. Let giant coneflower and gayfeather stand for their striking stalks, even after blossoms fade. Prairie goldenrod and purple coneflower each lend their distinct character for winter

Gayfeather seed stalks hold court well into fall

interest. When stems become rangy or fall akimbo, that's your cue to grab the shears. This task typically lands in late winter for summer and fall bloomers (inland sea oats, Gregg's mistflower), and during summer for spring performers such as winecup or cedar sage.

Preferences drive shaping. Sometimes intermingling plants reveal a clever design or happy accident, but most often, trimming plants away from one another avoids unintentional scruffiness. Gardeners control and redirect growth by understanding apical dominance, a phenomenon in which hormones in the terminal bud (or apex) of a branch inhibit side-branching. Clipping off leading tips removes these hormones and encourages lateral growth, creating a bushier overall form. Shearing and tipping are

Plants in groupings make a statement

the most common techniques to take advantage of this tendency. Light, frequent shearing results in tighter, denser foliage. If you prefer a more relaxed form, trim select branches a little less often. Regular "haircuts" eliminate the need for drastic correction and keep plants from looking like a second-grader after a play session of hair salon.

Not all troubles are solved by cutting: If mature plants wax too large, replace them with more appropriately sized species. And shearing, unfortunately, cannot correct habitual legginess caused when plants stretch toward more sunlight. Find alternatives better suited for shade. However, if conditions change for the better, say, a tree fall allows more light to reach a misfigured lantana, rehabilitate the lantana by lopping it to nubs and letting it resprout. It sounds extreme, but it usually works.

After the sharp tongue of a hard freeze licks your deciduous herbaceous perennials, such as river fern or tropical sage, give them a trim close to the ground. For Turk's cap, shrubby boneset, Texas lantana, and other woody or semi-woody plants, leave 2 to 6 inches of stem. Or wait until leaves emerge in spring before nipping off dead tips, so as to yield overall larger plants.

What about ornamental grasses? Manage them according to two categories: muhlys and everything else. Everything else includes little bluestem, switchgrass, inland sea oats, and most other clump grasses that die completely to the ground in winter. Leave them standing as long as they appeal. Then, before fresh spring blades emerge, snip last year's tired growth to a few inches above ground.

Muhlys, including Lindheimer muhly and Gulf muhly, comprise the second group. Since they maintain some evergreen foliage during winter, thus continuing photosynthesis, a hard military cut may overly stress plants (and, the ghostly silhouettes look weird). Yet old decadent grasses are weakened by years of accumulated dead material. Ideally, burn them. Built for fire, they respond quickly and vigorously to such treatment. Otherwise—assuming you do not have professionally trained fire management staff—the next best option involves breaking off brittle flower stems low in the plant with a gloved hand, followed by a combing of loose foliage with a leaf rake, taking care to groom "under the skirt." Conduct this cleanup in late winter or early spring ahead of new growth.

Cautious gardeners prefer to postpone most cleanup tasks until late winter with the theory that uncut stems help insulate plants. There is certainly no harm in waiting, but for native cold-hardy plants, cutting back unsightly foliage is a safe practice (emphasizing cold adapted). However, for vegetation that harbors wildlife through winter (skipper butterfly larvae in grass clumps, for example), grooming later is less likely to do damage. Bear in mind that overly tidy gardens may have reduced habitat value, but it isn't necessary to have a jungle of frozen mush, either.

Purple coneflowers, prickly pear, and big muhly socializing in an intimate vignette

Watering and Irrigation

It is possible to grow a garden with well-selected native plants that need no supplemental irrigation to survive. However, to encourage coloring of the garden, most of us opt to add water at least during seasons with the stingiest skies. You'll also need to pamper newly planted starts until they get established. How long this takes depends on multiple factors including plant size and species, soil type, temperatures, available moisture, time of year, and exposure to sun and wind.

Various irrigation methods include a hose with a handheld nozzle or sprinkler at the end, soaker or drip hoses, or in-ground systems (often dubbed "irritation" systems when pipes get nicked or their complexity requires complicated or frequent repairs). Avoid water waste and gaps in coverage by adjusting heads and run times according to the season, and check regularly for leaks and misangled heads. Schedule overhead application for early morning just before sunrise so water has time to infiltrate before breezes pick up and carry droplets away. Additionally, fungal-inducing humidity drops and leaves dry off with the sun, reducing the time foliage sits wet.

Saturate the ground enough to encourage roots to stretch downward and reach deep moisture. This makes plants more resilient during dry spells. Ideally, give good soakings less frequently instead of a little bit every day. Desiccated plants in containers require thorough drenching by passing over multiple times or placing pots in shallow water for a while to ensure the rootball is resaturated. Wetting until water runs out of the drainage holes isn't always enough. Like a dehydrated sponge, water rolls off the sides until it is slowly quenched.

Watering tip: We usually assume drooping leaves indicate a thirsty plant. But tender and vulnerable young leaves wilt during the first warm and sunny days of spring as a way of minimizing surface area exposed to the sun's intensity. Symptoms are the same, so avoid drowning your plants by probing the soil before deciding to douse.

Using This Book

Texas is huge. Gardening here is not like anywhere else, and cultivating gardens here can be tricky. The 225 official plant entries in this book (plus a few others that somehow snuck in when I wasn't looking) include gems from all areas of the state. Regardless of where you garden—sunny beds to woodland retreats, desert sites to ponds, sticky gumbo to chalky caliche—you'll find useful suggestions.

Use these native plants to glue the soil against erosion, cool your neighborhood as they transpire or provide shade, escort floodwaters back into the ground and aquifers, and inhale carbon dioxide and exhale oxygen. The plants you choose will support wildlife in great need of boosting. In exchange, these animals will reward you with funny and astounding stories. Ultimately, these elegant, quirky, resilient, mysterious, healing, inspiring, calming, and thrilling plants will deepen your curiosity and point you, dear gardener, toward years of blissful (occasionally wretched) gardening with your native green neighbors.

◀ Hill Country Meadow Garden with gayfeather and partridge pea

I'm thrilled to have this platform to highlight standard reliable garden workhorses, and with luck, pique some excitement for the lesser knowns of the bunch. Some of these currently elude the trade, and I invite you to share your interests and requests with your local growers and garden retailers. They'll listen and respond if we shout loud enough! In the meantime, collect seeds (ethically, of course) and swap plants and experiences with members of the Texas Native Plant Society, garden clubs, and all of your plant geek buddies. Visit the Wildflower Center's gardens, explore the searchable database at wildflower.org, and come to the Wildflower Center's plant sales.

Use the following pages to knock some of the guesswork out of the experiment we call gardening in Texas. The plant profiles will guide you to the best plants for your site and provide tips for an informed gardening practice—and it is a practice. After all, dead plants teach us lessons, and I've killed gardensful!

Theme Garden water tank

Reading the Plant Profiles

The next part of the book is divided into seven chapters beginning with Groundcovers and Turf, followed by Perennials and Annuals, Grasses and Grasslike Plants, Cacti and Other Succulents, Shrubs and Small Trees, Large and Shade-Producing Trees, and lastly, Vines. Each starts off with an overview of the plant category, with individual plant profiles for each species following in alphabetical order by botanical name. Each profile includes the following information:

Botanical names are listed first in the standard convention of italics, using the names currently listed on the Wildflower Center website: wildflower.org.

Common names listed are those with which I am personally most familiar. Since we're all in Texas, there is a good chance you use many of them too. I acknowledge that other names are in circulation, so if you know a plant by another title, by all means, call it what you will.

Size reflects the usual height and width under typical growing conditions. Deeper, wetter, and richer soils usually yield larger plants. Shade may stretch plants taller than normal.

Flowers are described by color, size, and fragrance when applicable. Typical bloom period is indicated.

Fruits are included when especially noteworthy, described by color, size, and edibility where applicable. Approximate season of ripening is indicated.

Duration qualities are described as deciduous or evergreen, woody or herbaceous, and perennial, biennial, or annual.

Light requirements for optimal growth during the growing season are listed in order of general preference for each plant:

    sun—at least six hours of total sunlight daily

    part shade—mostly sunny, with some shade or lightly dappled light

    part sun—mostly shady, with some sun or moderately dappled light

    shade—very little sun, heavily dappled or filtered light

Soils are described as sand, loam, and clay. When significant, calcareous/limestone or igneous/granite parent material is identified. Acid or basic/alkaline pH is noted where plants grow in one or the other preferentially or exclusively; where pH is not indicated, plants prefer neutral or tolerate wide-ranging conditions. Preference for high organic matter/rich or lean/poor soils is indicated.

Moisture and drainage requirements for optimal growth during the growing season are listed in order of general preference for each plant:

    dry—low moisture

    mesic—medium or moist

    wet—continuous moisture or saturation

    good or fast drainage—excessive amounts of water retained for a day or less

    poor or slow drainage—soggy conditions persisting for a day or longer

Habitats describing the environmental conditions where a plant naturally grows are listed.

Ranges in which the plant is found in Texas are listed (ranges outside of the state are not included).

Wildlife sections include information about pollinators, caterpillars, songbirds, and other interesting fauna served by the plant, as well as deer palatability.

In addition, symbols can be found to the right of plant names to indicate which groups of wildlife birds 🐦, hummingbirds 🐦, bees 🐝, butterflies 🦋, large moths 🦋, or caterpillars 🐛—directly benefit by using the plant as a food source, for shelter, or for nesting materials.

Maintenance sections describe how to manage for plant health and aesthetics, as well as the best methods for propagation.

Notes sections provide other useful and remarkable information about the species, including edibility. Caution: Never eat any wild plant unless you are 100 percent certain of its identity as a safe thing to eat. Remember: You can eat anything . . . at least once!

Happy Gardening

Groundcovers and Turf

Most people define groundcovers as plants maturing at heights below 12 inches, with trailing, creeping, dense, or mat-forming foliage. These characteristics informed the plant selection for this chapter. Larger plants—zexmenia, Gregg's mistflower, and Jimsonweed for example—can function as groundcovers too, but are treated under subsequent categories since they play different primary roles. Groundcovers often perform as excellent living mulch under and around bigger plants by outcompeting weeds, insulating bare soil, and providing habitat for small animals and soil microorganisms.

The classic groundcover is lawn. In the United States, lawns cover about 50,000 square miles (the size of Mississippi!). On average, Americans use 200 gallons of water per person per day in order to maintain this "crop" that we can't even eat! Water conservation is the single most critical conservation issue in Texas, and yet residential and commercial lawns and golf courses represent the largest area of irrigated crop in America. It may not be financially or otherwise practical to uproot existing thirsty turf, but when planning a new lawn, buffalograss alone, or mixed with blue or Texas grama and curly mesquite (*Hilaria belangeri*), provides a drought-tolerant native turf option. You might even add a few flowering forbs such as rain lilies to accommodate pollinators.

As responsible citizens, we need to consider what type of turf, if any, we choose to occupy our yards. Is it necessary? Some cite the need for a lawn to accommodate kids and pets. Many animals happily romp on mulch or paths between flowerbeds (albeit, some are too rambunctious to tolerate in a garden). Maybe a dog park exists in your area? And what better place for kids to explore and engage than in a garden habitat full of interesting seeds, tendrils, caterpillars, and lizards? Send them to the neighborhood park to play football or to hurl a Frisbee.

Lawns can provide a neutral canvas or welcomed palette cleanser for transition areas within a garden, but other groundcovers here can also satisfy such design requirements.

Bacopa monnieri

Coastal Water-hyssop

1–8 in. tall; mat forming

flowers white, ¼ in. diameter; April–September

deciduous herbaceous perennial

sun, part shade | sand, clay, loam; mud | moist, wet; poor drainage

wet meadows, pond and stream margins | southern half of Texas

Wildlife: Nectar nourishes butterflies and bees. Larval host for white peacock butterfly. Pill bugs may inflict significant damage. Moderate deer palatability.

Maintenance: Trim off dead foliage before new spring growth. Trim stolons that creep into unwanted areas. Propagate by division, layering, and seed.

Notes: This easy-to-grow, bright green stoloniferous spreader roots along the stem where it contacts the soil. Stems dripping from hanging baskets or edges of pots add a touch of elegance. Rain and bog gardens, or areas that get regular irrigation, provide perfect growing conditions. Limited scientific research supports its use in Ayurvedic medicine for improving memory and cognition.

Bouteloua dactyloides

Buffalograss

3–12 in. tall; turf forming by stolons

flowers on 4–8 in. tall spikes, dioecious; April–September

herbaceous perennial; semievergreen to dormant in winter and during drought

sun, part shade | loam, clay; caliche or limestone, sand not preferred | dry; well drained

grasslands | most of Texas except the far eastern counties

Wildlife: Provides food for grazers. Supports green skipper butterfly caterpillars. Low deer palatability.

Maintenance: Mow at 4 in. setting once or twice a year before spring or summer dormancy breaks, more often for lawns as desired. Frequent mowing and short settings invite weeds, remove them swiftly. Leave completely unmown for a meadow. Avoid summer dormancy with irrigation and deep soil. Propagate by seed (resulting in female and male plants) and stolon layering.

Notes: Many available sod cultivars offer various merits, some proving tolerant of light foot traffic or deeper drought. In tallgrass prairies, wild types form part of the understory, while dominating in shortgrass prairies. Buffalograss provides a loose matrix in which wildflowers can grow. In cultivation, these openings allow for weed invasions. Be vigilant!

Calyptocarpus vialis

Horseherb, Prostrate Lawn Flower

3–8 in. tall; spreading to 18 in. wide
flowers yellow, ¼ in. wide; April–November
herbaceous perennial; evergreen in mild settings
shade, part shade, sun | sand, loam, clay; caliche, calcareous preferred | mesic, dry; well drained
woodlands, meadows, disturbed areas | throughout Texas except Panhandle

Wildlife: Small butterflies take nectar. Moderate to low deer palatability.

Maintenance: If grown as a lawn substitute, mow as desired. Cut back plants damaged by frost. Soak periodically through drought or allow summer dormancy. Propagate by seed, division, layering, and cuttings.

Notes: If you have a shady plot, chances are you already have horseherb. Encourage it. It accepts moderate foot traffic and blankets the ground with foliage soft enough to sit on. And it has flowers to boot! Seeds are hard to collect in quantity but seedlings transplant easily.

Dichondra argentea

Silver Ponyfoot

2–4 in. tall; mat forming

flowers greenish yellow, minute; April–November

cold-tender herbaceous perennial, sometimes used as an annual

sun, part shade | loam, sand; loose limestone or igneous-based soils, susceptible to rot in heavy clay | dry; well drained

rocky mountain slopes, desert grasslands | far western Texas

Wildlife: Low deer palatibility.

Maintenance: Provide winter protection in northwestern half of state. Propagate by layering and cuttings.

Notes: Silver silky sheened foliage might be all that needs to be said! You've seen it everywhere draping down the side of a planter or hanging from a basket. As a groundcover, it suppresses weeds while complementing plants with contrasting foliage. Trivia: It belongs to the morning glory family (Convolvulaceae) and shares the same genus as dichondra, the maligned lawn weed. 'Silver Falls' is a common cultivar.

Dyschoriste linearis

Snake Herb

6–10 in. tall; spreading indefinitely by rhizomes

flowers lavender, purple, up to 1 in. across; April–October, mostly spring and after rains

deciduous herbaceous perennial

sun, part shade, part sun, shade | sand, loam, clay; limestone | dry, mesic; good drainage

rocky, grassy slopes, silty flats, open woodlands | throughout Texas except Panhandle and east

Wildlife: Provides nectar for pollinators. Host plant for common buckeye butterfly larvae. Low deer palatability.

Maintenance: Cut back or mow during the growing season, and after first hard frost, to keep mats tidy. It creeps slowly, giving you time to control its spread. Propagate by division, cuttings, and seed.

Notes: Snake herb is subtle, but its quiet charm and versatility under various light and soil conditions makes it a useful, if underappreciated, living carpet. Its thick weave efficiently squeezes out weeds, and pretty flowers and butterflies add a little frosting to the cake. In spite of its name, it attracts snakes no more than other plants.

Hydrocotyle umbellata

Water Pennywort

3–10 in.; colonizing indeterminately

flowers white, tiny, on rounded heads; April–October

deciduous herbaceous perennial

sun, part shade, part sun, shade | sand, loam, clay; mud | wet, mesic; adapted to poor drainage or shallow water no deeper than 4 in.

mud and shallow water along edges of streams, wet meadows | southeastern two-thirds of Texas

Wildlife: Flowers attract tiny insect pollinators. High deer palatibility.

Maintenance: Remove from unwanted areas. Trim away freeze-damaged foliage. Propagate by division and layering.

Notes: The long petiole (leaf stem) attaches to the middle of the circular leaf, creating a mini parasol. Or maybe the shiny round leaves remind you more of coins. Stems cuddle the ground, rooting into the soil at each node and allowing plants to spread vigorously. If water pennywort looks familiar, it's probably because you've seen it, or its close relatives in the genus *Hydrocotyle*, in moist, sandy lawns as dollarweed. It might gain more favor in or around a pond, or highlighted in decorative pot.

Indigofera miniata

Scarlet Pea

3–8 in. tall; spreading to 3 ft. wide
flowers salmon pink, ¾ in. long; April–October
deciduous herbaceous perennial
sun, part shade | sand, loam, clay; caliche | mesic, dry; well drained
open grasslands | throughout Texas except west

Wildlife: Nectar attracts butterflies. Larval host for gray hairstreak, common dogface, and Reakirt's blue butterflies. Moderate deer palatability.

Maintenance: Trim back leggy stems and frostbitten foliage. Propagate by seed.

Notes: This largely overlooked darling tucks nicely between other plants in the garden. Flowers show heaviest in spring, then on and off during the rest of the season, especially after rains. The unusual coral-colored flowers work particularly well with purples and blues such as wild petunias and bushy skullcap. Plant with bluebonnets or Texas yellowstar for winter cover and early spring color.

Marsilea macropoda

Bigfoot Water-clover, Clover-fern

6–10 in. tall; colonizing by rhizomes
deciduous herbaceous perennial; drought and winter dormant
part shade, part sun, sun, shade | sand, loam; mud | moist, wet; adapted to slow drainage
swamps, wet woodlands, ditches, margins of water bodies | central and southern Texas

Wildlife: Low deer palatability.

Maintenance: Cut back when ragged or dormant, plants rejuvenate quickly during the growing season. Beware that these robust and tenacious plants may pose a management challenge. Propagate by division.

Notes: You could be fooled into thinking you've found a four-leaf clover when coming across this plant. No relation to true clovers, water-clover falls into the nonflowering fern division. Ideal for pots with or without drainage holes, or a pond edge. Sibling to the Texas-endemic bigfoot water-clover, hairy water-clover (*Marsilea vestita*) has a broader geographic range and similar growing characteristics.

Mimosa roemeriana

Sensitive Briar

6–10 in. tall in bloom, up to 6 ft. wide; may form extensive colonies by stolons

flowers pink, showy, 1 in. globes, fragrant; April–July

deciduous semiwoody perennial

sun, part shade | sand, loam, clay, rocky; caliche, limestone, or granite based | dry, mesic

rocky slopes and grasslands | north-central Texas through the Edwards Plateau

Wildlife: Lures butterfly and bee pollinators. Moderate deer palatability.

Maintenance: Prevent stems from rooting into unwanted areas. The "briar" part of the name indicates prickles, so fondle with caution. It's tenacious once established and difficult to remove. Propagate by seed, division, and layering.

Notes: Enchanting features beyond the blanket of pink powderpuffs include sensitive briar's high heat tolerance, and the touch-sensitive nature of the leaves. Adults like to say that kids enjoy watching the thigmonastic movements of the leaves folding in after being touched (well, maybe not those exact words), but in my maturity, I'm not bored with them yet! Botanists speculate that this adaptation may reduce water loss or defend against herbivory.

Packera obovata

Golden Groundsel

1–1½ ft. tall in bloom; forming extensive colonies by rhizomes, stolons, and seeds

flowers yellow, ¾ in. diameter; February–May

herbaceous perennial with evergreen winter rosette

shade, part sun | loam, clay; humus rich, calcareous | mesic; well drained

rich woodlands and slopes | mostly central and eastern Texas

Wildlife: Flowers attract bees, butterflies, and other pollinators. Moderate deer palatability.

Maintenance: For a tidy appearance, cut back spent flower stalks once seeds have dispersed. Propagate by seed and division.

Notes: Golden groundsel stands as one of the first Texas wildflowers to bloom each year. A cheerful harbinger of spring, it provides much-needed fuel for early-emerging pollinators. Plant in expansive colonies for the greatest visual and wildlife-supporting impact. Note the foliar variability where tooth-edged, rounded basal leaves become deeply indented on flowering stalks.

Phyla nodiflora

Frogfruit

3–6 in. tall; spreading vigorously by stolons

flowers white with puce centers, ½ in. diameter heads; May–October, especially after rains

herbaceous perennial; evergreen in protected areas

sun, part shade | sand, loam, clay; caliche, limestone, salt tolerant | mesic, wet, dry; tolerates poor drainage

grasslands, fields, beaches, edges of water bodies | throughout Texas

Wildlife: Nectar nourishes small butterflies and other pollinators. Larval host for Phaon crescent, buckeye, and white peacock butterflies. Moderate to low deer palatability.

Maintenance: Plants establish best in loose soil, but tolerate tight or compacted sites (as under moderate foot traffic) once well rooted. Light fertilizing and watering during dry periods increases flowering. Sun and drought render plants dense and ground hugging. Propagate by division, layering, and cuttings.

Notes: Frogfruit proves remarkably versatile. Its flood tolerance makes it ideal for rain gardens, and its acceptance of drought allows it to thrive near pavement while laughing at the radiating heat. Trailing stems pour nicely over edges of planters or from hanging baskets.

Rubus trivialis

Southern Dewberry

arching or trailing canes 1–3 ft. high; indeterminate stoloniferous spreader
flowers white, 1 in.; March–April
fruits black when ripe; April–June
deciduous woody perennial
sun, part shade, part sun | sand, loam, clay; limestone, caliche | dry, moist; seasonally wet, otherwise well drained
open woodlands, grasslands, sand dunes, roadsides | southeastern half of Texas

Wildlife: Flowers feed insect pollinators, while fruits feed humans and a variety of other animals. Wiry stems with prickles provide shelter for birds, rabbits, and other wildlife. Moderate to low deer palatability.

Maintenance: Ensure adequate ventilation and water early in the day to avoid fungal blackspot. Irrigate if conditions are dry during fruit set. During attempts to remove them, strong roots put up a fight. Propagate by seed, division, cuttings, and layering.

Notes: Elegant flowers last only a few weeks. Delicious blackberry-like fruits make excellent pies and cobblers, or eat them fresh off the plant. Take care harvesting around the grabby prickles. When grown in full sun, fall foliage colors range from burgundy to crimson to purple.

Salvia lyrata

Lyreleaf Sage

1–2 ft. tall in bloom, rosettes 6–12 in. across
flowers sky blue, white, 1 in. long, tubular; March–May
herbaceous perennial with evergreen winter rosette
shade, part sun, part shade, sun | loose sand, loam, clay; acidic or alkaline | mesic; tolerates poor drainage
open woodlands, alluvial areas, wet or dry meadows | eastern third of Texas

Wildlife: Blossoms invite bees, hummingbirds, and small butterflies. Moderate deer palatability.

Maintenance: If desired, cut back spent flower stalks after seeds drop. Propagate by seed and division.

Notes: Remarkable lyre-shaped basal foliage with burgundy leaf veins is most pronounced in winter and resembles the non-native *Ajuga*. Flowers show best in large patches, and rosettes add winter greenery under deciduous plants such as possumhaw, American beautyberry, or chile pequin. Plants reseed readily, forming extensive colonies. Stress from cold or drought sometimes turns foliage brilliant reds or purples.

Stemodia lanata

Woolly Stemodia

4–6 in. tall; stolons form a thick mat, spreading indefinitely
flowers lavender, blue, ¼ in. wide; spring–frost (particularly after rains)
deciduous herbaceous perennial
sun, part shade | sand, loam, clay; saline tolerant | dry, mesic; well drained
sand dunes, plains, scrublands | far southern Texas

Wildlife: Small butterflies nectar on blossoms. Low deer palatability.

Maintenance: Cut back to nubs after killing frost and trim anytime stolons sneak into unwanted areas. Propagate by layering and cuttings.

Notes: Creeping tightly to the ground, this opulent, silver-leaved spreader takes to cultivation more readily than the similar looking, sometimes temperamental silver ponyfoot. Soft silvery fingers drop roots to the ground from each node. It calls for a double take rambling across gravel mulch or dribbling over the lip of a pot or a wall. This heat-tolerant trailer dies back in cold winters, but may remain evergreen—or evergray—in protected areas.

Perennials and Annuals

The herbaceous layer supplies most of our garden color. But more than mere jewelry and accessories, herbs compare more closely to flesh on a skeleton. ("Herb" as used here is shorthand for "herbaceous plant," not necessarily for culinary use, although some are edible and delicious.) If trees and shrubs form the framework of a landscape, herbs serve as connective tissue. They tie surrounding plants together for a wildlife corridor and to visually unify a composition. Flowers bring joy to human eyes, but their biological roles support wildlife, particularly pollinators, in more vital symbiotic relationships.

As a maintenance activity, deadheading—the removal of spent flower heads before seed maturation—not only keeps a garden looking groomed but in many cases prompts further flowering for pollinators and people to enjoy. Allowing seeds of many herbs to ripen before cutting down old stems is a way to assist our seed-eating avian friends. Or, when trimming, you may want to shake seeds back onto the ground to renew the crop, especially for annuals, ensuring full stands continue year after year. You may also collect and store them for future sowing. Cutting plants back after frost, or for aesthetic shaping, is largely optional and doesn't usually affect the health of the plant. Wild plants clearly thrive without that kind of treatment. So you'll have to decide whether to cut or leave seed heads according to what fits the circumstance.

Note that the true annuals included below go through their entire life cycle in just a few months before expiring after seeds set, differing from tropicals, often falsely described as annuals, that die due to cold temperatures but are long-lived when protected. Since annuals and many perennials have "off" seasons when they are dormant, absent, or don't look so great, timesharing (where plants trade seasons, as discussed in the "Seasonal Succession" section of the Using Native Plants in the Garden chapter) is an important technique for maximizing color and habitat throughout the year.

Whether the goal is an organized garden, wildflower meadow, restoration, or naturalized area, there exists an herbaceous native plant to fit the circumstance. Allow me to introduce you to some of my favorites.

Adiantum capillus-veneris

Maidenhair Fern

12 in. tall, 12–18 in. wide; spreading by rhizomes

winter- and drought-deciduous herbaceous perennial

part sun, part shade, shade | sand, loam; limestone | mesic, wet; well drained

crevices along streamsides, shady cliffs and canyons on limestone | Edwards Plateau to Big Bend

Wildlife: Very low deer palatability.

Maintenance: Plants appreciate constant moisture in the stone crevices of their native habitat. When grown in soil, avoid keeping plants soggy, but don't let them dry out either. Trim away dead foliage after dormancy. Propagate by division and spores.

Notes: Any rock-rimmed pond appears lusher, greener, and even wetter with the emerald green lacy leaves and contrasting black stems of maidenhair ferns sprouting from crannies between the stones. But you don't need a pond to enjoy cultivating them in patio containers, hanging baskets, or in the ground. Lightweight fern spores lift into the higher levels of the atmosphere and spread globally, resulting in a native range that spans Eurasia and South America as well as North America.

Allium candense var. candense

Canada Wild Onion

8–18 in. tall, 6–12 in. wide
flowers white, ¼–½ in., in clusters; April–June
winter-evergreen, summer-deciduous herbaceous perennial
sun, part shade | sand, loam, clay; calcareous | mesic
open woodlands, along streams, swales and ponds, prairies, meadows, pastures | eastern two-thirds of Texas

Wildlife: Flowers draw insect pollinators. Bulbs and leaves eaten by wild turkeys. Very low deer palatability.

Maintenance: Cutting back spent foliage is optional. Plants spread prolifically under ideal conditions, weed them out (share or eat) as necessary. Grasshoppers and snails sometimes mar the leaves. Propagate by bulbils, division, and seed (seed production is rare depending on the variety).

Notes: Our native onions lie dormant much of the year, sprouting foliage in winter and receding in late spring, making them ideal timesharing fillers underneath warm-season species like devil's claw or tropical sage. If you've ever witnessed a plant emerging straight from the top of a flower stalk, you likely saw *Allium canadense* var. *canadense* with its strange and novel habit of sprouting vegetatively from bulbils in the heads. Eat the abundant leaves and bulbs like other onions or chives, but *do not eat anything if you have any hesitancy in your identification skills.* Many look-alikes contain strong toxins. If you detect an unmistakable onion odor, you're in the clear.

Allowissadula holosericea

Velvet Mallow

3–5 ft. tall, 2–3 ft. wide
Flowers saffron, ¾–1½ in.; May–November
deciduous or evergreen semiwoody perennial
part shade, part sun | sand, loam, clay; limestone | mesic; well drained
openings and edges of dry woodlands | Edwards Plateau, Trans-Pecos

Wildlife: Larval fodder for several skipper butterflies. Nectar feeds a number of butterflies. Occasional host for the brilliant, indigo sawfly larvae (*Neoptilia tora*). Low deer palatability.

Maintenance: Trim lightly as needed, heavy cutting during the growing season leaves awkwardly stubby plants. Propagate by seed and semi-softwood cuttings.

Notes: Irresistible to touch, the velvety soft, heart-shaped leaves span up to 7 in. long, contrasting well against shrubby boneset, chile pequin, and similar plants with fine-textured foliage. Use these plants to cover for the velvet mallow when it loses its lower leaves as summer progresses. Flowers with unusual saffron color resemble miniature hibiscus. No surprise here since they share membership in the mallow family (Malvaceae).

Aquilegia canadensis

Red Columbine

8–18 in. tall (2½ ft. in bloom), 10–18 in. wide
flowers red with yellow, 1½–2 in.; February–May
herbaceous perennial; winter evergreen, dormant during summer drought
part shade, part sun, shade | gravel, sand, loam, decomposed leaf litter; calcareous | mesic; well drained
crevices along streamsides, shady limestone cliffs, boulders and canyons | Edwards Plateau

Wildlife: Hosts columbine duskywing butterfly caterpillars. Blooms attract hummingbirds, butterflies, and sphinx moths. Seeds nourish some songbirds. High deer palatability.

Maintenance: Red columbine tolerates similar, yet slightly drier conditions to maidenhair fern. It appreciates constant moisture in the stone crevices of its native habitat. When grown in soil, avoid keeping plants soggy but don't let them dry out. For a tidier appearance, remove spent flower stalks and dead foliage. In ideal conditions it may seed out heavily, but not aggressively. Propagate by seed.

Notes: Nodding blossoms appear in coordination with hummingbird spring migration. Flowers require pollinators with tongues or proboscises able to stretch deep enough to reach into the long nectar-filled spurs. Featured in pots with loose, fast-draining potting mix, red columbine's excellent cool-season foliage holds its own even when out of bloom. Texas harbors a few mostly yellow *Aquilegia* species, which seem more susceptible to leaf miners. *A. canadensis* hybridizes readily with these, forming intermediate sizes with pink and peach flowers.

Asclepias asperula ssp. *capricornu*

Antelope Horns Milkweed

12–18 in. tall, 18–30 in. wide

flowers green, in rounded clusters 3–4 in. across; March–May

herbaceous deciduous perennial

sun, part shade | rocky, sand, loam, clay; caliche, calcareous | dry, mesic; well drained

prairies, savannas, pastures, brushlands, open woodlands | mostly central and western Texas, scattered throughout

Wildlife: Nectar source for bees and a range of butterflies. Larval host for monarch and queen butterflies. Very low deer palatability.

Maintenance: All milkweeds eventually host aphids, but these pests usually pose no major threats and ladybugs help keep them in check. If plants appear stressed by aphids, support the plant with your hand while washing them away with a blast of high-pressure water. Or spray aphids on foliage, including stems and undersides of leaves, with soapy water. Cut back frost- or drought-killed foliage. Propagate by seed.

Notes: One spring, while exploring McKinney Roughs near Bastrop, I came upon a colony of what looked like scoops of pistachio ice cream densely dotting a meadow. Dancing upon these intricate and bizarre flower heads were monarchs and other pollinators feasting on the nectar confection. It was breathtaking! Fragile plants are slow to establish, but tough once they get going. Milky sap may irritate the skin of sensitive people or be toxic if ingested.

Asclepias tuberosa

Butterfly Milkweed

1–2½ ft. tall, 2 ft. wide

flowers orange to yellow, 2–4 in. heads; May–September

herbaceous deciduous perennial

sun, part shade, part sun | sand, loam, clay | dry, mesic; well drained

prairies, open woodlands, canyons, hillsides | central, eastern, and northern Texas

Wildlife: Nectar source for bees, hummingbirds, and a range of butterflies. Larval host for monarch and queen butterflies. Very low deer palatability.

Maintenance: See antelope horns milkweed. Propagate by seed and root cuttings.

Notes: The saturated color of butterfly milkweed in bloom dazzles the eyes like no other! And witnessing so many happy pollinators sipping on nectar is a bonus. In spite of being a milkweed, this plant has no milky sap. Thanks to its taproot, it grows best in sand or loose soils and endures drought well. All parts are toxic in large amounts, so leave the noshing to the monarchs and queens.

Asclepias viridis

Green Milkweed

1–2½ ft. tall and wide

flowers green, 3–5 in. wide inflorescences; April–September

herbaceous, deciduous perennial

sun, part shade | sand, loam, clay | dry, mesic; well drained

prairies, pastures, glades, ditches, disturbed ground | eastern half of Texas

Wildlife: Nectar source for bees and a range of butterflies. Larval host for monarch and queen butterflies. Low deer palatability.

Maintenance: See antelope horns milkweed. Propagate by seed.

Notes: If antelope horns milkweed is out of your range, I'm so sorry! But green milkweed is an admirable alternative. Showy blossom heads prove just as attractive to pollinators, and make nice cut flowers if you are willing to sacrifice them from the garden. As with other milkweeds, sticky sap presumably gums up the mouthparts of herbivorous caterpillars (queens and monarchs), making it cumbersome for them to inflict much damage. Open seed pods (follicles) of any milkweed before they explode to see the beautifully fascinating silk and seed packing job.

Astrolepis sinuata

Wavy-leaf Cloakfern

8–18 in. tall and wide

semiwoody, semievergreen perennial

sun, part shade | rock, gravel, sand, loam | dry; well drained

rocky slopes, outcrops and crevices, cliffs, brushlands, ravines | western Edwards Plateau, Trans-Pecos into southern Texas

Wildlife: Plants offer cover and nesting supplies. Very low deer palatability.

Maintenance: Trim out dead fronds to keep tidy. Protect from prolonged periods of sogginess. Propagate by division and spores.

Notes: Minds are blown with the realization that more xerophytic (drought- and sun-loving) ferns grow in Texas than woodland species. (The Trans-Pecos boasts eighty, sixty-three occur in the Edwards Plateau, and eastern Texas claims sixty-two total species of ferns and allies.) Wavy-leaf cloakfern nestles among boulders, grasses, cacti, and agaves. Pots make good homes, and their mobility allows for easy sheltering from too much rain, particularly in winter. Grayish scales shield leaves from the harsh sun, and roots appreciate cool protection from a rock. Unfortunately, all but the most common native fern species are hard to come by in the trade. Create more demand by asking your local nursery for more ferns.

Baileya multiradiata

Desert Marigold

9–18 in. tall, slightly wider than tall

flowers yellow, 1–1½ in. across; March–November, especially after rain

annual or short-lived herbaceous perennial with winter rosette

sun, part shade | sand, loam, clay, gravel; caliche | dry; well drained

desert flats and grasslands, disturbed areas along roadways | Trans-Pecos

Wildlife: Bees and butterflies take nectar. Plants are reportedly toxic to sheep. Low to moderate deer palatability.

Maintenance: Deadhead plants to increase flowering, or allow seeds to drop for next year's crop. Avoid overwatering or heavy mulch, which increase risk of rot. Propagate by seed.

Notes: Lemony flowers top stems rising above the gray clumps, blooming prolifically over a long season. Short-lived plants reseed readily if not heavily mulched (which they shouldn't be). They grow and bloom rapidly from seed, filling gaps between larger plants, or comingling with penstemons, verbenas, or other wildflowers under dry, hot conditions.

Berlandiera betonicifolia

Texas Greeneyes

2–4 ft. tall, 1–3 ft. wide

flowers yellow with green centers, 1–2 in. wide; April–November

herbaceous perennial with evergreen winter rosette

sun, part shade | sand, loam, clay; caliche | mesic; well drained

sloped meadows, edges of thickets and woodlands, lightly shaded riverbanks | Panhandle, northern and central Texas

Wildlife: Nectar nourishes many pollinators. Seed-eating birds consume seeds. High deer palatability.

Maintenance: Deadhead plants to increase flowering, or allow seeds to drop for next year's crop. Supplemental watering extends blooming. Propagate by seed.

Notes: With its long, sumptuous season of uplifting green and yellow blossoms, Texas greeneyes merit more prominent and extensive use in gardens. Those flirtatiously winking green eyes are particularly sweet fronting switchgrass or sided up next to mealy blue sage. And the butterflies never stop their continuous parade!

Berlandiera lyrata

Chocolate Daisy

1–2 ft. tall, similarly wide
flowers yellow with maroon center, 1½ in. across; April–November (heaviest in spring)
herbaceous perennial with evergreen winter rosette
sun, part shade | sand, loam, clay; rocky limestone, caliche | dry, mesic; well drained
savannas, plains, mesas | northwestern third of Texas

Wildlife: Blossoms attract insect pollinators; seeds nourish birds. Low deer palatability.

Maintenance: Deadhead plants to increase flowering and keep plants tidy, or allow seeds to drop for next year's crop. Too much water produces floppy plants. If you've ever pegged a rose, you can use the same technique on a smaller scale with chocolate daisies: Stretch stems out parallel to the ground and "peg" them with landscape pins or rocks. Flowers and leaves will sprout along the arching stem, offering up more blossoms. Propagate by seed.

Notes: If you're nimble enough to stoop down close to the flowers, the sweet chocolate scent is your reward. While you are down there, turn over a ray flower to observe prominent maroon veins on the undersides. For the not-so-bendy folks, chocolate daisies do well in elevated planters and pots, too.

Callirhoe involucrata

Winecup

6–12 in. tall, 2–3 ft. wide
flowers magenta, 2–2½ in. across; March–June
herbaceous perennial with evergreen winter rosette; summer dormant
sun, part shade, part sun | sand, loam, clay | dry, mesic; well drained
meadows, prairies, open woodlands, rocky hills, scrublands, thickets | throughout Texas

Wildlife: Larval host for gray hairstreak butterflies. Bees and butterflies relish its nectar. Rabbits nibble relentlessly. High deer palatability.

Maintenance: Trim tired rambling stems to the base by summer. Conceal the stump while prolonging the botanical display with companion plantings such as partridge pea. New leaves emerge with fall rain and remain through winter. Ensure well-drained soil, good ventilation, and early morning watering to avoid fungal maladies. Propagate by seed and softwood cuttings.

Notes: Attractive, dark green, deeply lobed leaves dress the ground in winter. During spring, the richly hued winecup will hold your attention hostage. This hardy performer spills delightfully out of a hanging basket, drapes over walls, or rambles along a walkway at the front of a border. It is a visually sweet and tangy addition to a hellstrip (that torrid narrow bit of dirt between the street and sidewalk).

Callirhoe involucrata var. lineariloba (*white*) with C. involucrata var. involucrata (*magenta*)

Calylophus berlandieri ssp. berlandieri

Square-bud Primrose

6–18 in. tall, 15–24 in. wide
flowers lemon yellow, 2 in. across; March–July
deciduous semiwoody perennial
sun, part shade | sand, loam; caliche | dry, mesic; well drained
plains, woodland edges, roadsides | throughout Texas, less in the eastern edge

Wildlife: Nectar source for moths, butterflies, bees. High deer palatability.

Maintenance: Trim to shape in late summer or late winter ahead of the following growing season. Propagate by seed and cuttings.

Notes: Square-bud primrose puts on quite a show with its large, saturated yellow blossoms. You are most likely to find the compact version of square-bud primrose (*Calylophus berlandieri* ssp. *berlandieri*) commercially, but the subspecies (*C. b.* ssp. *pinifolius*) with a more upright stature, reaches up to 3 ft. tall, sometimes with black centers inside the flowers, giving a striking contrast. Either of these make a wonderful contribution to the hot and arid conditions of a rock garden. Why the common name? Find the square flower bud before it opens.

Canna glauca

Water Canna

3–5 ft. tall; colonizing by rhizomes
flowers soft yellow, 2–4 in. long; April–October
herbaceous, deciduous perennial
sun, part shade | sand, loam, clay; mud | shallow water, wet, mesic; poor drainage is fine
around coastal marshes, lakes, and swamps | south Texas coast

Wildlife: Host for Brazilian skipper butterfly larvae (caterpillars known as canna leafrollers). Nectar attracts butterflies. High deer palatability.

Maintenance: Cut plants back after hard frost. Plants colonize by rhizomes, but are easy to control. Perforations in rows perpendicular to the leaf midvein is a sign of squishy, translucent canna leafrollers (a.k.a. skipper butterfly caterpillars). Grasshoppers also damage foliage. Organic treatment options are available for both. Should you decide to treat for caterpillars, be aware that products, including Bt, may affect nontarget butterfly caterpillars, so apply with caution. Propagate by seed and division.

Notes: If you have a pond, moist garden soil, or any container with or without drainage holes, water cannas offer a long season of gentle butter yellow flowers and upright tropical blue-gray foliage. Native cannas are difficult to come by in nurseries. Making requests increases the likelihood of them becoming more available.

Capsicum annuum

Chile Pequin, Chile Petin, Bird Pepper

2–4 ft. tall and wide
flowers white, ½ in.; May–November
fruits red, ¼–¾ in. long; July–November
herbaceous, deciduous perennial; cold tender in northern range, evergreen in the Rio Grande Valley
sun, part shade, part sun, shade | sand, loam, clay; caliche, limestone | mesic; well drained
ledges along rivers, thickets, groves, arroyos, airy understory | central, southern, and eastern Texas

Wildlife: Fruits invite mockingbirds (and parrots and people). Tiny flowers attract small insect pollinators. Moderate deer palatability.

Maintenance: Cut back ahead of new spring growth. Propagate by seed and cuttings.

Notes: In mostly sun, the naturally rounded form is full and dense. In mostly shade, plants reach taller with an open crown. I don't even bother growing jalapeños anymore. The beauty, versatility, and ease of cultivation bumps chile pequins to my top ten. They are water thrifty, perennial in the southern half of Texas, grow in sun or shade, and will adequately burn holes in your tongue in spite of their misleading size. Enjoy them fresh when green or red. Crush them into scrambles, a pot of beans, or anywhere you want some heat. Preserve them in vinegar or dry them for future use. Many cultivars originate from *Capsicum annuum*, including jalapeños, serranos, and bell peppers.

Chamaecrista fasciculata

Partridge Pea

1–3 ft. tall, 1–2 ft. wide
flowers yellow, 1 in. across; June–October
herbaceous warm-season annual
sun, part shade | gravel, sand, loam, clay | dry, mesic; well drained
disturbed areas, open woodlands, prairies, fields, riverbanks | southeastern half of Texas, scattered elsewhere

Wildlife: Provides caterpillar food for sleepy orange and orange sulphur butterflies. Extrafloral (outside of the flower) nectaries arising in glands at leaf bases attract ants and other insects seeking nectar, and are the sole source of nectar from this plant. Flowers entice bees with fertile and sterile "food" pollen. Gallinaceous birds consume seeds. Provides cover. Moderate to high deer palatability.

Maintenance: Allow seeds to ripen and fall before removing spent plants. Propagate by seed.

Notes: Airy, warm-season partridge pea is exceedingly useful for concealing dormant cool-season species such as winecup and square-bud primrose during their offseason while allowing light and airflow underneath, preventing suffocation. Leaves fold together at night, reopening each day. Roots fix nitrogen, thus improving the soil for future vegetation.

Chrysactinia mexicana

Damianita

1 ft. tall, 1–2 ft. wide

flowers yellow, ½–⅔ in. across; April–May, occasionally after fall rain

evergreen woody perennial

sun, part shade | gravel, sand, loam, clay; caliche, limestone | dry; well drained

rocky outcrops, desert plains and mountains | Edwards Plateau, Trans-Pecos

Wildlife: Goldfinches and other seed-eating birds enjoy ripe seeds. Insect pollinators take nectar from flowers. Very low deer palatability.

Maintenance: Work with the gnarly natural shape of mature specimens (they make good candidates for bonsai), or remove thick, woody stems and shape what remains in mid-February. Light shearing after flowering keeps plants compact and encourages more blossoms, but waiting a few weeks (but before the wind carries them off like dandelions) allows seeds to ripen for birds to enjoy. You decide. Propagate by seed and softwood cuttings.

Notes: If the flowers are fragrant, it is hard to tell next to the powerfully aromatic foliage. I find the scent softens from sharp (yet pleasant) up close to sweet at a distance. The compact-sized billowing mounds of this subshrub nicely fill small spaces, and acceptance of intense heat, sun, and drought earns it a place in a xeric rock garden.

Conoclinium greggii

Gregg's Mistflower, Palm-leaf Mistflower

1–2 ft. tall; colonizing by rhizomes
flowers lavender-blue, rarely white, in 2–3 in. clusters; April–November
herbaceous, deciduous perennial
sun, part shade | gravel, sand, loam, clay; calcareous | dry, mesic; well drained
streambeds, plains | southern and western regions of Texas

Wildlife: Hosts Rawson's metalmark butterfly caterpillar. Various insect pollinators delight in nectar throughout summer, particularly queen butterflies, whose numbers peak in fall. Male queens glom onto nonblooming plants, sequestering pheromone-building compounds from the leaves through their feet— stranger than fiction! Low deer palatability.

Maintenance: Keep overrunning rhizomes in check. To counter legginess, give more sun and pull back on moisture. If you cut plants back to encourage fuller growth, consider trimming only part of the stand, leaving the rest to support pollinators. Once the first section begins reblooming, shear back the remaining section. Propagate by seed, division, and cuttings.

Notes: Easy cultivation and reliable and continuous all-summer blooming earn Gregg's mistflower a favored reputation. Use as filler between larger plants or enjoy them in containers. The related blue mist-flower (*Conoclinium coelestinum*) prefers more shade and moisture—sometimes colonizing wet stream banks—but blooms only for a month or so in fall.

Cooperia pedunculata

Rain Lily

6–12 in. tall and wide

flowers white, pink, 2 in. across, fragrant; April–June after rains

herbaceous, deciduous perennial

sun, part shade | sand, loam, clay; caliche, limestone | dry, mesic; well drained

prairies, shortgrass meadows and savannas, open woodlands | southern two-thirds of Texas

Wildlife: Flowers entice insect pollinators. Low deer palatability.

Maintenance: Avoid crowding from larger neighbors. Propagate by seed and bulb offsets.

Notes: Like ethereal angels on the prairie, ephemeral rain lily flowers epitomize purity and are most impactful en masse. Grasslike strappy leaves hide in lawns or among other low-growing plants such as four-nerve daisy or prairie verbena. Then, as perhaps a forgotten surprise, the milky white trumpets burst out of seemingly nowhere after rain, lasting only a couple of days before withering to translucent pink. Flowers with such a fleeting nature delightfully change a garden composition, even if temporarily. The nearly identical *Cooperia drummondii* turns up in summer and into fall and bloom seasons may overlap.

Coreopsis tinctoria

Goldenwave, Plains Coreopsis

1–3 ft. tall, similarly wide

flowers yellow and maroon with brown, sometimes all one color, 1 in.; May–August

herbaceous annual with winter rosette

sun, part shade | sand, loam, clay | mesic; tolerates poor drainage

grasslands, roadsides, pond banks | throughout Texas

Wildlife: Nectar supports bees, butterflies, and other insect pollinators. Birds appreciate the nutritious seeds. Moderate to low deer palatability.

Maintenance: To ensure next year's display, allow seeds to mature completely and drop before cutting or mowing. Propagate by seed.

Notes: Goldenwave, also called calliopsis and tickseed, commonly fills roadsides with copious blossoms on upright, branching plants. Widely cultivated throughout the United States, most folks plant them in wildflower meadows, but they fit nicely in regular garden settings, too. Closely related *Coreopsis basalis* grows in similar conditions, but its range covers less of the state, sticking to the southeastern half.

Cucurbita foetidissima

Buffalo Gourd

½–1½ ft. tall, trailing stems 10–20 ft. long

flowers orange-yellow, 3–4 in. long and wide; May–September

fruits green and yellow striped, round, 3–4 in. across; toxic when ripe

herbaceous, deciduous perennial

sun, part sun | gravel, sand, loam, clay; caliche, calcareous | dry, mesic; well drained

open plains, savannas, roadsides, dry streambeds, disturbed sites | central and western Texas, Panhandle

Wildlife: Flowers appeal to pollinators. Small mammals nibble fruits. Low deer palatability.

Maintenance: Cut stems to base after hard freeze. Massive mature tubers are difficult to remove. Trim away branches rambling into unwanted areas. Propagate by seed.

Notes: If you are looking for something heat and drought tolerant with an aesthetic flair, buffalo gourd might be your bag—if you can tolerate its slightly malodorous foliage, which only offends when wet or crushed. Its strongest feature lies in the large, course, and bright silvery leaves that tend to line up into an organized pattern, contrasting perfectly with most other plants if they don't become smothered by it. Flowers provide an extra bonus. The world would be more interesting if buffalo gourd increasingly adorned our gardens!

Dalea frutescens

Black Dalea

1–3 ft. tall, 3–4 ft. wide

flowers purple-magenta, tiny, in ¾ in. clusters; primarily September–October

deciduous semiwoody perennial

sun, part shade | sand, loam, clay; caliche, limestone | dry; well drained

scrubby limestone hills, washes, and uplands | central, north-central, and western Texas

Wildlife: Deer and rabbits browse this plant, as do caterpillars of Reakirt's blue and several other blue and sulphur butterfly species. Flowers provide outstanding fodder for bees. High deer palatability.

Maintenance: Excess moisture or shade causes weak and leggy growth. Trim plants to shape as needed. Protect from freezes below 15°F. Propagate by seed, layering, and cuttings.

Notes: Tiny, fine leaflets and mounding form of black dalea contrast with bolder shapes of prickly pears and fountain forms of grasses. Though pretty, flowers are not showy until fall, when the whole plant exudes purple. Perhaps even more engaging are the tiny blue butterflies flashing their cerulean upperwings when startled or laying eggs. Its excellence as a low-maintenance filler or frothy massed planting earns it its garden worthiness. Try dropping one into a rustic or ornamented pot.

Dalea greggii

Gregg's Dalea

1 ft. tall; spreading indeterminately by self-layering

flowers purple, in ½ in. clusters; March–November

semiwoody perennial; evergreen in south, deciduous in north

sun, part shade | sand, loam, gravel; limestone, granite | dry; well drained

rocky, limestone hills | Trans-Pecos

Wildlife: Caterpillars of Reakirt's blue and several other blue and sulphur butterfly species feed on the leaves while flowers provide excellent forage for bees. Low to moderate deer palatability.

Maintenance: While virtually maintenance free once established, supplemental watering during drought prompts lusher foliage. Hold off watering during winter to reduce rot. Trim away winter damage in early spring in colder areas, and prune off wandering stems as desired. Propagate by layering and cuttings.

Notes: Similar to those of its close relative black dalea, the flowers of Gregg's dalea might underwhelm. But the low silver mounds are a knockout! Trailing stems accent a planter or make a suitable soil-stabilizing groundcover. Sprightly bees and butterflies are great fun to watch.

Datura wrightii

Jimsonweed, Datura

3–4 ft. tall, 6 ft. or larger spread

flowers white, occasionally lavender tinged, 6–9 in. long, 4–6 in. across, perfumed; May–November

herbaceous, deciduous perennial

sun, part shade | sand, loam, clay; deep soils preferred | dry, mesic; well drained

washes, desert flats, roadsides, floodplains, bottomlands | scattered throughout Texas

Wildlife: Larval host for multiple sphinx moths, its primary pollinators, but bees also visit flowers, knocking impatiently on the door just before they unfurl. Low deer palatability.

Maintenance: Monitor remarkably fast growth and prune to prevent it from overtaking its neighbors. Cut back to the base after hard freeze. Wear long sleeves, pants, and gloves when working with this plant. Extensive exposure to all parts may produce skin rashes, nausea, hallucination, and other more serious conditions. Ingesting may be lethal in large doses. Propagate by seed and root division.

Notes: Night-blooming plants display prolific, large, trumpet-shaped fragrant flowers that last into the next morning. If that's not stunning enough, try watching a night-flying sphinx moth with its nearly foot-long proboscis extended to take nectar. Plants grow extremely fast and easily from small transplants or seed. They hog real estate in the summer garden, leaving gaps in winter to be filled with giant spiderwort, wild onions, or other cool-season species. Attractive, grayish foliage smells of stale peanut butter, but keep children and pets from ingesting or overexposure to skin due to the toxins.

Echinacea purpurea

Purple Coneflower

1–3 ft. tall, 1–2 ft. wide

flowers cerise, pink, with orange heads 2–4 in. across; April–September

herbaceous, deciduous perennial, sometimes with evergreen winter rosette

sun, part shade | sand, loam, clay | mesic, dry; well drained

rocky open woodlands, thickets, prairies | far northeast part of Texas

Wildlife: Nectar source for butterflies, bees, and hummingbirds. Seeds sustain finches and other seed-eating birds. High to moderate deer palatability.

Maintenance: Deadhead spent flowers to encourage continuing blooming, or leave for seasonal interest or for wildlife fodder. Propagate by seed and division.

Notes: Purple coneflower is already well documented in horticultural literature, but it's such a garden overachiever that I couldn't leave it out! Pretty enough on its own, it's even prettier topped with a red admiral or fat bumblebee. Flamboyant flowers last seemingly forever (up to ten days with no sign of fading, even in a vase). Plants colonize abundantly by seed, countering any hesitation you might have to harvest purple coneflower for medicinal use (tinctures of *Echinacea purpurea* and *E. anqustifolia* roots, flowers, and seeds purportedly boost immunity). Breeders have conjured cultivars with various plant and petal forms, and colors including white, pink, orange, and yellow.

Engelmannia peristenia

Engelmann Daisy

1½–3 ft. tall, 1–2 ft. wide

flowers yellow, 1–1½ in. across; March–July and again October–November

herbaceous perennial with evergreen rosette

sun, part shade, part sun | sand, loam, clay; caliche, limestone | dry, mesic; well drained

open, calcareous fields, grasslands, roadsides | throughout Texas except Pineywoods

Wildlife: Favored by painted buntings and other seed-eating birds. Entices butterfly and bee pollinators. Moderate deer palatability.

Maintenance: Cut spent stems back beginning in June after flowers fade or seeds ripen, and remove remaining stems in winter to keep neat. Drought-tolerant plants bloom more with added water during dry spells. Propagate by seed and division.

Notes: Engelmann daisy's upright form during the growing season looks right at home with mealy blue sage, winecup, and *Echinacea* spp. in wildflower meadows and gardens. Deeply lobed winter leaves with white midveins hold interest in winter. Robust taproots support drought resistance.

Erigeron modestus

Prairie Fleabane

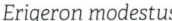

6–12 in. tall and wide

flowers white with yellow centers, ¾ in. heads; February–November

herbaceous, short-lived perennial with winter rosette

sun, part shade, part sun | gravel, sand, loam, clay; calcareous | dry, mesic; well drained

open uplands, rocky outcrops, shortgrass meadows | western, central, and north-central Texas

Wildlife: Bees, beetles, flies, and small butterflies gather pollen and nectar. Moderate deer palatability.

Maintenance: Short-lived plants reseed readily. Transplant small seedlings to fill in gaps. As desired, cut back wiry stems if new growth appears at the base. Propagate by seed.

Notes: Unopened flower heads blush pink on petal undersides and nod modestly, hence the species name, *modestus*. Strongest flowering occurs in spring and fall, with summer blossoms prompted by rain. Plant for easy color in pots, as filler between other plants, or in a "short garden" with winecup, prairie verbena, sneezeweed, bushy skullcap, black dalea, four-nerve daisy, and scarlet pea.

Euphorbia cyathophora

Wild Poinsettia

1½–3 ft. tall, similarly wide

flowers insignificantly tiny, subtended by flashy red-orange blotched bracts; May–November

herbaceous, warm-season annual

sun, part shade, part sun | sand, loam, clay loam | mesic, dry; well drained

stream banks, fields, roadsides, open and disturbed sites | Trans-Pecos, central and northeastern Texas

Wildlife: Beetles, bees, flies, and other small insects visit the minute flowers. Moderate to high deer palatability.

Maintenance: Allow seeds to drop, or collect by hand and plant elsewhere for the following year's crop. Optionally, remove frost-killed plants in winter for a well-groomed garden. Propagate by seed.

Notes: What most viewers assume to be flowers are technically colorful modified leaves called bracts. These inspire the alternate moniker of fire on the mountain. Leaf outlines vary from narrowly linear to wide and fiddle shaped, and plants make excellent fillers between larger bodies such as Lindheimer muhly, prickly pears, and fragrant sumac. All parts of this self-sowing annual exude milky sap that can irritate sensitive skin. Wearing sleeves and gloves, and washing after handling is recommended.

Gaillardia pulchella

Firewheel, Blanketflower

1–2 ft. tall and wide

flowers combinations of red, orange, and yellow, 1–2 in. heads; April–July

herbaceous annual with winter rosette

sun, part shade | sand, loam, clay | dry, mesic; well drained

savannas, prairies, plains, roadsides, open areas | throughout Texas

Wildlife: Flowers draw bees and butterflies. Low to moderate deer palatability.

Maintenance: Collect seeds or allow them to drop for the following year. Plants grow quickly and seeds may be planted from fall to as late as March for a later bloom. Optionally, remove spent plants at the end of the season, usually July or August. Most folks don't bother, but deadheading prolongs flowering. Propagate by seed.

Notes: It's nearly impossible to be sad when viewing firewheel. Bring some of that joy indoors; they last well in a vase. Observe the massive spectacle of reds and yellows on roadsides, or directly sow these easy-to-grow wildflowers into your garden. Color patterns vary, and breeders take advantage of this to create fancy cultivars.

Glandularia bipinnatifida

Prairie Verbena

4–12 in. tall; spreading 1–2 ft.

flowers lavender, purple, pink, 1–2 in. clusters; March–October

herbaceous annual to short-lived perennial, usually with evergreen winter rosettes

sun, part shade, part sun | sand, loam, clay; caliche, limestone | dry, mesic; well drained

open grassy areas, disturbed sites | throughout Texas except Pineywoods

Wildlife: Nectar provides excellent forage for butterflies and bees. Hummingbirds also take sips. Very low deer palatability.

Maintenance: Occasionally cut back leggy stems as needed. Spread ripe seeds to replenish the crop. Propagate by seed, cuttings, and layering.

Notes: Prairie verbenas reward gardeners with their long season of colorful flower clusters adorned with dancing butterflies. Even though plants typically live only one season, they readily reseed, grow, and bloom quickly. Tuck them into potted arrangements, or plant them as a low filler in a bed or wildflower planting.

Helenium amarum

Sneezeweed

6–12 in. tall and wide
flowers yellow, 1 in. heads; April–November
herbaceous, warm-season annual
sun, part shade | sand, loam, clay | dry, mesic; well drained
low grasslands, roadsides, rocky outcroppings, woodland edges, disturbed sites | throughout Texas

Wildlife: Flowers draw bees and butterflies. Plants host butterfly larvae including dainty sulphur. Very low deer palatability.

Maintenance: Remove spent plants in fall as desired. Allow seeds to drop for the next year's display. Propagate by seed.

Notes: Heat-loving sneezeweed delivers strong color in perfectly formed bouquets all summer. Intersperse it among a mix of wildflowers, or pair it with early spring bloomers like Texas yellowstar and large buttercup for a useful timesharing combination. Insects, not wind, transfer the heavy pollen, so *sneezeweed* is misleadingly bad advertising. Plants contain toxins that discourage browsing and produce bitter honey and milk from foraging bees and cows, hence the alternate name of bitterweed. The genus *Helenium* is rumored to be named after Helen of Troy.

Helianthus annuus

Common Sunflower

4–8 ft. tall, 3–5 ft. broad
flowers yellow, 2–4 in. heads; May–November
herbaceous, summer annual
sun | sand, loam, clay | dry, mesic
disturbed areas | throughout Texas

Wildlife: Open-branched architecture offers cover for various wildlife. Flowers attract bees, butterflies, and an occasional hummingbird. Fat-rich seeds nourish finches, buntings, and other birds. Butterfly species including bordered patch, painted lady, and several checkerspots eat *Helianthus* as caterpillars. Low to moderate deer palatability.

Maintenance: Towering plants may list after wet weather, requiring staking. Let spent plants stand in autumn to feed seed-eating birds, or remove them by the stalk and prop upright in a less visible, yet bird-accessible location. Propagate by seed.

Notes: Common sunflower is parent to the countless cultivars extensively developed as ornamentals with enormous, variously colored heads, or as food crops with plump seeds. But the wild form is far from humble, growing tall in remarkably fast order. Flowers in a vase brighten an entire room (but will drop pollen on your table). Observe the mesmerizing Fibonacci spirals in the flower heads. Its sibling silverleaf sunflower (*Helianthus argophyllus*) from coastal Texas, grows similarly but flaunts silky haired, frosty white leaves.

Helianthus maximiliani

Maximilian Sunflower

4–8 ft. tall; clump spreading indefinitely by rhizomes

flowers yellow, 3–4 in. heads; August–November

herbaceous, deciduous perennial

sun, part shade | sand, loam, prefers clay | dry, mesic

rich prairies and grasslands | throughout Texas except south, west, and Pineywoods

Wildlife: Same as for common sunflower except plants are unbranching. Moderate deer palatability.

Maintenance: Seedlings and rhizomes pull or dig up reasonably easily, keep in check as needed. Wet weather or excess irrigation leads to taller stalks needing staking. Or cut plants to the ground before summer encroaches, allowing them to bloom as normal later in the season. This keeps plants shorter while minimizing the "bare legs" that form as old leaves slough away from older stems. Propagate by seed, softwood cuttings, and division.

Notes: Spectacular flower heads stack up along unbranched stems like multiple lemony sorbet scoops balanced on a cone. Thanks to Maximilian sunflowers' upright habit and ever-increasing rhizomatous base, large landscapes accommodate it best. Against a wall or fence in narrow locations also works. Plant with Lindheimer muhly, switchgrass, or other robust plants with ground-sweeping foliage covering the leafless stalk bases.

Hibiscus laevis

Halberdleaf Hibiscus

6 ft. tall, 5 ft. across

flowers white or blushed pink, crimson throat, 4 in. across; May–November

deciduous semiwoody perennial

sun, part shade | sand, loam, clay; mud | mesic, wet; happy with slow drainage

marshes, edges of water bodies | eastern third of Texas

Wildlife: Butterflies, bees, and hummingbirds come to flowers. High deer palatability.

Maintenance: Cut plants to 4 to 6 in. above ground before new spring growth emerges. Optionally, trim or tip branches every so often to keep plants compact. Propagate by seed and cuttings.

Notes: Halberdleaf hibiscus, as well as its other native wetland *Hibiscus* siblings, grow well aside narrow-leaf water primrose and Jamaica sawgrass flanking a pond (a fitting partner as *jamaica* is Spanish for "hibiscus"), or in irrigated garden soils. They'll provide highly ornamental, dramatic flowering all summer. Following leaf drop after cold weather, dried seed pods ornament the rounded shrubs, provided you leave stems standing through winter.

Hibiscus martianus

Heartleaf Hibiscus, Tulipán del Monte

1–2 ft. tall and wide

flowers blood red, 2 in. across; May–October, especially after rain, year-round in frost-free areas

deciduous semiwoody short-lived perennial; cold tender north of Austin

part shade, part sun, sun | sand, loam; caliche | dry; well drained

canyons, talus slopes, gravelly hillsides, chaparral | Rio Grande Plains from Val Verde to Corpus Christi

Wildlife: Attracts butterflies, bumblebees, and hummingbirds. Moderate to high deer palatability.

Maintenance: Protect from deep cold. Will rot and mildew in clay soils, poor ventilation, or with too much moisture. Clip out dead stems after winter and prune to shape as needed. Propagate by seed.

Notes: When in bloom, heartleaf hibiscus gets everyone's gaze! It is compatible and lovely with feathergrass, even though their native ranges don't overlap. It's an excellent potted plant, particularly where it is too cold to survive unprotected and can be sheltered indoors or for those of us who have clay-based soils. The Spanish common name means "tulip of the mountain."

Hymenocallis liriosme

Spiderlily

1–3 ft. tall and wide

flowers white, 4–6 in. across, fragrant; April–September

deciduous herbaceous perennial

part shade, part sun, sun | sand, loam, clay | wet, mesic; mature plants tolerate poor drainage (young plants may rot)

floodplains, bottomlands, ditches, marshes, stream banks, wet grass-lands | Pineywoods and along the coast

Wildlife: Insect pollinators, including night-flying sphinx moths, visit flowers. Toxicity makes it browse and pest resistant. Low deer palatability.

Maintenance: Cut back spent flower stalks as you wish and frozen winter foliage before sour vegetation gets funky. Keep plants from drying out. Propagate by bulb division and seed.

Notes: Strappy, dark green, glossy leaves lend a tropical flavor to a moist garden bed, rain garden, pot with no drain-age, or at a downspout or pond edge. Plants play nicely with water canna, obedient plants, Virginia blue flag, and cardinal flower. They often form stunning and extensive colonies in wet areas, with their bulbous roots stabilizing water banks from erosion. Blossoms are a little bit weird and very elegant. Spiderlily has only six "legs" whereas true spiders have eight.

Ipomopsis rubra

Standing Cypress

2–5 ft. tall, 1–2 ft. wide

flowers red, orange, rarely yellow, 1 in., on long spires; May–August

herbaceous annual to biennial with evergreen rosette in first winter

sun, part shade | gravel, sand, loam, clay | dry, mesic; well drained

open grasslands, woodland edges | eastern, northeastern, and central Texas

Wildlife: Nectar nourishes hummingbirds, large butterflies, and occasionally bees. Moderate deer palatability.

Maintenance: Allow seeds to fully ripen and fall before removing spent plants. Propagate by seed.

Notes: Standing cypress is loved for its striking flower color, distinctive threadlike foliage, strong vertical form with unbranched stems, and easy cultivation. Allow enough space for seedlings to form colonies at least 20 square ft. for a small garden, and more for larger spaces. Its hot colors stand out among soft grasses like switchgrass and bluestems. Or surround it with mealy blue sage and partridge pea to hit the primary colors. For landscapes in the Trans-Pecos, plant scarlet gilia (*Ipomopsis aggregata*).

Iris virginica

Virginia Blue Flag

1½–3 ft. tall, half as wide

flowers purple, violet, rarely white, 3–5 in. wide; March–June

herbaceous perennial; evergreen in mild winters, summer dormant in dry weather

sun, part shade, part sun | sand, loam, clay; mud | wet, mesic; fine with slow drainage

swamps, ditches, wet meadows, marshes, stream edges, lake and pond shores | Big Thicket, Pineywoods

Wildlife: Hummingbirds, bees, and other pollinators visit flowers. Low deer palatability.

Maintenance: Grow in moist or wet soil. Plants like wet feet and dry ankles. Cut off dead or yellowing leaves and flower stalks as desired. Propagate by rhizome division and seed.

Notes: Texas claims a handful of lovely *Iris* species, all with similar growing conditions that would ornament a pond edge or container. As beautiful as it is, please avoid cultivating the invasive yellow iris (*I. pseudacorus*) with diagnostic pink-fleshed rhizomes. Irises contain toxins that repel herbivores such as deer. All parts, especially rhizomes, should be handled with caution due to their toxicity.

Kosteletzkya virginica

Saltmarsh Mallow

4–6 ft. tall, 3–4 ft. broad

flowers light pink with yellow stamen column, 2–3 in. across; June–October

deciduous semiwoody short-lived (approximately 5 years) perennial

sun, part shade | prefers sand, tolerates clay; moderately salt tolerant | wet, mesic

brackish marshes, swamps, shallow standing water, wetland margins | coastal plains

Wildlife: Flowers frequented by bees, butterflies, and hummingbirds. Moderate deer palatability.

Maintenance: Remove frost-damaged tissue before new growth sprouts in spring. Occasionally trim wayward branches from pathways or to keep them from smothering other plants nearby. Plants prefer wet feet and dry ankles. Easily grown from seed to replace senescent plants. Propagate by seed and softwood cuttings.

Notes: Saltmarsh mallow and others in the mallow family (Malvaceae) generally thrive in warm and hot weather, so enjoy the soothing, soft pink blossoms that adorn the open-branched plants when many other flowers take their summer vacation. Plant alongside lizard tail and pickerelweed in moist soil skirting a pond for fast growth and prolific flowers. Many taxonomists recognize the synonym *Kosteletzkya pentacarpos.*

Lantana achyranthifolia

Desert Lantana

1–3 ft. tall, 3–4 ft. wide

flowers lavender, pink, white, violet, in 1 in. clusters; March–November

deciduous semiwoody perennial

sun, part sun | sand, loam, clay; calcareous | dry, mesic; well drained

rocky limestone hills, scrublands, arroyos, roadsides | southern and western Texas

Wildlife: Hummingbirds, butterflies, and other insect pollinators eagerly imbibe nectar. Low deer palatability.

Maintenance: Cut back to stumps after hard freeze for compact growth come spring, then trim plants to shape throughout the growing season as desired. Propagate by seed, semi-hardwood cuttings, layering, and division.

Notes: Currently a missed opportunity, this species is barely in the trade. But heat tolerance, prolific blooming, and carefree cultivation make it a promising addition to gardens throughout Texas, particularly as an alternative to the similar non-native, and sometimes invasive, purple trailing lantana (*Lantana montevidensis*). Plant form and multicolored flowers pair handsomely with velvet mallow, desert marigold, doctorbush, or autumn sage. An alternative name, Mexican marjoram, nods to its culinary usage.

Lantana urticoides

Texas Lantana

3–5 ft. tall, similarly wide

flowers red-orange, gold, small, in 1–2 in. clusters; April–frost

deciduous woody perennial

sun, part sun | sand, loam, clay; caliche | dry, mesic; well drained

fields, thickets, rich sandy woodlands, scrub, gravelly hills, flats, chaparral, roadsides | southeastern two-thirds of Texas

Wildlife: Hummingbirds, butterflies, and other insect pollinators swarm flowers for nectar. Low deer palatability.

Maintenance: Shear lightly after each flowering cycle to encourage blooming and bushy growth. Cut plants to 6 in. stumps in winter to make room for new spring foliage. Monitor for spider mites in summer and protect from extreme cold north of its native range. Propagate by seed, softwood or semi-hardwood cuttings, layering, and division.

Notes: This plant is found in gardens everywhere for good reason: It's reliable, durable, and deer don't like it! Since heat-loving Texas lantana sprouts hesitantly in spring, underplanting with cool-season pink evening primrose or baby blue-eyes supplies green through winter and early spring flowers. These fade away with encroaching hot weather just as Texas lantana gets going again. Be aware of sharp prickles on stems of mature plants; toxic fruits resemble blackberries, so keep children away.

Liatris punctata

Gayfeather, Liatris

1–3 ft. in height, 1–1½ ft. apart

flowers purple, lavender, 4–9 in. spikes; August–October

deciduous herbaceous perennial

sun | gravel, sand, loam, clay; caliche, calcareous | dry, mesic; excellent drainage needed

open fields, prairies, savannas, uplands | throughout most of Texas

Wildlife: Flowers entice bees and butterflies, especially swallowtails. Moderate deer palatability.

Maintenance: Excess moisture, heavy gumbo clay, or shade leads to sprawling, almost vinelike stems and, in worst cases, rotting corms. Trim winter-dead stems to the ground once the fluffy seeds leave stems bare. Level of exposure to wind determines how early stalks shatter. Propagate by seed and corm division.

Notes: In punishingly hot, nonirrigated locations such as a hellstrip, branches grow attractively stiff and upright with slender wands of flowers in late summer. Cut for fresh or dried flower arrangements combined with prairie goldenrod, which blooms around the same time and delivers complementary color. Seeds on bottlebrush-like stalks remain attached, offering interest through winter. Come spring, lush, dark green, needlelike basal growth inspires constant comment. Its sibling *Liatris pycnostachya* grows in acidic soils. According to the USDA, some plants live thirty-five years or more.

Lindheimera texana

Texas Yellowstar, Lindheimer Daisy

6–24 in. tall, 1–2 ft. wide

flowers yellow, 1–1¼ in. heads; March–May

herbaceous annual with winter rosette

sun, part shade | sand, loam, clay; limestone | dry, mesic; well drained

grasslands, roadsides, woodland edges | central two-thirds of Texas

Wildlife: Nectar source for pollinating insects. Seeds attract birds. Moderate to low deer palatability.

Maintenance: Pull out plants after ripe seeds drop. Propagate by seed.

Notes: Here is a satisfyingly reliable, fast-growing cool-season wildflower to plant with warm-season scarlet sage or devil's claw. Cute young plants begin to bloom at a mere couple inches tall, branching widely as they age and delivering copious golden five-pointed stars. Ferdinand Lindheimer collected many hundreds of plant specimens and identified hundreds of species, dozens tagged with his name (including this entire genus), earning him the honorific Father of Texas Botany.

Lobelia cardinalis

Cardinal Flower

1–4 ft. tall, 6–24 in. across

Flowers scarlet, 2 in., on 8 in. spike; May–November

herbaceous short-lived perennial with or without winter rosette

sun, part shade, shade | sand, loam, clay; humus rich | moist, mesic; poor drainage is fine

swamps, ravines, swales, wetland margins, wet or moist grasslands and woodlands | throughout Texas except southern tip

Wildlife: Hummingbirds perform primary pollination services, but large butterflies with proboscises long enough to reach deep nectar also visit flowers. Bumblebees are known to "rob" nectar by chewing a hole at the flower base to take nectar from the side without transferring pollen for the plant, thus breaking the handshake deal. High deer palatability.

Maintenance: Ensure adequate moisture and allow plants to reseed to replenish the population. Cut back frozen stalks as desired. Propagate by seed and layering.

Notes: These upright, unbranched stalks lift the brilliant crimson flowers high to facilitate hummingbird visits. The best floral displays develop with autumn as plants have amassed some size, and timing tracks the fall hummingbird migration.

Ludwigia octovalvis

Narrow-leaf Water Primrose

1–5 ft. tall and wide

flowers soft yellow, 1–1½ in. wide; June–November

deciduous herbaceous perennial

sun, part shade, part sun | gravel, sand, loam, clay; mud | wet, mesic; slow drainage is ideal

wetland margins, swamps, ditches | southeastern two-thirds of Texas

Wildlife: Flowers offer nectar and pollen to bees, moths, and butterflies. Caterpillar host for the banded sphinx moth (*Eumorpha fasciatus*); both adult and larvae are impressive in size and colors. Moderate deer palatability.

Maintenance: Prune back frost-killed foliage, and give a light trim periodically to keep plants from getting too rambunctious. It's a prolific seeder, so you may need to thin out a few new recruits. Propagate by seed.

Notes: Unknown to most folks, narrow-leaf water primroses and several other water primroses in the genus *Ludwigia* provide steady summer color with minimal meddling from the gardener. Yellow blossoms of most species tend toward gold or lemon colored, so the soft buttery tones of the water primroses provide a welcomed opportunity to harmonize with other pastels around the pond such as the light pink saltmarsh mallow and the blue-hued pickerelweed.

Lupinus texensis

Bluebonnet

12–18 in. high, 18 in. wide

flowers deep blue, occasionally pink, white, or pale blue, with white tips, 2–4 in. spikes, fragrant; March–May

herbaceous annual with winter rosette

sun, part shade | sand, loam, clay; caliche, limestone | dry, mesic

open grasslands and roadsides | throughout Texas except Panhandle and far west

Wildlife: Bees eagerly collect pollen. Caterpillars of gray hairstreak and eastern tailed-blue butterflies eat plants, as do the less welcomed and more common genista broom moth larvae. Moderate to low deer palatability.

Maintenance: Mow or remove spent plants only after seed pods have matured to tan, allowing them to drop for next year's crop. Propagate by seed.

Notes: Why do Texans lose their minds over bluebonnets every spring?! Well, *Lupinus texensis* and the other five Texas *Lupinus* species combined are recognized as our official state flower, reminding us of how special we are to live here. Or maybe it results from the great work by Lady Bird Johnson to enrich our roadsides and landscapes with wildflowers. Else, could it be that only a rare flower can pull off such a true blue? And in such vast swaths to boot! Don't overlook the handsome palmate leaves. One of the loveliest sights I've ever seen is a bead of water like a crystal ball cupped in the palm of each leaf after heavy dew.

Malvaviscus arboreus var. *drummondii*

Turk's Cap, Wax Mallow

3–5 ft. tall and wide

flowers red, 1–2 in. long; May–November

fruits red, ½ in. diameter; June–November

deciduous semiwoody perennial

part sun, part shade, shade, sun | sand, loam, clay; limestone | dry, mesic; well drained

open woodlands, woodland edges, wooded slopes, streamsides | eastern half of Texas

Wildlife: Hummingbirds, large butterflies (with proboscises long enough to reach deep into flowers), bumblebees, and other insects appreciate its nectar. Fruits appeal to birds and mammals. Moderate deer palatability.

Maintenance: Snip off uneven tips for a tidier appearance. Cut back to a few inches after hard freeze (it may stay evergreen in the southern part of Texas). Propagate by seed, softwood cuttings, root division, and layering.

Notes: With a long season of continuous, reliable blooming, Turk's cap is a staple for shaded gardens. Copy nature by timesharing it with giant spiderwort for all-season interest. The showy but shy hibiscus-like flowers appear to never fully open. The bland-tasting edible flowers and fruits are more rewarding as colorful garnishes than for flavor.

Marshallia caespitosa

Barbara's Buttons

6–18 in. tall, two-thirds as wide
flowers white, pale pink, 1½ in. heads, fragrant; April–May
herbaceous perennial with winter rosette
sun, part shade | sand, loam, clay; caliche | dry; well drained
rocky hillsides, road cuts, open short grasslands | east, northeastern, and central Texas

Wildlife: Flower heads attract small butterflies and bees. Rabbits browse leaves. Moderate deer palatability.

Maintenance: If faded flower stalks aren't to your liking, cut them back after seed falls or earlier if you don't need the seeds. Propagate by seed and root division.

Notes: Puffballs of flowers hovering above upright unbranched stems are sure to turn the corners of your mouth into a smile. These polite garden plants take easily to cultivation, reseeding readily, but not too aggressively. Their small stature fits between brick or rock, or at the front of a border. Fold them in with small- or medium-sized warm-season grasses like sideoats grama, windmillgrass, or little bluestem for a nice floral display before the grasses gain in size. Cut a bouquet to continue enjoyment indoors.

Melampodium leucanthum

Blackfoot Daisy

6–12 in. tall, 10–20 in. wide
flowers white with yellow centers, lightly scented, 1 in. across; March–November
evergreen to deciduous semiwoody perennial
sun, part shade | gravel, sand; caliche, limestone; alkaline | dry; well drained
short grasslands, bare rocky soils and slopes | Trans-Pecos, Panhandle, Edwards Plateau

Wildlife: Bees, butterflies, and other insects are drawn to the flowers. Low deer palatability.

Maintenance: The biggest complaint about blackfoot daisy is its propensity to rot during wet weather, particularly in summer. Don't be fooled into giving wilting plants more water, as wilting also indicates rotting and you'll make the problem worse. Use mineral mulches to reduce humidity and moisture at plant bases. Propagate by seed and cuttings.

Notes: Rounded mounds smothered in white frothy flowers bring a cool illusion of snow drifts in warm weather. Flowering is strongest in spring and fall, with sparse flickers in summer. Plants grow lush and floriferous in typically rich and irrigated gardens, but live shorter lives than those in leaner terrain. Blackfoot daisy works well in a rock garden or hellstrip, where heat limits other options.

Melochia tomentosa

Pyramid Bush

3–6 ft. tall and wide (can reach 10 ft.)

flowers hot pink, ½ in. across; April–November

deciduous to evergreen woody perennial

sun, part shade | sand, loam; limestone, calcareous | dry, mesic; good drainage

open areas on rocky limestone hills, coastal thorn thickets, grasslands, roadsides | Hidalgo County

Wildlife: What a powerful bee attractant! Small butterflies such as hairstreaks, blues, skippers, and the like also find themselves partaking of the abundant flowers. Low to moderate deer palatability.

Maintenance: Prune away frost-damaged vegetation ahead of new spring growth. Plants stay compact with enough sun, but take a light trimming periodically. Propagate by seed, cuttings, and root division.

Notes: This is one of our best flowering natives! It's electric next to flowering Texas lantana, flame acanthus, or yellow bells. Even though it only grows wild in far southern Texas (and south into Mexico to Brazil), it cottons to landscapes at least as far north as Austin without trouble. If cold hardiness is of concern, grow it in a large pot that can be protected. Formerly placed in what was the cacao family (Sterculiaceae, from the Latin *stercus* meaning "manure," referring to the malodorous flowers of some species), pyramid bush now resides with the mallow family (Malvaceae).

Monarda citriodora

Horsemint, Lemon Beebalm

1–3 ft. tall, 10–24 in. wide

flowers lavender, purple, white, ¾ in. long with colorful bracts stacked on long spikes; May–July

herbaceous annual with winter rosette

sun, part shade | sand, loam, clay; limestone | dry, mesic; well drained

grasslands, disturbed sites | throughout Texas

Wildlife: Provides excellent bee forage. Hummingbirds and butterflies also visit flowers. Very low deer palatability.

Maintenance: Pull out plants after ripe seeds fall, or leave dried plants standing longer for their curious tiered whorls. Easy to grow, but ensure good ventilation and drainage to avoid mildew. Propagate by seed.

Notes: Flowers borne in tiers resembling rounded pagodas. Plants, individually or in small groupings, hold their own in small gardens, but look best in generous stands to scale. The appealingly pungent and spicy aroma, similar to oregano with a lemony tinge (hence the species name, *citriodora*), can flavor stews and teas or perfume potpourri. Use other Texas monardas similarly. Cut flowers for fresh or dried arrangements.

Nelumbo lutea

American Lotus

leaves on water surface to 3 ft. above, flower stalks up to 6 ft.; unchecked rhizomes spread indeterminately

flowers pale yellow, 8 in. across, fragrant; May–September

deciduous herbaceous perennial

sun, part shade | muddy pond bottoms | in water

still or slow waters of shallow ponds, marshes, and sloughs | eastern half of Texas

Wildlife: Bees and various beetles pollinate flowers. Waterfowl nosh on seeds. Surface leaves with small triangular notches along the margins implicate foraging turtles. Moderate deer palatability.

Maintenance: Manage this aggressive spreader by giving it its own trough or large container, or by wading into the pond to cut and pull it away from other plants. Propagate by root division and seed.

Notes: The soft yellow, velvety textured petals remind me of luxuriously well-worn cotton bedsheets. Matte-textured, dinner plate–sized leaves (sometimes up to 2 ft. diameter!) convey strength and spectacle on a water body. Edible seeds and tubers are tasty, and woody honeycombed seed pods make an ornate shelf knickknack or rattle.

Nemophila phacelioides

Baby Blue-eyes

6–24 in. tall, slightly broader

flowers pale blue with whitish eyes, ½–1 in. across; March–May

herbaceous annual with winter rosette

shade, part shade, part sun | leaf litter over sand, loam, clay; rich, calcareous | mesic; well drained

open woodlands, woodland edges | central-southeastern Texas

Wildlife: These flowers are designed for bees, but moths and small butterflies like skippers take advantage of the resource. High to moderate deer palatability.

Maintenance: Pull out plants after ripe seeds drop. Propagate by seed.

Notes: Rosettes with deeply lobed bright green leaves make a good-looking groundcover for winter landscapes. Use them in pots, among other cool-season plants, or as a thick carpet under an open woodland garden canopy. In spring, their mirthful eyes twinkling back at you from a shady bed have surprisingly effective antidepressant properties. Since they peter out by mid- to late spring, combine them with wood fern or pigeonberry for summer cover.

Nymphaea mexicana

Yellow Waterlily

leaves floating, flowers rise 3–6 in. above water; spreading indeterminately by stolons

flowers pale yellow, 3–5 in. across; May–October

deciduous herbaceous perennial

sun, part shade | muddy pond bottoms | in water

quiet waters of shallow ponds, marshes, and sloughs | mostly along the coast

Wildlife: Bees and beetles pollinate flowers. Water fowl consume fruits and seeds that mature underwater. Moderate deer palatability.

Maintenance: Manage this moderately aggressive spreader by planting it alone in a container. Periodically pull it away from other plants if it's sharing a pond. Unlike tropical waterlilies, our native species are cold hardy. Propagate by stolon division and seed.

Notes: Yellow waterlily delivers delightful flowers all summer, and glossy, leathery leaves provide resting places for frogs and small turtles. Plants resemble American lotus, but waterlily leaves are deeply cleft to the center. Its sibling white waterlily (*Nymphaea odorata*) sports pure white blossoms with yellow centers and grows less vigorously, making it a little easier to manage in a smaller pond.

Oenothera lindheimeri

Butterfly Gaura

2–4 ft. tall, two-thirds as wide

flowers white-pink, 1 in. across; April–October

herbaceous perennial, sometimes with winter rosette

sun, part shade | sand, loam, clay | mesic; poor drainage okay

coastal prairies, pinelands | mostly along the upper Gulf Coast

Wildlife: Bees and butterflies tend the flowers. Host plant for white-lined sphinx moth caterpillars. Moderate deer palatability.

Maintenance: After many weeks of blooming, plants get wiry. Address this by cutting spindly flower stalks to foliage near the base. New growth will present flowers quickly with favorable weather conditions. Propagate by seed and division.

Notes: With flowers like swirling butterflies, butterfly gaura's open, lissome form and delicate texture make a complementary filler between and among plants such as Gulf muhly and Brazos penstemon. Cultivars with darker pink flowers and burgundy-tinted foliage are attractive and commonly grown. Surpassing the long anther filaments, the single pistil terminates with a cross-shaped stigma typical of the genus *Oenothera*.

Oenothera macrocarpa

Fluttermill, Missouri Primrose

6–12 in. tall; spreading 1–2 ft.

flowers yellow fading to peach, 3–4 in. across; April–June

deciduous herbaceous perennial

sun, part shade | sand, loam, clay; caliche, limestone | dry; well drained

bluffs, roadsides, rocky prairies and hillsides | Edwards Plateau through Blackland Prairies, Rolling Plains, and High Plains

Wildlife: Pollinated by sphinx moths, butterflies, and bees. Moderate to high deer palatability.

Maintenance: Snip off foliage killed back by frost or to tame sprawling stems after seeds set. Propagate by seed.

Notes: Disproportionately large flowers put a high demand on fluttermill at garden centers during bloom season. Plant them into a chalk prairie or rock garden, where their low profile is not threatened by larger plants. Rock penstemon, winecup, and prairie verbena make good neighbors. The species name, *macrocarpa* (literally meaning "large fruit"), nods to the intriguing, outsized capsule comprised of four broad wings acting as sails in the wind to disperse seeds. The subspecies *Oenothera macrocarpa* ssp. *incana*, native to the Panhandle, has striking silver foliage.

Oenothera speciosa

Pink Evening Primrose

1–2 ft. tall; colonizing extensively by rhizomes

flowers pink, white, 2–3 in. across; March–June

herbaceous perennial; winter evergreen, often dormant in summer

sun, part shade | sand, loam, clay; caliche | mesic, dry; fast draining

prairies, roadsides, plains, meadows, savannas, hillsides, slopes, woodland edges | throughout Texas

Wildlife: Bees, butterflies, and sphinx moths nectar at flowers. Small mammals, finches, and other birds nibble on seed capsules. Caterpillars of white-lined sphinx moths feed on plants. Low to moderate deer palatability.

Maintenance: When unchecked, plants spread aggressively into massive mats. Flea beetles sometimes make problems. Water periodically in summer during drought to prevent dormancy, if you wish. Propagate by seed, root division, and cuttings.

Notes: Take advantage of this winter groundcover under Texas lantana or other robust, winter-dormant plants. However, cultivate with caution! In a small garden bed, it behaves like a thug. In the right setting like a roadside, wildflower planting, the back forty, or wherever enthusiastic expansion is welcomed (or possible to be kept in bounds), drifts of luxurious flowers are dreamy. Hanging baskets or flower pots offer smart seasonal options too. Fresh leaves offer a mildly spicy addition to salads or sandwiches, and cooked, can enhance egg dishes or stir-fries.

Onosmodium bejariense var. *bejariense*

False Gromwell, Marbleseed

1½–3 ft. tall, similarly wide

flowers white and green, ⅔ in. long, on uncoiling spikes 3–6 in. long; March–May

herbaceous perennial, sometimes with winter rosette

part shade, part sun, sun, gravel, sand, loam | dry, mesic; well drained

open woodlands, roadsides, pastures | eastern two-thirds of Texas

Wildlife: Bees and butterflies visit flowers. Important spring nectar source for monarchs. Low to moderate deer palatability.

Maintenance: Cut back dormant plants in winter to tidy up. Propagate by seed and cuttings.

Notes: Smallish, spindle-shaped flowers likely won't knock anyone's socks off, but the unfurling scorpioid flower stalks and prominently pleated leaves add interest to a shaded garden or woodland edge. They are lovely in masses alongside lyreleaf sage and inland sea oats. They'll even grow in a sunny bed with false foxglove. You and the butterflies will really appreciate them during monarch spring migration. The species name presumably references Bexar County, where it occurs at its nearly southernmost location.

Oxalis drummondii

Drummond's Wood-sorrel

3–6 in. tall and wide, flower stems up to 12 in. tall

flowers pink, lavender, ½–¾ in. across; September–November

herbaceous, deciduous perennial; mostly dormant outside of bloom season

sun, part shade, part sun | sand, loam, clay; calcareous | dry, mesic

grassy areas, open woodlands | most of Texas except Panhandle and Pineywoods

Wildlife: Syrphid flies, ants, bees, and small butterflies such as skippers serve as pollinators. Low to moderate deer palatability.

Maintenance: Tiny young plants tend to show up anywhere, often being transported from reused potting soil. No problem. They pull out easily where you don't want them. Note that they lie dormant most of the year. Propagate by seed and division.

Notes: Dainty flowers begin blooming before foliage emerges in the fall from dormant bulbs. Fun little surprise! Boomerang-shaped leaflets, often mistakenly identified as clover, exhibit sleep behavior, folding down at night and during overcast weather. I've not seen this plant available commercially outside of periodic offerings at the Wildflower Center, but it grows easily from seed. All parts are edible, with a sour flavor imparted by the eponymous oxalic acid. Excessive quantities of oxalic acid–rich rich foods can cause problems for some people.

Pavonia lasiopetala

Rock Rose Pavonia

2–3 ft. tall and wide

flowers pink, 1½ in. across; April–November

semievergreen woody perennial

sun, part shade, part sun | gravel, sand, loam, clay; prefers limestone, caliche | dry, mesic; well drained

rocky open woodlands and slopes, savannas, ravines | Rio Grande Plains, Trans-Pecos, Edwards Plateau

Wildlife: Butterflies, moths, bees, and hummingbirds regularly drop by for a nip of nectar. Moderate deer palatability.

Maintenance: Clip off dead stems after winter, trim growing tips periodically to encourage bushy growth. Protect from extreme cold in northern parts of Texas. Ensure adequate air circulation, use drip irrigation, or water early in the morning to limit the time foliage is wet and minimize mildew. Propagate by seed and softwood cuttings.

Notes: This member of the mallow family (Malvaceae) brandishes rich, clear pink, miniature hibiscus-like flowers that unfurl with sunrise, curling back with the waning of the day. A short-lived but eager reseeder, this garden workhorse plays perfectly with neighbors such as zexmenia and black dalea to flesh out the interior or front edge of a bed.

Penstemon baccharifolius

Rock Penstemon, Cut-leaf Penstemon

10–18 in. tall and wide

flowers coral red, pink, 1–1½ in. long, on spikes; May–October

semievergreen herbaceous perennial

sun, part shade | gravel, sand; limestone, caliche | dry; well drained

limestone crevices and bluffs | Western Edwards Plateau, Trans-Pecos

Wildlife: A classic hummingbird pleaser, butterflies and bees enjoy it too. High to moderate deer palatability.

Maintenance: To address legginess after several weeks of blooming, take flower stems down to foliage or allow seeds to form. Avoid overwatering, especially in summer and winter. Apply a mineral mulch to remind them of their dry ancestral homelands, and add rocks over the root zone help keep them cool. Propagate by seed and cuttings.

Notes: Aptly named, rock penstemons grow straight out of caliche or tight cracks in stone, and fit the style and conditions of a rock garden or dry area in the landscape. Their summerlong steady blooming, upright bushy form, and not-too-giant size make them ideal for a pot, alone or with friends like candellia, paper-flower, and windmillgrass.

![Rock Penstemon plants with coral red flowers growing in gravel]

Penstemon cobaea

False Foxglove, Prairie Beardtongue

1½–2½ ft. tall, 12–18 in. wide
flowers pink, rose, lavender, white, 2 in. long; April–May
herbaceous perennial with sparse rosette in dormant seasons
sun, part shade | sand, loam, clay; limestone | dry, mesic; well drained
rocky limestone outcrops, open hillsides, roadsides | north-central, central, and south-central Texas

Wildlife: Flowers provision bees, butterflies, moths, and hummingbirds. Hosts dotted checkerspot butterfly larvae. High deer palatability.

Maintenance: Prune away spent stems after collecting seeds as desired. Propagate by seed.

Notes: Generously sized blossoms vary in color, so select a source in bloom if you are particular about such things. Since bloom window is short and plants take up little room, plant a good number of them in combination with bluebonnets, clammyweed, and small- to medium-sized warm-season grasses for a succession of flowers. *Beardtongue* refers to the fuzzy strip that lines the bottom of the flower mouth, while the name *false foxglove* derives from its likeness to the unrelated true foxgloves (*Digitalis* spp.).

Penstemon tenuis

Brazos Penstemon, Gulf Penstemon

1½–2 ft. tall, 1–1½ ft. wide

flowers lavender, pink, 1 in.; March–May

herbaceous perennial with evergreen rosette

part shade, part sun, sun | sand, loam, clay | mesic, wet; accepts poor drainage

Gulf prairies, marshes and riparian areas | Gulf Coast

Wildlife: Bees, butterflies, other insects, and hummingbirds enjoy the blossoms. High to moderate deer palatability.

Maintenance: Cut spent flower stalks to emerging rosettes, or later for seed collection. Deadheading early enough after the first flower flush may induce a second wave of flowering. Reseeds easily. Propagate by seed.

Notes: Profuse bell-shaped flowers lend a cottage garden feel to a spring bed. Plants have excellent winter and good summer foliage, but locate them strategically as the odor of wet leaves has been compared to cat urine. It shares space nicely with scarlet sage and inland sea oats.

Phacelia congesta

Blue Curls

2–4 ft. tall, 2–3 ft. broad

flowers blue, lavender, ⅓ in., on spiraled curls; March–May

herbaceous annual or biennial with winter rosette

part sun, part shade, sun | gravel, sand, loam, clay | mesic, dry; well drained

woodland edges and openings, open grasslands and ditches | north north-central and southwestern half of Texas

Wildlife: Bees love blue curls. Butterflies and other insects also visit flowers. High to moderate deer palatability.

Maintenance: Remove spent plants after seeds mature. Collect seeds to sow in fall, or cast them onto the ground as you pull out the plants. Mildew thwarts in rainy years, under too much irrigation, or in areas with poor ventilation. Propagate by seed.

Notes: Handsome flower inflorescences unfurl like octopus arms to grab your attention. The deeply lobed foliage also attracts one's gaze, if a bit more subtle. Colonies stand out, but small groupings work well in more intimate spaces. Bring them to an indoor table where their curious form can be admired up close, but flowers drop each day, making a minor—but worthwhile—mess.

Phlox drummondii

Drummond Phlox

6–12 in. tall, 8–18 in. wide

flowers red, light to neon pink, white, peach, lavender, ½–1 in.; March–June

herbaceous annual with sparse winter foliage

sun, part shade | sand, loam | mesic, dry; well drained

grasslands, open woodlands | southeastern two-thirds of Texas

Wildlife: Butterflies enjoy the flowers at least as much as humans. High deer palatability.

Maintenance: Allow seeds to mature and fall (or save to sow later) before removing spent plants. Propagate by seed.

Notes: Vast colonies along quiet roadsides make an excellent excuse to stop the car for a more thorough gawk. The widely adaptable plants are equally gaze-worthy in cultivated gardens, even well beyond their natural range. As far away as England, the naturally eclectic array of colors has inspired further development since the mid-1800s into various cultivars for worldwide distribution. Drummond phlox grows easily in most gardens and is primarily know in sandy regions, but several varieties occur throughout the state including *Phlox drummondii* ssp. *mcallisteri*, which can grow in calcareous soils.

Physostegia spp.

Obedient Plant, False Dragonhead

2–4 ft. tall, 1–3 ft. wide; often merging into large colonies by rhizomes
flowers lavender, pink, 1 in., on 4–6 in. spikes; April–July (August–September for *Physostegia virginiana*)
herbaceous, deciduous perennial
sun, part shade, part sun | sand, loam, clay; mud | mesic, wet; happy with poor drainage
stream banks, floodplains, marshes, bottomlands, wet meadows | eastern half of Texas

Wildlife: Flowers entice hummingbirds, butterflies, bees, and other insects. High to moderate deer palatability.

Maintenance: Depending on species, plants may spread vigorously by rhizomes. Dig them out when they unwelcomely expand their territory. Propagate by division and seed.

Notes: Adorn your pond edge, moist bed (containment recommended), or pot with the luminous blossoms of one of several highly ornamental *Physostegia* species of our state, all known as obedient plants. *P. intermedia*, *P. pulchella*, and *P. virginiana* occur in east Texas, but *P. angustifolia* creeps into the central parts. All bloom in spring and early summer except for *P. virginiana*, which blooms from August to October. Why the odd name? Push individual flowers sideways around the stem where they'll stay put. Try it, it's fun!

Plumbago scandens

Doctorbush, White Plumbago

2 ft. tall, 3 ft. wide

flowers white, 1 in.; May–November

deciduous semiwoody perennial; cold tender in norther half of Texas

sun, part shade | sand, loam, clay; responds well to compost | dry, mesic; well drained

washes, canyons, and brushy slopes from 2,500 to 4,000 ft. elevation | southern tip of Texas, Big Bend

Wildlife: Nectar is a hit with butterflies. High to moderate deer palatability.

Maintenance: Trim lightly through the growing season for bushier growth. Water periodically during drought. Protect roots below 20°F and cut back before spring growth. Propagate by seed and semi-softwood cuttings.

Notes: Heavily donned with pointy tipped, phloxlike blossoms continuously all season, doctorbush truly outperforms! Scarlet new growth greens up quickly in spring, reverting to an even richer burgundy following the first solid cold front in fall. Stark white flowers atop brilliant red foliage is a showstopper. Sticky seeds innocuously latch on to clothes, hair, and fur. Broadly arching to trailing stems make doctorbush a great choice for planters. Plants are toxic to people, but others in the genus have been used medicinally for a multitude of ailments.

Polanisia dodecandra

Clammyweed

1–3 ft. tall and wide

flowers white with purple to orange stamens, 1–1½ in. long; May–October

herbaceous warm-season annual

sun, part shade | gravel, sand, loam | dry, mesic

washes, plains, sandy stream banks, roadsides, disturbed areas | throughout most of Texas

Wildlife: Flowers provision bees and butterflies. Low deer palatability.

Maintenance: Allow seeds to ripen before collecting, or let them fall directly to the ground before removing exhausted plants at the end of their season. Propagate by seed.

Notes: The splendor and intricacy of clammyweed flowers are highlighted when grown next to the contrasting forms and textures of Lindheimer muhly, Gregg's mistflower, and purple coneflower. Glands on the three-lobed leaves and stems secrete a sticky substance, giving plants a decidedly green pepper aroma and inspiring the common name. The easily cultivated clammyweed deserves more prominence in Texas gardens.

Pontederia cordata

Pickerelweed

2–4 ft. tall; colonizing by rhizomes

flowers sky blue to lilac, violet, white, tiny, densely packed on 4–6 in. spikes; June–September

herbaceous, deciduous perennial

sun, part shade | sand, loam, clay; mud | mesic, wet

mud and shallow calm waters in marshes, ponds, and ditches | eastern into central Texas

Wildlife: Bees and butterflies take nectar and pollen. Stiff, vertical foliage provides good perching sites for territorial male dragonflies. Waterfowl readily feed on seeds. Moderate deer palatability.

Maintenance: Cut back frost-injured vegetation after first hard freeze. Propagate by division.

Notes: Upright plants with heart-shaped leaves attractively foil saltmarsh mallow and narrow-leaf water primrose along pond margins, and the pastel flower combinations on continuously blooming plants are easy on the eyes. Cultivars offer assorted sizes and flower colors such as pink or white. Seeds and tender leaves may be eaten raw or cooked.

Proboscidea louisianica

Devil's Claw

2–3 ft. tall; spreading 3–4 ft.

flowers lavender, pink, cerise, with orange throat; June–September

fruits 4–6 in. long, splitting into two sharp claws when mature; July–November

herbaceous, warm-season annual

sun, part shade | sand, loam | mesic, dry; well drained

river banks, meadows, pastures, fields, disturbed sites | throughout Texas

Wildlife: Pollinated by bees. Low deer palatability.

Maintenance: Remove fruits before they split to avoid injuring pets and to collect seeds for next year's crop or for snacking. Take out finished plants at the end of the season. Propagate by seed.

Notes: The innocent orchidlike blossoms of devil's claw stare unflinchingly into the wicked, burning eyes of summer. The not-so-innocent sharp hooks of mature hitchhiking seed pods can pierce the hides of domestic and wild animals, so take care with placement when planting. Prepare young pods as you would okra for a summer treat (try a classic dill pickle recipe). Plants are related to sesame and tender seeds are delicious raw or toasted. Pods supply an important textile fiber for Indigenous people of the Southwest. The curiously greasy fruits and foliage have a mild but distinctive aroma detectable from several feet away. Fast and easy to grow, alternate them with bluebonnets, large buttercup, or other cool-season species to extend the seasons of interest.

Psilostrophe tagetina

Paperflower

6–18 in. high; spreading 6–24 in.

flowers yellow, 1 in.; March–October

herbaceous biennial or short-lived perennial

sun, part shade | rock, gravel, sand, loam, clay; limestone, igneous, gypsum | dry; well drained

open plains, mesas, grasslands, desert scrub, mountains, salt flats | Trans-Pecos, Rolling Plains, High Plains

Wildlife: Flowers feed butterflies and bees. Low to moderate deer palatability.

Maintenance: A little supplemental irrigation during drought prolongs flowering, but excess moisture leads to lush foliage and fewer flowers. Propagate by seed.

Notes: Plants are smothered with long-lasting blossoms that turn pale and papery over time. Heat tolerance, long flowering season, and low, mounded form make paperflower ideal for a rock garden, hellstrip, flower pot, or other dry location.

Pycnanthemum albescens

Whiteleaf Mountain Mint

1½–2½ ft. tall; spreading indeterminately by stolons and rhizomes

flowers white to lavender, tiny, in ½–1 in. clusters subtended by showy snowy white bracts; June–September

herbaceous, deciduous perennial

sun, part shade | sand, loam, clay | mesic

rocky woodlands, woodland edges, along streamsides | Pineywoods

Wildlife: It's a party! When in bloom, everyone from butterflies, bees, wasps, flies, and moths join in the blissful revelry. Low deer palatability.

Maintenance: Like the related true mints (*Mentha* spp.), unfettered runners run amok. Planters, sidewalks, or walls help with containment. Give old stems a winter trim for an orderly look. Plants easily tolerate heat with adequate moisture. As bracts begin to silver up, you might think powdery mildew is encroaching, but most likely all is well. Propagate by division, layering, and seed.

Notes: Rounded purplish tinged leaves emerge in spring. As foliage matures, it develops pointed tips and frosty white tops. Not only is whiteleaf mountain mint a handsome addition to a garden, the deliciously strong peppermint-flavored leaves can be used like any mint in the kitchen.

Ranunculus macranthus

Large Buttercup

12–18 in. tall and wide

flowers yellow, 1½ in. across, fragrant; March–April

herbaceous perennial with winter rosette

sun, part shade | sand, loam, clay; rich | mesic

moist grasslands, woodland edges and openings, ditches, seeps, ravines | south-central Texas

Wildlife: Blossoms attract bees and butterflies. Rabbits consume foliage. Low deer palatability.

Maintenance: Plants may develop powdery mildew under irrigation, but this usually occurs shortly before summer dormancy, so many gardeners ignore it. Good ventilation and appropriate irrigation practices limit the problem. Trim away decaying foliage as plants shut down for summer. Propagate by seed.

Notes: Easy to grow and underused, large buttercup graces a garden during the peak of spring with a spectacular floral show before completely disappearing into summer dormancy. With this in mind, overseed with clammyweed or devil's claw to hold the hot season until growth resprouts in fall. Plants readily reseed, forming a dense groundcover with appealing winter foliage. The species name, *macranthus*, means "large flower," and it is indeed the largest-flowered native *Ranunculus* in North America.

Ratibida columnifera

Prairie Coneflower, Mexican Hat

2–3 ft. tall, 1–2½ ft. wide
flowers combinations of dark red, yellow, brown, and orange, 2 in. long; May–July or later with rains
herbaceous perennial with winter rosette
sun, part shade | sand, loam, clay; caliche, limestone | dry, mesic; well drained
grasslands and roadsides | throughout Texas

Wildlife: Bees and butterflies frequent blossoms, and seed-eating birds pluck at ripe seed heads. Foliage repels cattle, deer, and other herbivores. Very low deer palatability

Maintenance: Cut spent stems to rosettes any time after leaves appear at the base. Plants in the wild commonly stay short, whereas in richer, irrigated garden soils, they may reach over 3 ft. and bloom later into the year. Avoid mildew by ensuring good ventilation, adequate sun, and not overwatering, particularly in clay soils. Propagate by seed.

Notes: This easily cultivated common wildflower is overrepresented in overgrazed pastures due to its unpalatability and strength to outcompete weaker species. Flower colors vary from all yellow to all red, or some of each. Deeply cleft leaves impart an interesting, lacy texture. Plants grow well in pots.

Rivina humilis

Pigeonberry

1–3 ft. tall and wide

flowers light pink, ⅛–¼ in., on 2–4 in. spikes; June–October, longer in mild weather

fruits red, ⅛–¼ in.; July–November

herbaceous, deciduous to evergreen perennial

shade, part shade, part sun | sand, loam, clay; calcareous, rich, alluvial; mesic; well drained

woodlands, thickets, pockets between rocks, stream valleys | throughout Texas except Panhandle, rare in the east

Wildlife: Bees and small butterflies enjoy flowers. Fruits attract birds. Moderate to high deer palatability.

Maintenance: Soak well periodically during droughts to keep plants perky. Cut back after hard frost. Propagate by seed and cuttings.

Notes: Stalks topped with flowers subtended by cherry red translucent berries displaying simultaneously all summer long make for a particularly cute shady groundcover, filler, border, or specimen for a container. Pigeonberry timeshares well with baby blue-eyes, which provide winter cover and spring flowers. It is also called rouge plant in recognition of its historic cosmetic use; however, plants are toxic, so such use is discouraged.

Rudbeckia hirta

Brown-eyed Susan

1½–2½ ft. tall, 1–2 ft. wide

flowers yellow, sometimes with maroon, brown, or orange splotches near the brown central cone, 2–3 in. diameter; April–July, through September with extra moisture

herbaceous annual or short-lived perennial

sun, part shade, part sun | sand, loam, clay | dry, mesic; well drained

grasslands, roadsides, woodland edges and openings, disturbed areas | eastern two-thirds of Texas

Wildlife: Butterflies and bees enthusiastically tend the flowers. Larval host to gorgone checkerspot and bordered patch butterflies. Seeds bring in birds. Moderate to low deer palatability.

Maintenance: Plants are drought tolerant, but supplemental watering extends the flowering season. Allow seeds to ripen for collecting or feeding birds before removing tired plants. Propagate by seed.

Notes: When viewed in masses, contrasting yellow ray flowers and brown disc flowers leave one bedazzled! Intermingle them with purple coneflower for a classic combination using analogous flower forms and complementary colors. Cultivars with larger flowers and various shades of gold, orange, brown, and red are available, and all varieties make fabulous cut flowers.

Rudbeckia maxima

Giant Coneflower

6 ft. tall, 2–3 ft. wide

flowers yellow with brown cones, 3–5 in. tall; April–June

herbaceous perennial with winter rosette

sun, part shade | sand, clay, silt | mesic; tolerates slow drainage

moist open grasslands, roadside ditches | northeastern Texas

Wildlife: Bees and butterflies feed on flowers. Birds take ripe seeds. Low deer palatability.

Maintenance: Cut down old flower stalks after seeds have nourished birds, and once their angles disagreeably clash akimbo (perhaps August or September). Groom an occasional yellowing leaf. Propagate by seed and division.

Notes: I'm thrilled to see this outstanding plant gaining more horticultural attention! The bold-textured silvery leaves of winter and early spring are splendid, even if plants didn't later bolt into bloom. As a bonus, unbranching flower stalks deliver striking vertical form, even after the golden rays have dropped. Plant in groups of a minimum 20 square ft. to balance the scale of their size—more is better. Although its native range is reserved to east Texas, it does well in landscapes with enough moisture. Try giant coneflower in a swale or rain garden.

Ruellia nudiflora

Wild Petunia

1–1½ ft. tall, 1 ft. wide

flowers violet, lavender, occasionally white, 2 in. across; March–November

herbaceous, deciduous perennial

sun, part shade, part sun, shade | sand, loam, clay; limestone | dry, mesic; well drained

woodland edges and openings, meadows, thickets | throughout Texas except Panhandle

Wildlife: Nectar source for butterflies. Larval host for malachite, crescent, common buckeye, and peacock butterflies. Moderate deer palatability.

Maintenance: Cut back now and then to stimulate fresh flowering all season long. Most native and non-native *Ruellia* species seed out vigorously, and tenacious roots resist pulling, making them difficult to control. Be warned. Propagate by seed and division. Ruellias sometimes exhibit cleistogamy, in which flowers self-pollinate and don't open.

Notes: Though in a completely different plant family, flowers of wild petunias (the genus *Ruellia* broadly) resemble actual petunias. They grow easily as showy, durable groundcovers and regrow reliably after deer browsing or mowing. Most *Ruellia* sold in garden centers, such as Mexican petunia (*R. simplex*) are invasive, not native to Texas, and escape cultivation. Please avoid planting them.

Sagittaria spp.

Arrowhead

2–4 ft. tall, 1–3 ft. wide; some colonizing by rhizomes, stolons, or tubers

flowers white, 1–2 in.; June–November

herbaceous, deciduous perennial

sun, part shade | mud | wet; up to 12 in. underwater

still waters of marshes and sloughs | mostly eastern and central Texas

Wildlife: Ducks, turtles, and other animals forage for fleshy tubers of some species. Bees and other insects pollinate flowers. High deer palatability.

Maintenance: Remove plants that wander out of bounds. Cut back any foliage browned by age or weather. Propagate by rhizome division and seed.

Notes: Native *Sagittaria* species grow similarly with clear white, three-petaled flowers in aquatic habitats, and are at home around a pond. Some species have separate male and female flowers with furry yellow stamens or green rounded centers respectively. Leaf shape varies (a.k.a. polymorphism), with submerged vegetation appearing grass-like, surface foliage more rounded, and emerging leaves taking on the characteristic arrowhead form. *Arrowhead* refers to the leaf shape common in the genus, but several species native to Texas exhibit lance- or grass-shaped aerial leaves. Duck-potato (*S. latifolia*) is named for its starchy edible tubers.

male flowers

female flowers

Salvia coccinea

Scarlet Sage, Tropical Sage

1–3 ft. tall, 1–2 ft. across

flowers red, sometimes white or pink, 1 in.; March–November

herbaceous perennial or annual

shade, part shade, part sun, sun | sand, loam, clay | mesic; good drainage

thickets, chaparral, open woodlands, woodland edges | eastern and southern Texas

Wildlife: Nectar attracts hummingbirds, butterflies, bees, and other pollinators. Pungent foliage repels herbivores. Moderate to low deer palatability.

Maintenance: Trim tips to keep plants compact, cut to stubs after frost. Collect seeds to replant in case they do not resprout after winter. Propagate by seed and cuttings.

Notes: The continuously blooming, blood red, tubular-shaped flowers make scarlet sage a reliable summer color source. White forms gleam in shady settings, but over time revert to red from seed. New plants replenish their freely seeding parents.

Salvia farinacea

Mealy Blue Sage

2–3 ft. tall, 1½–2½ ft. wide

flowers deep to light blue, white, on 3–9 in. spikes; April–June, intermittently through October following rain or irrigation

herbaceous perennial with thin winter rosette

sun, part shade | sand, loam, clay; calcareous | mesic, dry; fast draining

grasslands, roadsides, woodland edges and openings | throughout Texas except Panhandle

Wildlife: Bees constantly visit flowers; hummingbirds and butterflies less frequently. Low deer palatability.

Maintenance: Plants tolerate dry conditions but bloom longer through summer with irrigation. However, excess moisture produces weak plants. To encourage extended flowering, cut leggy stalks back to basal foliage. You might sacrifice a few flowers, but new ones will follow more densely in short order. Propagate by seed, cuttings, and division.

Notes: The fresh blue flowers cool down plantings of hot pinks, yellows, oranges, and reds. They balance nicely with purple coneflower, Engelmann daisy, and Texas lantana. Aromatic foliage typical of the mint family (Lamiaceae) deters herbivores and adds flavor to beverages and cooked dishes. Cultivars bring versions with larger flower spikes, compact growth, prolonged bloom periods, and different shades of blue to white.

Salvia greggii

Autumn Sage, Cherry Sage

2 ft. tall and wide

flowers red, pink, white, purple, 1 in. long; March–November

semievergreen woody perennial

sun, part shade, part sun | sand, loam, clay; limestone | dry, mesic; well drained

rocky slopes and hillsides | Trans-Pecos, Edwards Plateau

Wildlife: Flowers attract bees, butterflies, and hummingbirds. Low deer palatability.

Maintenance: Around Valentine's Day clip out the thickest woody stems, then shape the remaining greenery. After each bloom cycle, lightly shear finished flower stems to the leaves, and continue shaping periodically throughout the growing season to keep plants fresh and maximize blooming. Propagate by seed, softwood or semi-hardwood cuttings, and layering.

Notes: Copious flowering occurs in spring and fall, with a scattering of blossoms during summer, particularly after rain. The type form is red, but sports and cultivars provide other colors. Those tinged with orange or yellow tend to struggle, whereas red, pink, and white versions prove quite hardy, with white accepting the most shade. The aromatic, usually evergreen shrubs suffer from brittle stems, so situate them away from heavy activity.

Salvia roemeriana

Cedar Sage

1–1½ ft. tall and wide

flowers scarlet, 1–1½ in. long, on 2–4 in. spikes; March–May

herbaceous perennial with winter rosette

part sun, shade, part shade | sand, loam, clay, rocky; limestone based | dry; well drained

rocky cedar breaks and oak woodlands | Edwards Plateau, Trans-Pecos

Wildlife: Plants bloom concurrently with spring hummingbird migration. Butterflies and bumblebees also visit flowers. Low to moderate deer palatability.

Maintenance: No maintenance is necessary, but some folks prefer to trim old flower stalks down to medium-sized leaves. Shake out seeds for new recruits to fill in any gaps between plants. Propagate by seed and cuttings.

Notes: Adapted to thick shade and dry duff under *Juniperus* species, colloquially called cedars, this plant is right at home in a rocky woodland garden or any bed in dry shade. Enjoy it alongside twist-leaf yucca and cedar sedge, which have well-matched growing conditions and complementary foliage. Cedar sage's short stature makes a good pathway planting, and cracks between stones or bricks catch seeds that sprout and fill in.

Saururus cernuus

Lizard Tail

2–3 ft. tall; colonizing by stolons and rhizomes

flowers white, tiny, on bending spikes 5–8 in. long; April–August

herbaceous, deciduous perennial

part shade, part sun, shade, sun | muds of most kinds | mesic, wet; up to 4 in. underwater

still water, wet lowlands, marshes, stream and lake edges | mostly Pineywoods and Post Oak Savanna

Wildlife: Waterfowl value seeds. Small insects, including bees, come to flowers, but wind is the plant's main pollinator. Low to moderate deer palatability.

Maintenance: Cut back frost-damaged tissue if desired. Keep roots wet. Propagate by division and seed.

Notes: Whether planted along a path for close-range observation or in large colonies, the novel form of lizard tail flowers rouses curiosity, if not appreciation. One of the most shade-accepting plants for water gardens and moist areas, highlight them in a pot (no drainage holes needed) or use them to stabilize a pond edge. Pleasantly aromatic foliage, leaf shape, and slender white flower spikes resemble the unrelated rootbeer plant (*Piper auritum*) of Central America. In Greek, *sauros* means "lizard" and *oura* translates as "tail." *Cernuus* is a Latin word meaning "drooping," and describes the nature of the flower stalks.

Scutellaria ovata

Heart-leaf Skullcap

1½–2½ ft. tall; colonizing by tuberous roots

flowers blue, purple, lavender, 1 in., on 3–4 in. spikes; April–June

herbaceous, summer deciduous perennial, new foliage emerges late winter

part sun, part shade, shade | sand, loam, clay | mesic; good drainage

open woodlands, woodland edges, thickets | eastern and central Texas

Wildlife: Flowers attract hummingbirds, butterflies, and bees. Moderate deer palatability.

Maintenance: It's not hard to keep plants in check, but pull them as they creep into other plants' territories. By June heart-leaf skullcap transitions into summer dormancy. Clearing away old flower stalks is optional. Avoid overwatering. Propagate by division, cuttings, and seed.

Notes: Blue spires similar to salvias command attention at their peak. Due to their colonizing habit, they flow into voids between other plants. Since they are dormant for half of the year (roughly July to January), plant them in front of inland sea oats or Turk's cap, which will grow over the gap left by the skullcap. Many subspecies range into Canada, so select local plants for best adaptability.

Scutellaria wrightii

Bushy Skullcap

6–12 in. tall and wide

flowers purple, violet, usually with white tongue, ½ in.; March–June

evergreen semiwoody perennial

sun, part shade | gravel, sand, loam; limestone, chalk | dry, mesic; well drained

grasslands, roadcuts, caliche banks, open woodlands | scattered throughout the northwestern two-thirds of Texas

Wildlife: Bees and butterflies frequent blossoms. Moderate deer palatability.

Maintenance: Lightly shearing plants right away after blooming encourages a second flush, or leave alone, allowing seeds to set. Propagate by seed and cuttings.

Notes: Plant bushy skullcap close together for a solid massing, or a little farther apart to reveal it's compact, rounded form. Too much shade or moisture gives leggier plants. Cute and perfectly suited for rock gardens, at the front of a border, or in containers, it shares space well with prairie fleabane, four-nerve daisy, and sneezeweed for extended color.

Solidago nemoralis

Prairie Goldenrod

1–2 ft. tall, 1–1½ ft. wide

flowers yellow, tiny, on 4–8 in. open sprays; September–October

herbaceous perennial with winter rosette

sun, part shade | sand, loam, clay; caliche | dry; well drained

grasslands, uplands, open woodlands | south-central to north-eastern Texas

Wildlife: Flowers draw in bees and butterflies; seed-eating birds follow. Moderate deer palatability.

Maintenance: Even after losing color, spent flower stalks remain attractive, but eventually you'll probably want to cut them back. Transplant seedlings in winter to fill in any gaps in the stand. Propagate by seed and division.

Notes: Not to be confused with prohibitively aggressive tall goldenrods (*Solidago altissima, S. canadensis*), prairie goldenrod has great manners. It occasionally seeds out, but you won't be endlessly digging up runners! Importantly, goldenrods are not to blame for respiratory allergies. They bloom coincidentally with ragweeds, whose wind-carried pollen is a known allergen. Goldenrod pollen is heavy and must be transported by animal pollinators, so it's not likely to accidentally float into your nostrils. Prairie goldenrod makes beautiful flower arrangements, particularly combined with its complementary purple playmate, gayfeather, whose habitat preferences and range overlap closely.

Sphaeralcea spp.

Globemallow

height varies by species
flowers orange, pink, lavender, ¾–1 in. across; mostly April–October, year-round depending on species and location
deciduous or evergreen semiwoody perennial
sun, part shade | sand, loam, clay | dry, mesic; well drained
grasslands, scrublands, high and low deserts | southern and western Texas

Wildlife: Bees and butterflies value flowers. Moderate deer palatability.

Maintenance: Clip away dead stems and snip tips to encourage more compact growth. Avoid excess water and overly rich soils. Propagate by seed and cuttings.

Notes: Native to the southwestern United States, with Texas boasting around a dozen species primarily in the Trans-Pecos, globemallows are exquisite in a rock garden or desert planting. The unusual orange to grenadine flowers of most species set off against the grayish foliage. Flowers of *Sphaeralcea angustifolia* can be pink, lavender, or orange. If lower leaves of shrubbier species thin out, plant them behind a shorter plant like desert lantana to deemphasize that feature. Lindheimer globemallow (*S. lindheimeri*) of southern Texas—and endemic to the state—tops at about 1 ft. tall with 3 ft. long trailing stems. It makes a fabulous groundcover or hanging basket.

Sphaeralcea lindheimeri

Symphyotrichum drummondii var. *texanum*

Texas Aster

2–5 ft. tall, 1–4 ft. wide

flowers light blue, lavender, yellow centers turning purple with age, ½–⅓ in. across; September–November

herbaceous perennial with winter rosette

part shade, part sun, shade, sun | sand, loam, clay; calcareous, rich | dry, mesic; good drainage

open deciduous woodlands, woodland edges | northeastern third of Texas

Wildlife: Flowers are valuable to bees and small butterflies. High to moderate deer palatability.

Maintenance: Plants spread vigorously by seed but not so much by rhizomes like other asters, making them more manageable for a cultivated setting. Seedlings that show up unwelcomed are easily pulled and transplanted to a more favored location. Cut back in winter by hand, or with a line trimmer for large areas. Propagate by seed and division.

Notes: The upright, branching stems of Texas aster bear baby's breath–like blossoms in fall that vibrate with pollinators. Use it as a filler, or naturalized in large swaths for a woodland garden (or back forty) requiring minimal attention. Unfortunately, you'll be hard-pressed to find them currently available commercially, so collect your own. Check with local Native Plant Society chapters or the Wildflower Center for sources.

Symphyotrichum oblongifolium

Fall Aster

1–2 ft. tall; colonizing indefinitely

flowers lavender-purple, in 1½ in. masses; October

herbaceous perennial with winter rosette

sun, part shade | sand, loam, clay; limestone | dry, mesic; well drained

thorn woodlands, desert scrublands, shady spots, dry eroded banks | central and north-central Texas

Wildlife: Bees, butterflies, and other insects come to flowers. High deer palatability.

Maintenance: Trim tips periodically through spring and summer, especially during wet years, to keep plants compact and from splaying out. In worst cases, cut stems to the ground to resprout. Leave plants alone after mid-August to allow flowers to develop for fall. Dark-colored frozen foliage provides precious texture and form throughout winter; cut them back only after they look scruffy, but before new spring growth emerges, typically in March. Propagate by division and semi-softwood cuttings.

Notes: The flowering period is sadly short, but during their dazzling October peak, you'll find the happy lilac mounds boiling with butterflies and other pollinators. Even out of bloom, the billowing form fills spaces between shrubs and other plants.

Tetraneuris scaposa

Four-nerve Daisy, Bitterweed

10–15 in. tall and wide

flowers yellow, 1–1½ in. across; March–June, October

herbaceous to semiwoody perennial with winter rosette

sun, part shade | sand, loam, clay; caliche, limestone | dry, mesic; well drained

dry plains, rocky hillsides, chalk prairies | western two-thirds of Texas

Wildlife: Flowers nourish bees and butterflies. Moderate to low deer palatability.

Maintenance: Avoid overwatering, especially in summer. Lay a mineral mulch around plants to keep humidity low. Clip tired flower stalks as you wish. Propagate by seed.

Notes: The species name, *scaposa*, refers to the long unbranching scapes (flower stems) that hold flower heads singularly. As one of the most endearing features of the plant, the flowers magically hover above the pincushion-like foliage below. Plants grow with tightly compact, needlelike leaves that look best as individual plants plugged in among other species, rather than in solid plantings, which inevitably develop bald patches. Intermingle with prairie fleabane and bushy skullcap in a rock garden. Ray flowers sporting four veins inspire the common and genus names.

Thalia dealbata

Powdery Thalia

4–8 ft. tall, 3–5 ft. wide

flowers purple, frosted white, 4–6 in. spikes; May–October

herbaceous, deciduous perennial

part shade, sun | mud, saline tolerant | wet; poorly drained substrates or shallow water

cypress swamps, marshes, ponds | north and east from Houston

Wildlife: Dragonflies enjoy tall stalks for perch sites. Larval host for the Brazilian skipper butterfly. High to moderate deer palatability.

Maintenance: If you're keen on provisioning Brazilian skippers, take note that the translucent caterpillars, also known as canna leafrollers, leave leaves of plants in the family Marantaceae perforated horizontally, or with entire chunks missing. Bt (*Bacillus thuringiensis* var. *aizawai* and *B. t.* var. *kurstaki*) is an effective biological treatment that is nontoxic to everyone except moths and butterflies. Use with caution to prevent damaging nontarget butterfly species. Propagate by root division and seed.

Notes: Powdery thalia grows tall, with stalks of purple flowers shooting dramatically beyond the leaves. All above-water parts are coated with a white powdery substance, which informs its common name and lends a distinctive aesthetic quality to a pond or other container.

Thelypteris kunthii

Wood Fern, River Fern

1½–3 ft. tall; colonizing by rhizomes

herbaceous, deciduous perennial

part sun, part shade, shade | sand, loam, clay; calcareous | mesic; tolerates poor drainage

swamps, canyons, stream banks, low woodlands, seeps on limestone | northeastern third of Texas

Wildlife: Low deer palatability.

Maintenance: Wood fern tolerates some drought in shade, but more sun requires heavily composted soil and extra water. Trim away winter-killed tops whenever they become irksome and before new growth of spring. Propagate by division and spores.

Notes: When one visualizes a typical fern, the image of something quite like wood fern comes to mind. In the drier, western reaches of its range (from Wise to Goliad counties), plants usually stay in place, but in wetter areas, they can run vigorously. The psychologically cooling wood fern is very suitable for woodland gardens, pond edges, and containers. Plants are often confused with the closely related Lindheimer shield fern (*Thelypteris ovata* var. *lindheimeri*), which looks and grows exceedingly similarly, but occurs naturally in the Edwards Plateau and Trans-Pecos.

Tinantia anomala

False Dayflower

1½–2½ ft. tall, 1–2 ft. wide

flowers lavender, blue, 1 in. across; March–June

herbaceous annual with evergreen winter tufts

shade, part shade, part sun | loose gravel, sand, loam, clay; calcareous, humus rich | mesic; well drained

ravines, open woodlands, floodplains | Blackland Prairies west to Edward Plateau, along southern coast

Wildlife: Bees descend on flowers. Seeds draw squirrels and turkeys. Rabbits eat foliage. Low to moderate deer palatability.

Maintenance: Readily self-sows. Small plants transplant easily. For a neat appearance, remove or cut plants after seeds mature. Allow seeds to drop to replenish the next generation. Propagate by seed.

Notes: False dayflowers naturally grow in thick colonies in woodland settings winter through spring and serve a similar function in a shaded garden. Winter's grasslike foliage makes a cheerful bright green groundcover. Merriment continues into spring with flowers resembling laughing faces with thick eyelashes and furry noses. Since plants fade by summer, plant them with inland sea oats and plateau goldeneye to extend the show.

Tradescantia gigantea

Giant Spiderwort

2–3 ft. tall, 1½–2 ft. wide
flowers blue, purple, lavender, pink, white, 1–1½ in. wide; March–May
herbaceous perennial with winter rosette
shade, part sun, part shade, sun | sand, loam, clay; calcareous | mesic
woodland edges and openings | central to north-central Texas

Wildlife: Bees, butterflies, and sometimes hummingbirds visit flowers for a li'l nip. High deer palatability.

Maintenance: Don't fret, all aboveground parts normally disappear around May until fall growth reappears. Neaten up by cutting faded foliage in late spring. Tenuous roots can be difficult to eradicate, particularly when growing between rocks or brick. Propagate by seed and division.

Notes: Giant spiderwort displays joyful, parti-colored patches in a single colony. To account for its warm-season absence, timeshare with scarlet sage or Turk's cap. Plants will also naturalize gracefully in an open woodland. Although essentially flavorless, flowers look amazing embedded into ice cubes or as a garnish, but note that they close at day's end. Use leaves as a potherb or thickener for stews. Other attractive spiderworts grow throughout Texas, including *Tradescantia occidentalis* and *T. ohiensis*.

Verbesina virginica

Frostweed

3–5 ft. tall, 2–4 ft. wide

flowers white, small, in 3–6 in. wide clusters; September–November

herbaceous, deciduous perennial

shade, part shade, part sun | sand, loam, clay; rich preferred | mesic, dry; well drained

open woodlands and stream banks | east and central half of Texas

Wildlife: Pollinators of all kinds mob the flowers, which are particularly important for fall migrating monarch butterflies. Very low deer palatability.

Maintenance: Although significantly drought tolerant, soaking during dry spells reduces wilting. Propagate by division and seed.

Notes: This large, coarse-textured plant contrasts agreeably with smaller-leaved species such as yaupon holly or coralberry. Some folks balk at including frostweed in a garden, but it really isn't a bad looking plant! In bloom, it absolutely quakes with pollinators. And there are the fascinating ice ribbons that appear after the first hard freeze of winter. You might think someone's lost track of their packing peanuts, but closer scrutiny reveals the oddity arising from the plants' bursting cells, which exude their sap slowly enough for elaborately curling ice to form.

Viguiera dentata

Plateau Goldeneye

3–5 ft. tall, 2–4 ft. wide

flowers golden yellow, 1–1½ in. heads; September–November

herbaceous, deciduous perennial

part shade, part sun, shade, sun | rocky, sand, loam, clay; caliche, calcareous | dry, mesic; well drained

woodland edges and openings | central Texas west to El Paso

Wildlife: Flowers bloom in parallel with the fall monarch migration and draw in other butterflies and bees. You'll find seed-eating birds foraging in late fall and early winter. Larval host for bordered patch and cassius blue butterflies. Moderate deer palatability.

Maintenance: Cut back winter-burned foliage after finches and friends get their fill of rich seeds. Plants spread by remaining seeds. They handle periods of scarce rain, but supplemental water remedies wilting. Propagate by seed, cuttings, and division.

Notes: Extensive, eye-catching colonies of plateau goldeneye naturalize in a woodland understory to brighten a fall landscape. In a cultivated shade garden, plants blend beautifully with shrubby boneset and frostweed, and in a bit more sun with fall aster and flame-leaf sumac in full fall regalia.

Wedelia acapulcensis var. hispida

Zexmenia

1–2 ft. tall, 1½–3 ft. wide

flowers orange-yellow, 1 in. daisies; May–November

herbaceous perennial; evergreen in south, winter dormant in north

sun, part shade, part sun | sand, loam, clay; caliche | dry, mesic; well drained

fields, savannas, open woodlands, woodland borders | Edwards Plateau, Rio Grande Plains to Big Bend

Wildlife: Butterflies find good meals at the flowers. Foliage hosts bordered patch and metalmark butterfly larvae. Seeds attract birds such as finches. Low deer palatability.

Maintenance: Light shearing after each bloom cycle keeps plants compact and in flower. Clip stems to the base following a hard freeze. Excess water or shade produces legginess. Propagate by seed and semi-hardwood cuttings.

Notes: Zexmenia loves heat, lives long, and grows easily. Forming low floral hummocks, it is well suited at the front of a border or as a filler between shrubs. Robust growth squeezes out most weeds, making it a great living mulch. Gaps resulting from winter cutbacks offer opportunities for early spring bloomers such as baby blue-eyes or large buttercup.

Grasses and Grasslike Plants

With its broad range of conditions, Texas is gifted with a diversity of grasses in every region. Historically, prairies blanketed most of the state, and every versed prairie ecologist can name the "Big Four" stalwarts of the North American prairie: switchgrass, little bluestem, big bluestem, and Indiangrass. Grasses establish the matrix in which wildflowers grow. They supply caterpillar food for a variety of skipper butterflies, and birds and other wildlife with nutritious seeds. Leaves provide nest-building materials. Avoid disturbing cocoons hibernating in the straw by delaying heavy grooming until spring. Although no credible person can promise a plant has full immunity from deer, the grasses listed here evade their browsing mouths . . . most of the time.

True grasses belong to the grass family (Poaceae). In this chapter you will find a few entries that technically fall outside of that category, but are included for their similar appearance and function. These grasslike plants are described as graminoids.

Andropogon gerardii

Big Bluestem, Turkeyfoot

4–8 ft. tall, 3–4 ft. wide

flowers red, purple, brown; August–November

warm-season herbaceous perennial

sun, part shade | deep sand, loam, clay; acid or calcareous | dry, mesic; tolerates periodic standing water

low meadows, prairies, savannas | throughout Texas

Wildlife: Provides seeds, cover, and nesting material for various wildlife, including many birds. Larval host for skipper butterflies. Very low deer palatability.

Maintenance: Cut to ground before new growth emerges in spring. Too much water, fertilizer, or shade causes plants to flop. Propagate by seed and division.

Notes: Garden with big bluestem for its tall stature, spiky form, and blue-green foliage that changes to a charming maroonish tan as temperatures cool in fall. Underplant with bluebonnets, pink evening primrose, and others to prolong interest into the cool season. Generally clumping, big bluestem sometimes forms rhizomes. Once dominant on Blackland Prairies, overgrazing and development have significantly reduced its range and density. Its presence in natural areas indicates a healthy landscape.

Andropogon glomeratus

Bushy Bluestem

2–5 ft. tall, 1½–3 ft. wide

flowers white, tan, on plumes; August–November

warm-season herbaceous perennial

sun, part shade | sand, loam, clay; moderately disturbed, salt tolerant | wet, mesic; poor drainage

low, moist swales and ditches; streamsides | throughout Texas except Panhandle

Wildlife: Provides seeds, cover, and nesting material for various wildlife, including many birds. Larval host for skipper and satyr butterflies. Very low deer palatability.

Maintenance: Cut to ground before new growth emerges in spring. Too much shade may cause plants to lean. Seeds germinate prolifically but excess plants pull out easily. Propagate by seed and division.

Notes: Grab this grass out of the pile of underappreciated plants! Its place in the garden is well-earned for heat tolerance, easy care, and spring green foliage that warms to copper in fall. Locate the cotton candy–like flowers where sunlight sets them aglow from behind. Perfect for rain gardens, pond edges, seasonally moist areas, and under air conditioner condensate drip, it combines well with swamp milkweed (*Asclepias incarnata*) or giant coneflower. Flower stalks cut while green dry nicely for arrangements.

Bouteloua curtipendula

Sideoats Grama

1–3 ft. tall and wide

flowers gray to tan with salmon colored anthers; June–November

warm-season herbaceous perennial

sun, part shade, part sun | sand, loam, clay; igneous or limestone based, disturbed | dry, mesic; well drained

prairies, woodlands, open brush, rocky slopes | throughout Texas

Wildlife: Seeds provide excellent bird food. Plants deliver nesting material and cover for various wildlife, including many birds. Larval host for skipper butterflies. Very low deer palatability.

Maintenance: If desired, cut to ground before new growth emerges in spring. Propagate by seed and division.

Notes: Sideoats grama has the honor of being the state grass of Texas. It grows in clumps, but sometimes spreads by stolons or rhizomes. Its relatively short stature and upright form allow it to play well alongside wildflowers such as rudbeckias, echinaceas, salvias, and penstemons. Blossoms dangling from one side of the stem look like Mexican party flags.

with brown-eyed Susans

Bouteloua hirsuta

Hairy Grama

1–1½ ft. tall and wide

flowers tan; March–May

warm-season herbaceous perennial

part shade, sun | prefers sand or loam, will grow in rocky, shallow clay; caliche and limestone based | dry, mesic; well drained

prairies, meadows, pastures, savannas, open woodlands, roadsides | throughout Texas

Wildlife: Seeds feed small mammals and granivorous birds. Foliage provides cover and nesting material. Larval host for skipper butterflies. Very low deer palatability.

Maintenance: If desired, cut to ground before new growth emerges in spring. Propagate by seed.

Notes: Regardless of whether or not your hairy grandma needs a shave, this hairy grama combines attractively with other plants of similar size such as rock penstemon or prairie goldenrod. Its cute seed heads curve slightly with a pointed tip, reminiscent of thick eyelashes or a pointing finger. Several other gramas, *Bouteloua gracilis, B. rigidiseta,* or *B. eriopoda,* for example, occur in various parts of Texas and also prove garden worthy.

Carex spp.

Sedge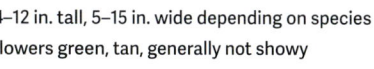

4–12 in. tall, 5–15 in. wide depending on species

flowers green, tan, generally not showy

evergreen herbaceous perennials

part shade, part sun | sand, loam, clay; rich, loose | dry, mesic, wet (depending on species); well drained

grasslands, dry woodlands, often found beneath *Juniperus* spp. | throughout Texas

Wildlife: Feeds seed-eating birds. Foliage used for nesting. Very low deer palatability.

Maintenance: Water during drought to keep foliage fresh. Propagate by seed and division.

Notes: Bad news first: few growers trade in sedges. Good news is you likely have one or two species already on your property. Once spotted, you can seed or transplant the miniature mop tops into beds and nooks to your desire. Texas boasts a number of sedges suitable for gardens. Texas sedge (*Carex texensis*), creek sedge (*C. blanda*), cedar sedge (*C. planostachys*), and others grow short and tufty, making an ideal matrix for cedar sage, golden groundsel, or pigeonberry to weave around. Substitute exotic monkeygrass or liriope with these evergreen natives. *Sedge* describes plants in the family Cyperaceae, which are not directly related to the grass family (Poaceae), although they generally appear similar. The adage "sedges have edges" refers to the triangular stems, which differ from the rounded stems of true grasses.

Carex emoryi

Emory Sedge

2–3½ ft. tall; colonizing
flowers white, cream; March–May
evergreen herbaceous perennial
sun, part shade, part sun, shade | various | wet; poorly drained
wet meadows, swales, ditches, gravel bars, pond edges, streamsides | northern and central Texas

Wildlife: Foliage offers cover and nesting supplies. Very low deer palatability.

Maintenance: Control colonizing clumps as needed. Groom leaf tips singed by winter. Propagate by division and seed.

Notes: Frequently selected for wetland restorations, emory sedge is equally appropriate for wet garden settings. It is grown less for its flowers than for its handsome evergreen, fine-textured foliage and fountain form that offers structure to pond edges, rain gardens, and wherever erosion control is needed in moist areas.

Chasmanthium latifolium

Inland Sea Oats

2–3 ft. tall and wide
flowers bright green becoming tan; emerge in May, persisting through December
warm-season herbaceous perennial
shade, part sun, part shade, sun (with ample moisture) | sand, loam, clay | mesic; tolerates seasonal poor drainage
woodlands, stream edges | northern, eastern, central, and into southern Texas

Wildlife: Small mammals and granivorous birds eat seeds. Foliage used for nesting and shelter. Very low deer palatability.

Maintenance: Cut plants to the ground once tattered or before emerging spring foliage grows too tall. In areas protected from wind, seed heads remain attractive into December. Seedlings spread enthusiastically in some situations and may require thinning. Propagate by seed.

Notes: One of only a handful of grasses that thrives in shade, inland sea oats lends a distinct form and pattern to a woodland garden. The gentlest of breezes stir the flower spikelets as they relax languidly on slender arching stems, adding a calm liveliness to the garden. Flower stems gracefully garnish arrangements when cut green.

Chloris verticillata

Windmillgrass

1–2 ft. tall and wide

flowers tan, in heads 2½–4 in. across; May–July, persisting through December

warm-season herbaceous perennial

sun, part shade | sand, loam, clay, gravel; caliche, compacted and disturbed soils | mesic, dry

prairies, disturbed areas, roadsides, lawns, parks | throughout Texas

Wildlife: Seeds eaten by waterfowl and other birds. Larval host plant for skippers and satyrs. Foliage lends shelter and nesting provisions. Very low deer palatability.

Maintenance: Cut dead foliage to the ground before new growth emerges in spring. Propagate by seed.

Notes: Looking like the end of a sparkler stick, flower tops and seed heads offer quite a long performance season. Closely related and very similar in appearance and preferred growing conditions, hooded windmillgrass (*Chloris cucullata*) differentiates itself with "arms" of tiny florets radiating from a tight point at the end of stems. With their compact forms, both species are suitable companions to rain lilies, false foxglove, gayfeather, and other plants with nominal foliage.

Cladium mariscus ssp. *jamaicense*

Jamaica Sawgrass

foliage 5–7 ft. tall, up to 10 ft. flower stalks; colonizing by rhizomes

seeds reddish brown; April–September

evergreen herbaceous perennial

sun, part shade | various wet soils, often limestone based | wet edges of streams, ponds, marshes, swamps, and lakes | eastern, central, and western Texas

Wildlife: Sharp-edged, dense foliage makes for good cover and nesting. Abundant and nutritious seeds feed ducks and other birds. Very low deer palatability.

Maintenance: Rein in plants that creep into unwanted areas. Leaf edges with sharp, fine teeth easily slice unprotected skin, so use caution when working nearby. Propagate by division and seed.

Notes: Iconic symbol of the Florida Everglades, sawgrass is not actually a grass; rather it's a large stately evergreen sedge. If you don't give it its own space, it will take it! Striking flower stalks emerge above the foliage and persist, embellishing the plant year round. Plant along pond edges or in rain gardens. In natural areas, it indicates moisture, such as a spring.

Elymus canadensis

Canada Wild Rye

2–4 ft. tall and wide
flowers green, turning tan; March–June
cool-season herbaceous perennial
part sun, part shade, sun | sand, loam, clay | mesic; well drained
prairies, open woodlands | northern, eastern, and central Texas

Wildlife: Provides seeds and forage for birds and small mammals. Leaves are used for denning and nesting. Supports skippers and most satyr butterfly caterpillars. Very low deer palatability.

Maintenance: Clear away spent foliage in summer as preferred. Propagate by seed and division.

Notes: Similar in size and form, both Canada wild rye and its sibling in the same genus, Virginia wild rye (*Elymus virginicus*), quickly and easily populate semishaded areas (Virginia wild rye prefers richer soils and tolerates shadier habitats). The blue-green foliage sets off against plants of other colors. Flowers of either species, when cut green, make elegant accents in fresh or dried arrangements. Take caution: Barbed awns on seed stalks may injure pets' eyes.

Equisetum hyemale

Horsetail

2–4 ft.; colonizing by rhizomes
evergreen perennial
sun, part shade | sand, loam | wet, mesic; tolerates poor drainage or shallow submergence
pond margins, swamps, floodplains, ditches | throughout Texas

Wildlife: Best dragonfly perch ever! Very low deer palatability.

Maintenance: Although not a speedy colonizer, its tenacious roots make it very problematic to remove, particularly from cracks between stones or other hard materials. Cut to nubs every year or two to allow for fresh new growth. Too much shade results in flimsy, lank plants. Propagate by division; it does not form flowers or seeds, but instead generates spores in cones.

Notes: Horsetail's pronounced vertical character nicely foils other garden residents. To prevent rampant invasion, it is safest grown in planters without drainage holes. Standing water poses no problem, and the sealed bottom prevents the captive from escaping. Beware of stems creeping over the container lip in search of a new place to root. Alternately called scouring rush, its abrasive silica-containing stems tied into bundles make effective pan scrubbers.

Muhlenbergia capillaris

Gulf Muhly

2–3 ft. tall and wide

flowers rose pink on airy branches; October

semievergreen herbaceous perennial

sun, part shade | sand, loam, well-composted clay | mesic; well drained

open pine forests, coastal and inland prairies | eastern and southeastern Texas

Wildlife: Birds consume seeds in fall. Small animals shelter under dense foliage. Leaves offer provisioning for nests. Very low deer palatability.

Maintenance: For a late winter cleanup, break off old brittle flower stalks by hand then gently comb plants with a leaf rake to remove dead foliage in preparation for fresh spring growth. Although commonly practiced, shearing or mowing is not recommended. Unlike deciduous grasses whose tops completely die in winter, many muhlys are semievergreen, with a few leaves remaining green and photosynthesizing through winter. Cutting limits their ability to garner energy, making them less vigorous come springtime. Aesthetically, the line created with shears seems oddly unnatural, taking many months to outgrow. Propagate by seed.

Notes: When backlit, clouds of pink mist fading to beige over the season are real conversation starters. The plant's size makes it easy to accommodate in most gardens or in pots. For fall displays, pair with pink autumn sage and Drummond's wood-sorrel. For spring, interplant with wildflowers for added color.

Muhlenbergia lindheimeri

Lindheimer Muhly, Big Muhly

4–5 ft. tall and wide

flowers silver to tan, on spikes 6–18 in. long; October

semievergreen herbaceous perennial

sun, part shade | sand, loam, clay; limestone based, often rocky | mesic, dry; well drained

limestone uplands and outcrops near streams | endemic to central Texas

Wildlife: Birds snack on ripe seeds. Small animals shelter under dense foliage. Leaves offer provisioning for nests. Very low deer palatability.

Maintenance: See Gulf muhly.

Notes: Light gray-green in color with a handsome fountain form, Lindheimer muhly punctuates a garden as a specimen, or it creates a moderately penetrable physical and visual barrier when planted densely. Open silvery flower plumes grace the month of October, folding in and becoming slender after pollination. Its elegant manner and lack of sharp slicing foliage make it a superior substitute for exotic (and invasive) pampas grass.

Nassella tenuissima

Feathergrass

1½–2 ft. tall and wide

flowers silvery green; April–May

semievergreen or deciduous herbaceous perennial

part shade, sun | sand, loam, clay; well drained | dry, mesic

open woodlands on rocky flats and slopes in mountains of the Trans-Pecos | western Texas

Wildlife: Small animals shelter under foliage. Leaves offer provisioning for nests. Very low deer palatability.

Maintenance: After winter, or if seed stems tangle unflatteringly, gently pull a leaf rake through. For the same reasons listed for muhlys, cropping plants is not suggested and plants will die if cut too short. Mulch with fine or medium-grade gravel to reduce rot in humid conditions. Ideally, offer afternoon shade and avoid overwatering. Excessive seeding may require control. Propagate by seed.

Notes: Lightest breezes lift feathergrass—and the garden—to life. In full bloom, it takes on a decidedly silky appearance and you may find the urge to fondle it irresistible. As enticing as it might be to transport such a beauty outside of the region, its invasive tendencies in some parts of the world (South Africa and Australia, for example) demonstrate the importance of cultivating plants native in your local region.

Nolina texana

Sacahuista, Basket Grass, Beargrass

1½–2 ft. tall, 3–4 ft. wide
flowers white-pink; April–June
evergreen woody perennial
part sun, shade, part shade, sun | sand, loam, clay; caliche, limestone | dry; well drained
open woodlands, brushlands, grasslands, rocky slopes and bluffs | western, central, and southern Texas

Wildlife: Nectar source for bees. Larval host for Sandia hairstreak butterfly. Shelter for various small animals. Very low deer palatability.

Maintenance: To tidy up, trim off spent flower stalks. In full sun, work extra organic matter into soil to improve drought tolerance. Propagate by seed.

Notes: Stout flower clusters cloister in the foliage, barely emerging above the fluid arching wave of leaves. Let them pour over boulders or a wall. In grand swaths sacahuista is graceful, firm, and confident. A pair in pots make a veritable welcoming committee flanking a lightly shaded front door. Strong ropey leaves are well suited for basketry, hence the common name of basket grass. Though resembling grass, sacahuista is a woody member of the lily family (Liliaceae). Devil's shoestring (*Nolina lindheimeriana*) is similar with sharp, serrated leaves and a more upright form.

Panicum virgatum

Switchgrass

3–6 ft. tall and wide

flowers green, reddish purple, on open panicles; July–October

warm-season herbaceous perennial

sun, part shade | sand, loam, clay; limestone based | mesic, dry; tolerates poor drainage

prairies, stream banks, open woodlands | throughout Texas

Wildlife: Seeds eaten by granivorous birds and other small fauna. Offers cover and nesting supplies. Larval host for Delaware skipper and other butterflies. Very low deer palatability.

Maintenance: Cut dead foliage to the ground before new growth emerges in spring. Too much shade causes gangly growth. Propagate by seed and division.

Notes: Many ecotypes and cultivars of switchgrass abound with varying blade and spray colors. They grow blue or gray-green in spring and summer, showing fantastic autumn hues ranging from rich yellow to copper and crimson. These fade as winter takes hold, but switchgrass still offers muted blonde tones and bold form. It happily inhabits seasonal creek beds and rain gardens, and lacy flower stems tucked into dried or fresh arrangements make good filler.

Poa arachnifera

Texas Bluegrass

1–2 ft. tall; colonizing by rhizomes

flowers silvery white or green, dioecious; March–May

cool-season herbaceous perennial

part sun, part shade, sun | sand, loam, clay | mesic; prefers good drainage but tolerates seasonal poor drainage

open woodlands, woodland edges, savannas, meadows | northern, central, and western Texas

Wildlife: Seeds eaten by granivorous birds and other small fauna. Offers cover and nesting provisions. Very low deer palatability.

Maintenance: May be mowed or cut back in summer or fall as preferred. Propagate by division and seed (female plants need male plants to produce fertile seed).

Notes: You guessed it! This grass sings in blues all year round. Its dense rhizomatous growth performs as a suitable groundcover for a bright woodland garden. Flowers invite attention when planted in large masses, and Texas bluegrass absolutely deserves more of our attention. Overgrazing has reduced this once common species.

Rhynchospora colorata

Star Sedge, White-topped Sedge

1–2 ft. tall; colonizing by rhizomes
flowers subtended by white bracts, 1–4 in. long; April–September
warm-season herbaceous perennial
sun, part shade | sand, loam, clay | wet; welcomes poor drainage, can grow in up to 1 in. of water
prairie swales, edges of water bodies | southern half of Texas

Wildlife: White bracts attract insect pollinators, which is unusual for the otherwise wind-pollinated plants of the sedge family (Cyperaceae). Very low deer palatability.

Maintenance: Clear away old foliage before spring pushes out new. Propagate by seed and division.

Notes: You'll find many uses for the glimmering star sedge in moist areas of the garden. It specializes in boggy areas, rain gardens, pond edges, in pots lacking drainage holes, and in garden beds with regular irrigation. This mostly summer bloomer buddies up agreeably with cardinal flower and spring-blooming irises.

Schizachyrium scoparium

Little Bluestem

2–4 ft. tall, 1–2½ ft. wide

flowers greenish yellow with rusty anthers, tan in seed;
June–November

warm-season herbaceous perennial

sun, part shade | sand, loam, clay; caliche, limestone based | dry;
well drained

grasslands, woodland edges | throughout Texas

Wildlife: Provides nesting supplies and cover for small animals. Feeds seed-eating birds. Larval host for some skipper butterflies. Very low deer palatability.

Maintenance: Thin out seedlings that proliferate more than you would like. Dead foliage may be trimmed away before new growth emerges in spring. Best with little or no supplemental irrigation outside of drought. Propagate by seed and division.

Notes: The silver-blue to blue-green foliage clearly inspire the common name. Depending on genetics, season, and growing conditions, purples and mahoganies may also appear. Seed heads sparkle when backed by the sun, and plants turn copper to blazing orange after first hard frost. For maximum impact, plant in groupings of five or more, depending on the scale of your space.

Sorghastrum nutans

Yellow Indian Grass

3–6 ft. (reaching 8 ft. tall), 3–5 ft. wide; colonizing by rhizomes

flowers golden yellow, sometimes with reddish brown, bronzing with age; August–October

warm-season herbaceous perennial

sun, part shade | rich, deep sand, loam, clay; calcareous | dry, mesic; tolerates seasonal poor drainage

rich grasslands, open woodlands | throughout Texas

Wildlife: Plants offer seeds, cover, and nesting material for various wildlife, including many birds. Larval host for skipper butterflies. Very low deer palatability.

Maintenance: Tenacious roots pose a moderate control challenge. Last year's growth may be trimmed away before new sprouts emerge in spring. Best with little or no supplemental irrigation outside of drought. Too much water or shade results in spindly, weak plants. Propagate by seed and division.

Notes: Yellow flowers of late summer contrast scrumptiously with basic green to metallic blue-gray foliage. Fall converts the grasses to deep orange ranging to purple, curing to flaxen in winter. Use yellow Indian grass as a fall accent around other tall plants, in masses for large spaces, or for erosion control.

Spartina spartinae

Gulf Cordgrass

3–5 ft. tall and 3–5 ft. wide

flowers pale yellow; June–September

semievergreen perennial

sun, part shade | sand, loam; saline tolerant | wet, mesic; easily accepts poor drainage

lagoons, tidal flats, marshes, moist prairies | predominantly along the coast

Wildlife: Provides cover, nesting sites, and seed snacks for many bird species. Geese graze on tender shoots. Very low deer palatability.

Maintenance: If desired, break off spent seed stalks and rake out dead, loose foliage. Propagate by seed and division.

Notes: If your garden grows along the Gulf Coast but you're sweet on Lindheimer muhly of the Edwards Plateau, Gulf cordgrass is a great alternative. Primarily used for coastal restoration and erosion control, its large, long-lived, dense clumps and tame temper (no suckers or heavy seeding) make it a fine addition to moist gardens where water gathers, including rain gardens. Stiff leaves with pointy tips can be a little prickly.

Sporobolus airoides

Alkali Sacaton

2–3 ft. tall, 1–2 ft. wide

flowers pink to cream, on open panicles; May–October

warm-season herbaceous perennial

sun, part shade | gravel, fine-textured sand, loam, clay; caliche, accepts high salinity and alkalinity | mesic, dry; well drained, tolerates occasional flooding

salt flats, sandy washes, floodplains | Panhandle, western and southern Texas, along the coast

Wildlife: Plants deliver seeds, shelter, and nesting supplies for various wildlife, including many birds. Very low deer palatability.

Maintenance: Dead foliage may be removed before new growth emerges in spring. Propagate by seed and division.

Notes: Held in a decorative planter, the cloudlike, frothy textured grass creates a striking focal point. En masse it settles over a garden like a luscious fog bank, while also providing effective erosion control. Its heat and drought resistance makes it an excellent candidate for xeric gardens.

Tridens flavus

Purpletop

2½–4 ft. tall, 1½–3 ft. wide

flowers purple in loose, drooping panicles; August–November

warm-season herbaceous perennial

part shade, part sun | sand, loam, clay | dry, mesic

open woodlands, woodland edges, roadsides, disturbed areas | northern, eastern, central, and into southern Texas

Wildlife: Seeds feed small mammals and granivorous birds. Foliage provides cover and nesting material. Larval host for skipper and wood nymph butterflies. Very low deer palatability.

Maintenance: Groom spent foliage to the ground before spring as desired. Propagate by seed and division.

Notes: Purpletop will not grab you by the collar, but its beauty becomes clear in colonies close enough for one to witness its lacy, delicate nature and deep purple flowers that would otherwise fade into the shadows. Adapted to bright, open shade mostly on poor sand, it also grows on other soil types. In addition, its fibrous roots anchor earth vulnerable to erosion, giving us an attractive and useful option for such demanding conditions. Flower stems are viscid, hence the alternate name of greasegrass.

Tripsacum dactyloides

Eastern Gamagrass

2–5 ft. tall, 3–6 ft. wide

flowers with bright orange anthers above and purple stigmas below, monoecious; April–June

warm-season herbaceous perennial

part shade, sun | sand, loam, clay; calcareous or acid | moist, mesic; accepts seasonal poor drainage

stream banks, salt marshes, prairies | throughout Texas

Wildlife: Plants lend protection and nesting materials for small animals. Larval host for skipper butterflies. Very low deer palatability.

Maintenance: Wear protective gloves and sleeves whenever cutting back foliage to avoid getting cut yourself. Propagate by seed and division.

Notes: Lush, spreading, dark green mounds cohabitate with buttonbush, American beautyberry, or other plants fitting for rain gardens, around pond edges, and in other moderately moist situations. Blades turn tawny after frost. Long flower stems rise above the clump, their bright orange anthers clinging loosely from the stalk reminiscent of chile ristras curing on a New Mexican patio. Roast mature kernels for a delicious cornlike snack.

Cacti and Succulents

***Succulent* describes plants with fleshy stems or leaves.** This adaptation to store moisture in their bodies allows them to thrive in dry landscapes. As the heat and drought of Texas summers take their toll, succulents make a lot of sense. Cacti are a family of succulent plants (Cactaceae), but not all succulents are cacti. Agaves, sotols, yuccas, and others suffer misidentification as cacti, presumably because of their thorns and prickles.

Many of these plants present strong visual personalities. The range of sizes and forms offer both subtle and dramatic design opportunities. Larger types make stately sculptural focal points or accents. Many others, including most cacti, grow relatively small. Lace cactus and claret cup, for example, hold steadfast against harsh climates and soils but remain vulnerable to crowding by larger plants. Although these garden pixies prefer an extra shower from time to time, withholding excess irrigation helps restrict competition from other vegetation. Crevices and thin, rocky soils in natural settings favor miniature plants. Mimicking these conditions in the garden advances both aesthetic and practical aspects of horticultural design. Overharvesting from wild areas poses a serious threat to many succulents, so when making choices for your property, harvest only from cultivated sites or salvage them from "doomed" (condemned for destruction) properties according to strict ethical standards.

And, of course, handle these plants with care! Wear eye protection and use thick gloves, wrap plants with newspaper, or handle them with tongs to avoid unnecessary injury.

Agave americana

American Century Plant

leaf rosette 3–5 ft. tall and wide; colonizing by rhizome pups
flowers yellow, on stalks up to 20 ft.; June–July
evergreen perennial
sun, light shade | sand, loam, clay, rocky | dry; well drained
grasslands, beaches, open woodlands, rocky slopes and cliffs | southern tip of Texas

Wildlife: Attracts insect pollinators and hummingbirds. Serves as protective habitat for birds and other small animals. Very low deer palatability.

Maintenance: Size and armament make removal of entangled weeds and dead or damaged parts challenging. Marred foliage does not rejuvenate and may need trimming. Propagation by seed and pup division.

Notes: Strikingly tall bloom stalks, curious teeth impressions on unfurling leaves, overall dramatic form, and extreme heat and drought tolerance make agaves excellent garden candidates. However, take care during placement to thwart the vicious defensive hardware from injuring people or pets. Folks once believed that century plants bloomed only after 100 years (hence the common name), but it turns out that each species flowers on its own cycle, with *Agave americana* maturing at about a decade. Mother plants die after blooming but pups appear at their base. Plants are strong enough to break out of pots. Other native agaves enjoy cultivation, but beware of cold-sensitive tropical species.

Dasylirion texanum

Texas Sotol

leaf rosette 2–3 ft. tall and wide, flower stalks up to 15 ft.

flowers light yellow clusters, on tall unbranched spikes; June–July

evergreen perennial

sun, part shade | sand, loam; caliche, igneous or limestone based | dry; well drained

prairies, plains, savannas, brush country, desert flats | endemic to central and western Texas

Wildlife: Bees, bees, bees. Very low deer palatability.

Maintenance: Grasshoppers sometimes get carried away with chewing on leaves. Remove spent flower stalks if desired. Pull or cut off dead leaves at base. Tip: Use a long handled tool to separate leaves for easier and less painful access. Propagate by seed.

Notes: Frequently misidentified as cacti, sotols may surprise you for being in the lily family (Liliaceae). Ordinarily requiring no supplemental irrigation, Texas sotol is a generously armed evergreen with a tidy, rounded form that serves as an attractive specimen or an impenetrable hedge. Flowers resemble cheese puffs without the orange food coloring. The closely related gray-leaved Wheeler's sotol (*Dasylirion wheeleri*) also makes a great landscape plant.

Echinocactus texensis

Horse Crippler

1–3 in. tall, up to 12 in. span; shrinks partially underground during drought

flowers rose to pale pink with red centers, 2–2½ in. across, lightly fragrant, open late morning to afternoon; April–May

fruits bright red, ½–1¼ in. wide, edible, slightly sweet

evergreen perennial

sun, part shade | sand, loam; igneous or limestone | dry; well drained

desert grasslands, scrublands, flats and lower mountain slopes and basins | along the Rio Grande and in central Texas, scattered elsewhere except Panhandle and eastern Texas

Wildlife: Bees pollinate flowers. Very low deer palatability.

Maintenance: Offer a fond gaze any time of year, particularly when plants are in bloom. Propagate by seed.

Notes: Tip a somber nod for all of the horses who have suffered at the spines of this plant with such a sad name! The cactus can likewise injure oblivious hikers, evading detection among grasses and other vegetation and even below ground during dry spells. Nowadays, they are uncommon due to eradication by ranchers. Give them a boost in a favored pot for a virtually zero-maintenance specimen.

Echinocereus coccineus

Claret Cup

12–18 in. tall; clumps of up to 100 stems or more

flowers red, orange, 2 in. across, dioecious; March–June

evergreen perennial

sun, part shade | rocky, gravel, sand | dry to mesic; well drained

mountains, hills, mesas, open woodlands, alluvial banks, grasslands, among scrub | central Texas, Trans-Pecos

Wildlife: You'll find bees and hummingbirds at flowers. Fruits feed small animals. Very low deer palatability.

Maintenance: Plants appreciate periodic blown kisses, just don't pucker up too closely! Propagate by seed and division.

Notes: As do other cacti on the small side, claret cup happily inhabits pots. In the ground, more stems occur in shallow, dry, and rocky conditions, while deeper soils produce fewer but larger stems. Rare among cacti, plants are dioecious, meaning female and male flowers occur on separate plants, with only female plants bearing fruit. Also unusual are blossoms that remain open overnight, blooming for two to four days. Individuals may vary in appearance, and they easily hybridize with other members of the genus *Echinocereus*. Note that a number of other species also go by the name of claret cup.

Echinocereus reichenbachii

Lace Cactus

5–8 in. tall, 3 in. across; sometimes forming large colonies

flowers deep magenta to rose-pink, 2–4 in. across; April–May

evergreen perennial

sun, part shade | gravel, sand, clay; caliche, pockets in rock outcroppings | dry; well drained

grasslands, scrub, oak-pine and oak-juniper woodlands | throughout Texas except Pineywoods

Wildlife: Insect pollinators, particularly bees, frequent the flowers. Small mammals nosh on fruits. Very low deer palatability.

Maintenance: Photograph the flowers for year-round enjoyment. Propagate by seed and division.

Notes: With one to several stems per clump, lace cactus fits perfectly in a planter or in a rock garden tucked around smaller plants that will not overwhelm it. Handsome even out of flower, but when it goes you'll want sunglasses to protect your eyes from all that pink brilliance!

Euphorbia antisyphilitica

Candelilla

1–1½ ft. tall; spreading slowly by rhizomes

flowers white, minute; May–October, year-round after rains

evergreen perennial; may freeze in extreme cold

sun, part shade | gravel, sand, loam, clay; caliche, limestone | dry; well drained

desert scrub, draws, rocky hillsides, ridges | west and southern tip of Texas

Wildlife: Look for tiny pollinators. Low deer palatability.

Maintenance: Trim out dead or broken stems, and reboot periodically by cutting to the ground in late winter if you wish. Protect from temperatures below the midteens Fahrenheit. Propagate by division.

Notes: Essentially leafless, pale gray-green vertical stems confusingly resemble the unrelated wetland horsetails (*Equisetum* spp.). Candelilla's extreme drought and heat tolerance render it well suited to neglected containers. In the ground, it moseys slowly, eventually forming a dense clump. Its high-quality wax is used for candles, waterproofing, soap, shoe polish, and other items. The common name means "candle" in Spanish. The species name, *antisyphilitica*, recognizes it as a purported remedy for venereal disease. Sadly, overharvesting from wild populations contributes to candelilla's decline. Many euphorbias are toxic—use caution.

Hesperaloe parviflora

Red Yucca, Coral Yucca

2–3 ft. tall and wide, flower stalks 4–5 ft. high

flowers on the red side of coral, sometimes yellow; 1–1⅓ in. long, on showy spikes; April–July

evergreen perennial

sun, part shade | sand, loam; caliche, limestone | dry; well drained

prairies, rocky slopes, limestone hills, arroyos, mesquite groves | central and southwestern Texas

Wildlife: Hummingbirds and butterflies nectar on blossoms. Low deer palatability (flower stalks edible).

Maintenance: Remove old stalks and leaves as desired. Propagate by seed and division.

Notes: Texas Parks and Wildlife currently ranks red yucca as "Vulnerable to Extinction" due to its restricted range and relatively few wild populations, often with eighty or fewer individuals. According to the Wildflower Center's Living Collection Policy, we normally would not recommend a vulnerable species for horticultural use out of concern for wild pilfering and potentially detrimental genetic mixing. However, red yucca already finds itself frequently in nurseries and enjoys popularity for its easy cultivation and heat and drought tolerance, making it well suited for dry gardens and containers. Not a true yucca, *Hesperaloe parviflora* sometimes goes by the name of false yucca.

Jatropha dioica

Leatherstem

1–3 ft. tall; colonizing by rhizomes
flowers white, pink, ⅓ in. long; April–June
deciduous perennial
sun, part shade | gravel, sand, loam, clay; caliche, limestone based | dry; well drained
desert scrub | endemic to western and southern Texas

Wildlife: Birds including white-winged doves eat seeds. Flowers provide nectar. Low deer palatability.

Maintenance: Trim out dead or broken stems. Protect from temperatures below the midteens Fahrenheit. Propagate by seed and division.

Notes: Plants are drought and cold deciduous. They may flush with foliage during warm weather after rain and defoliate during cold or scant precipitation. Either way, their odd character could spring straight from a Dr. Seuss book! Base-sprouting stems may colonize 6 square ft. or more over time, slowly traveling as older sections die out and new growth takes hold. Its Spanish name, *sangre de drago*, means "blood of the dragon," referencing the sap that runs clear, turning red upon oxidation. Feature leatherstem in a pot or rock garden. Female and male flowers sometimes occur on separate plants.

Mammillaria heyderi

Heyder Pincushion Cactus

ground grade up to 2 in. tall, up to 5 in. diameter
flowers cream with pink stripes, 1–1½ in.; March–April
fruits bright red, ½–1 in. long
evergreen perennial
sun, part shade | sand, loam; limestone, alluvial substrates | dry; well drained
scrubland, grassland, washes, piñon-juniper foothills | western, southern, and central Texas

Wildlife: Flowers attract insect pollinators. Small mammals eat fruits. Very low deer palatability.

Maintenance: Ensure it has its own space unfettered by more robust neighbors. Propagate by seed.

Notes: This tidy little cactus grows contentedly in a clay pot or in the ground. Bring it to eye level in a raised planter, or use it to fill a slot in a crevice garden. Its perfect geometric pattern, noticeably sunken top, and ring of flowers forming a circle around the stem resemble a pincushion. Plants may shrink at or below grade for protection of the soil during drought.

Manfreda maculosa

Spice Lily, False Aloe

2–4 in. tall, flower stalks 2–4 ft.
flowers cream white turning dark pink, 1–1½ in., in clusters; April–July
evergreen to deciduous herbaceous perennial
part shade, sun | sand, loam, clay | dry, mesic; well drained
prairies, thickets, chaparral | southern Texas

Wildlife: Nectar source for hummingbird and insect pollinators. Larval host for manfreda giant-skipper butterfly. High deer palatability.

Maintenance: Trim off spent flower stalks as desired. Propagate by seed and division.

Notes: What appears as a spiny, poky plant turns out to be surprisingly soft and fleshy. Strappy ground-hugging leaves blotched with purple-brown vary in spot size, density, and color intensity on different individuals. Plant several together for best impact. Called spice lily for its fragrance, and false aloe for its resemblance to the Old World genus *Aloe*.

Opuntia spp.

Prickly Pear

2–5 ft. tall, 3–8 ft. wide (depending on species)
flowers pale to rich yellow, orange, 2–4 in. diameter; April–June
fruits deep red or purple tunas, 2–3 in. long; summer–fall
evergreen perennial
sun, part shade | sand, loam, clay; caliche | dry; well drained
grasslands, deserts, scrublands | throughout Texas

Wildlife: Flowers lure bees and beetles. Many animals seek ripe tunas. Very low deer palatability.

Maintenance: No irrigation needed. Various fungal and bacterial diseases afflict plants when overwatered. Wipe off overly abundant cochineal cotton (a little is fine). Treat leaf-footed bug nymphs before maturation with soapy water. Decadent plants may be cut back to resprout. Propagate by calloused pads and seed.

Notes: Many prickly pears bless (or curse) our state. Cow tongue (*Opuntia engelmannii* var. *linguiformis*) gives "sharp tongue" a literal connotation, and spineless prickly pear (*O. ellisiana*) lacks sharp spines but sports glochids (minute irritating slivers), requiring careful handling. Thoroughly remove glochids before consuming the delicious fruits, called tunas. Eat tender spring pads (nopales) cut into strips, raw or cooked. Cochineal insects are inevitable, yet tolerable—even a conversation starter—in small amounts. Used commercially to color food and fiber, rich magenta pigment exudes from squished insects. See for yourself! In the landscape, prickly pears play with light to form dramatic patterns, complementing boulders, walls, grasses, shrubs, and any plant with contrasting form. Legend has it that their sunny blossom is the true yellow rose of Texas.

Portulaca pilosa

Chisme

1–3 in. tall; spreading to 1 ft. across
flowers pink, purple, ⅓–½ in. across; May–November
herbaceous warm-season annual
sun, part shade | sand, loam, clay | dry; mesic; well drained
gardens and turned fields, washes, desert grassland, scrub, urban and other disturbed areas | throughout Texas

Wildlife: Bees pollinate flowers. Low deer palatability.

Maintenance: To ensure its return, mulch area only lightly. Or collect seeds and replant. Propagate by seed.

Notes: Plants spread quickly like *chisme* (Spanish for "gossip"). It timeshares well with cool-season annuals such as bluebonnets and Texas yellowstar, or with large buttercup and other summer-dormant perennials. Easy to grow and easy to remove, it's useful in pots or as a colorful heat-tolerant seasonal groundcover under taller plants. Like other purslanes, you can eat all parts of the plant. It is described by Eric M. Knight and Stacy Coplin in their book *Foraging Texas* as "plump . . . [and] deliciously sour and cooling."

Yucca spp.

Yucca

varies, see details below

flowers white, bell-shaped, 1–2 in. long, in clusters; midspring–early fall

evergreen perennial

sun, part shade for most species (*Yucca rupicola* prefers part sun, shade) | rocky, sand, loam, clay; caliche, limestone | dry; well drained

deserts, grasslands, mesas, chaparral, savannas, woodlands | throughout Texas, see details below

Wildlife: Blossoms attract night-pollinating moths. Plants offer protected nesting habitat for birds and other animals. Hosts skipper and yucca moth caterpillars. Leaves highly unpalatable to deer, but flower stalks are relished.

Maintenance: Old leaves naturally senesce; remove them or leave to enhance habitat. Top-heavy plants sometimes pull out of the soil. Before this happens, stake or provide other support. For very heavy fallen specimens, cut stalks to the ground and allow plants to resprout. Propagate by seed; offsets of some species transplant successfully.

Notes: Yuccas provide security from intruders when deliberately located, all while appearing fabulous in silhouette. Smaller species look best in groupings large enough to hold the space. When properly sited and established, yuccas thrive in nonirrigated spaces and sunbaked rock gardens. Leaves provide fiber for textiles, and roots of some species make soap. Flowers and young stalks are edible, as are the fruits of some species. Texas native *Yuccas* include:

Arkansas Yucca *(Y. arkansana)*: 1–2 ft. tall and wide, flower stalks adding 3–4 ft. more height; eastern half of Texas. Thin curly filaments adorn leaf edges.

Plains Yucca *(Y. glauca)*: 3–4 ft. tall and wide, flower stalks 4–5 ft. tall; Panhandle. Roots used for soap.

Pale-leaf Yucca *(Y. pallida)*: 1–2 ft. tall and wide, flower stalks 4–6 ft. tall; Blackland Prairies. Sometimes considered synonymous with *Y. rupicola*, it differs in having gray-blue leaves and a preference for full to part sun.

Twist-leaf Yucca *(Y. rupicola)*: 1–2 ft. tall and wide, flower stalks 4–6 ft. tall; endemic to the Edwards Plateau. Leaves twist gently with age, combining aesthetically and horticulturally with other dry woodland plants.

Thompson Yucca *(Y. thompsoniana)*: 6–10 ft. tall, 3–5 ft. wide, flower stalks adding 2–3 ft. more height; Trans-Pecos. Leaves radiate symmetrically forming a neat head.

Torrey Yucca *(Y. torreyi)*: 3–10 ft. tall, flower stalks adding 2–3 ft. more height; Trans-Pecos, Edwards Plateau. Fleshy fruits reminiscent of dates. A favorite but seldom heard common name is old shag.

Spanish Dagger *(Y. treculeana)*: 10–12 ft. tall, 6–8 ft. wide at heads; southern Texas. Stiff pointed leaves inform the common name.

Shrubs and Small Trees

The line is blurry between this chapter of shrubs and small trees, and the next which addresses large shade trees. For our purposes, trees maturing roughly under 25 feet populate this chapter. But, of course, any given variety will range in size depending on individual genetics, available moisture, light, and soil depth and composition. With so many variables, mature size cannot precisely be predicted and some of the woody plants in this book could be placed in either chapter.

Medium-sized plants comprise important middle habitat layers and link shorter plants with the higher canopy. Many naturally branch low or, with periodic coppicing, can be maintained as dense shrubs. Plants tolerant of this treatment come from fire-adapted ecosystems, and the saw can have a similar effect as fire. "Fire sprouters" regrow vigorously with multiple, thin shoots, giving gardeners some options. Leave a few selected stems to dominate by removing the rest, or shear only the tops to encourage bushier plants.

Aside from their outstanding ornamental form and seasonal flowers and fruits, woody plants offer cover and fodder for wildlife. Evergreens function most effectively as windbreaks, visual screening, and to muffle noise from adjacent properties, but can feel heavy and dark in winter if overdone. Deciduous woodies better show off berries and seeds that persist after leaf drop.

Shrubs are particularly effective at providing privacy, foundation plantings, guiding pedestrian traffic, demarcating boundaries, and acting as living fences to gently contain dogs and children. Many can be sheared into loose or tight hedges, perhaps even into a fun puzzle maze, space permitting.

Aesculus pavia var. *pavia*

Red Buckeye

8–35 ft. tall; spreading 6–25 ft.

flowers pale to bright scarlet, 6–10 in. panicles; March–May

deciduous

part shade, part sun, shade | deep sand, loam, clay; limestone | mesic; well drained

woodlands, streamsides, canyons | eastern half of Texas

Wildlife: Flowering coincides with hummingbird spring migration. Bees also enjoy the blossoms. Moderate deer palatability.

Maintenance: Best protected from afternoon sun. Summer dormancy is normal. Propagate by seed.

Notes: These woodland residents sport handsome palmate, glossy foliage. Forms range from widely branching and multitrunked to more upright trees. All are fantastic during spring until midsummer leaf drop, when plants close shop for the year until new shoots appear the following spring. This normal "summer deciduous" behavior is no reason to fret, but you should position plants in your landscape accordingly. Roots and wood supply soap and black dye, respectively. Yellow buckeye (*A. pavia* var. *flavescens*) occurs in western counties, blooming yellow, with intermediate hues arising where ranges overlap. Caution: Young leaf shoots and seeds are poisonous.

Ageratina havanensis

White Mistflower, Shrubby Boneset

2½–4 ft. tall; spreading equally wide
flowers white to light pink, in clusters, fragrant; October–November
deciduous
part shade, sun, part sun | sand, loam, clay; limestone | dry, mesic; well drained
rocky hillsides, bluffs, ravines, woodland openings | Edwards Plateau

Wildlife: Nectar source for a wide array of pollinators. Moderate to high deer palatability.

Maintenance: Cut back before new growth emerges in the spring to keep plants compact. Propagate by seed and cuttings.

Notes: Prolific, fragrant, frothy white flowers present the best fueling stations for butterflies, moths, bees, and even hummingbirds come autumn. When not in flower, bushy blobs remain attractive but low-key during the growing season. Its billowing form dresses up cliffsides, and dense foliage at ground level smothers out most weeds. The deciduous habit allows for cool-season species such as large buttercup or giant spiderwort to share its space.

Aloysia gratissima

Beebrush, Whitebrush

4–10 ft. tall; thicket forming

flowers white, tiny, on spikes 1–3 in. long, heavily perfumed; March–November after rains

deciduous

sun, part shade | sand, loam, clay; caliche, limestone, granite; tolerates poor soils | dry, mesic; well drained

arroyos, desert grasslands, rocky outcrops, open woodlands | southern, central, and western Texas

Wildlife: Aptly named for making bees crazy for the flowers. Birds eat seeds. Thickets make great nesting habitat. Low deer palatability.

Maintenance: Cut back to encourage bushy growth. Plants suffering from chronic legginess likely need more sunlight. Propagate by seed and softwood cuttings.

Notes: No need to ring the dinner bell when these deliciously vanilla-scented blossoms get going! Throngs of bees home in to sip nectar, regurgitating it later into high-quality honey. A beebrush thicket effectively screens neighbors and takes well to loose hedging. Branches sometimes sport spiny tips. Similar in many ways, the closely related woolly beebrush (*Aloysia macrostachya*) flaunts purple flowers and hails from far southern Texas. Beebrush resembles the introduced invasive privet and serves as a fair substitute.

Anisacanthus quadrifidus var. wrightii

Flame Acanthus, Hummingbird Bush

3–5 ft. tall and broad

flowers red-orange, sometimes cantaloupe yellow, 1½ in. long, on spikes; June–October

deciduous

sun, part shade | sand, loam, clay; caliche, limestone | dry, mesic; well drained

grasslands, shrublands, dry arroyos, rocky banks and floodplains | southern Texas

Wildlife: Excellent for attracting hummingbirds and large butterflies. Larval host for janais patch and Texan crescent butterflies. Moderate to high deer palatability.

Maintenance: Takes well to shearing before flowers form in June; light tipping while blooming keeps plants compact and in flower. Cut back to nubs in late winter, or trim away dead stem tips after spring foliage emerges. Propagate by seed and softwood cuttings.

Notes: Aflame with flowers through the punishing months of summer when little else is willing, flame acanthus flushes lushly after rains while feisty, territorial hummingbirds orbit plants for hours. Though hailing from southern Texas, it grows easily under cultivation throughout the state, including in patio pots and planters.

Buddleja marrubiifolia

Woolly Butterfly-bush

3–4 ft. tall and wide

flowers orange, reddish orange, on globose 1 in. heads; June–November

evergreen to deciduous

sun, part shade | sand, loam, clay; calcareous | dry; well drained

desert ditches, ravines, gravelly slopes at high elevations | western Texas

Wildlife: Offers nectar for butterflies. Medium deer palatability.

Maintenance: Snip out frost-damaged tissue in late winter or early spring. Plants may succumb to cold in northern parts of Texas. Propagate by softwood cuttings and seed.

Notes: Various shades of orange dot the curiously shaped flower heads. Tiny hairs lend a woolly texture while protecting leaves from extreme heat and radiation from the sun. Its silvery appearance complements other desert denizens, such as desert lantana and skeleton-leaf goldeneye. The species name, *marrubiifolia*, refers to the resemblance of its leaves to those of Eurasian/African horehound (*Marrubium vulgare*).

Callicarpa americana

American Beautyberry

5–8 ft. tall and wide

flowers pale pink, small, in clusters; May

fruits magenta, in 2 in. clusters; August–January

deciduous

shade, part sun, part shade | rich sand, loam, clay; acidic or calcareous | moist, mesic

thickets, woodlands, bottomlands | eastern half of Texas

Wildlife: Bees and butterflies nectar on flowers. Fruits enjoyed by birds and people. Moderate deer palatability.

Maintenance: Arching stems are one of its best features, so avoid hard pruning. If plants grow too large for the space, make another selection. Leggy plants benefit from reduced competition and a one-time hard cutting back if necessary. Supplemental water during drought prevents fruit and leaf drop. Propagate by seed and soft- or hardwood cuttings.

Notes: Graceful bowing stems, weighed down further as fruits mature, present a distinct form for a woodland garden. As a harbinger of fall and standard go-to for reliable understory color—particularly once the aromatic leaves shed to reveal the ostentatious berries—the show continues into winter unless mockingbirds nab them earlier. A white fruiting form sparkles bright in the shade, but over-ripe berries turn dingy brown.

Cephalanthus occidentalis

Buttonbush

6–12 ft. tall and wide

flowers white, tiny, clustered in dense 1–1½ in. globes, fragrant; June–September

deciduous

sun, part shade | sand, loam, clay; limestone based | mesic, wet; thrives with poor drainage

necklacing water bodies, swales, marshes, and bottomlands | throughout Texas

Wildlife: Bees, butterflies, and a motley collection of insects relish nectar. Ducks and other wetland birds appreciate seeds. Moderate deer palatability.

Maintenance: Prune to shape as desired. Propagate by seed and semi-hardwood cuttings.

Notes: A continuous bloomer in sunny locations, buttonbush in blossom endlessly entertains. A diverse parade of pollinators swarms the honey-scented flowers, which inspire the alternate name of honeyballs. Exserted stamens fringe the globes like sparks spewing from a firework display. Even out of flower, the glossy leaves and bronze new growth remain attractive. Perfect for rain gardens. Caution: Plants reportedly contain glucosides, which may be toxic to people and other animals.

Chilopsis linearis

Desert Willow

15–25 ft. tall, 10–15 ft. wide

flowers pink, white, magenta, 1–2 in. long, perfumed; April–September, particularly after rain

deciduous

sun, part shade | gravel, sand, loam, clay, limestone or granite based, tolerates low organic content but prefers loose texture | dry, mesic; well drained

desert washes, arroyos, and river banks | mostly west, but grows throughout much of Texas

Wildlife: Mostly caters to bees, but other insects and hummingbirds sup on nectar. Seeds feed birds. Moderate to low deer palatability.

Maintenance: Best with minimal irrigation, allow to dry out between waterings. However, plants appreciate a deep soaking during drought. Prune to shape and remove dead twigs after winter. New wood bears flowers. Propagate by seed and semi-hardwood cuttings.

Notes: This low-branching, open-crowned small tree, clad with long narrow leaves resembling willows, belongs not to the willow family (Salicaceae) but to the catalpa family (Bignoniaceae). Best flowering occurs during hot weather, offering nectar that produces good honey. Many cultivars demonstrate a range of flower colors, leaf shapes, and plant sizes. One selection even boasts a lack of seed pods, but I would yearn for the long, slender fruits dangling like icicles in summer.

Cordia boissieri

Mexican Olive

15–25 ft. tall, 12–15 ft. wide

flowers white with yellow centers, 2 in. wide; year-round, heaviest late spring–early summer

evergreen to deciduous

sun, part shade | gravel, sand, loam, clay; caliche | dry, mesic; well drained

brushlands, chaparral, thickets, savannas, plains | southern Texas

Wildlife: Butterflies, moths, hummingbirds, and bees take nectar. Birds and mammals consume fruits. Low deer palatability.

Maintenance: Lightly prune to shape. Protect from extreme or prolonged cold; may freeze to the ground or perish in extremely cold weather. Propagate by seed and semi-hardwood or softwood cuttings.

Notes: It's a shame that not everyone can greet this fabulously ornamental tree at their front step every day. Most years it survives in Austin, particularly when grown against a south-facing wall, only to get knocked to the ground or even killed by exceptionally low temperatures every few years. The large crepe paper–like blossoms over a long season will steal your heart, and the stout, twisting trunk and densely pubescent leaves appearing gray with a silver lining are lovely too. Fruits make a sweet jelly.

Cotinus obovatus

Smoke Tree

15–30 ft. tall and wide

flowers pink, yellow, purple, tiny, with long, attractive filamentous petioles; April–May

deciduous

sun, part shade | rocky, sand, loam, clay; limestone | dry; well drained

hillsides, limestone outcrops, rocky woodlands | Edwards Plateau

Wildlife: Seed-eating birds consume fruits. Moderate to high deer palatability.

Maintenance: Rich soils and excess water result in weak plants. Take caution to cover bare skin when pruning or working with this plant if its relative poison ivy irritates you. Propagate by seed and semi-hardwood or softwood cuttings.

Notes: Trees with short trunks, open canopy, and gnarly branches demonstrate distinctive personalities. Flower and fruit clusters with rose-pink hairlike stems impart a smoky appearance, leading to the tree's common name. Autumnal leaves range from peach to yellow, orange, and red. Smoke tree is in the same plant family (Anacardiaceae) as cashews, mangoes, and poison ivy, and sometimes causes contact dermatitis in sensitive individuals.

Diospyros texana

Texas Persimmon

10–15 ft. tall, 8–12 ft. wide

flowers whitish, ⅜ in. wide, lightly scented, dioecious; March–April

fruits black, 1 in. round, delicious!; July–September

deciduous to semievergreen

sun, part shade | loam, clay; caliche, limestone based | dry; well drained

rocky, open woodlands, savannas, slopes, and arroyos | southern and central Texas, Trans-Pecos, along the coast

Wildlife: Butterflies and bees take nectar. Fruits are prized by birds and mammals. Larval host for gray hairstreak butterflies. Low deer palatability.

Maintenance: Lightly prune to clean up low branches and sculpt into a distinct form. Dropping fruits make a big mess. Sorry! Best planted away from walkways and parking areas. Propagate by seed.

Notes: Texas persimmon tops my list of favorites for its multicolored, sometimes peeling bark on muscular yet elegant trunks resembling crape myrtle. It fits into intimate spaces and an open canopy allows other plants to flourish beneath it. Astringent immature fruits are mouth puckering, but when plump and fully ripe, they sweeten a field hike with datelike pulp surrounding a bulk of seed. Inky flesh temporarily stains teeth, so wait a moment before flashing a smile.

Erythrina herbacea

Coralbean

6–10 ft. tall (15 ft. in the Rio Grande Valley); spreading equally wide

flowers scarlet to pink, tubular, 3–5 in. long, on 8–12 in. spikes; April–June, sporadically summer through fall

herbaceous or woody; deciduous

sun, part shade, part sun | mostly sand, also loam and clay; acidic or calcareous | mesic, dry

coastal plains and prairies, open woodlands, woodland clearings | central, eastern, and southern Texas along the coast

Wildlife: Hummingbirds consume nectar. Moderate deer palatability.

Maintenance: Cut to 6 in. above ground in late winter, or remove only frost-damaged stems after live growth becomes evident in spring. Propagate by seed and semi-hardwood cuttings.

Notes: The first flush of flowers appear before foliage in spring. Stems typically sprout from the base after winter, but may take on a tree form in southern Texas. Regardless of thorns and prickles scattered along stems and sometimes the undersides of leaflets, and in spite of the poisonous bright red beans encased in long black pods, coralbean's elegance earns regard in the garden. Just keep plants away from the kids.

Eysenhardtia texana

Texas Kidneywood

5–12 ft. tall, 4–8 ft. wide

flowers white, tiny, in showy spikes 1–4 in. long, intensely fragrant; May–September, especially following rain

deciduous

sun, part shade | rock, gravel, sand, loam, clay; caliche, calcareous | dry, mesic; well drained

brushlands, chaparral, brushy hills and canyons | central, southern, and western Texas

Wildlife: Excellent nectar source for a range of pollinators including butterflies and bees. Host for dogface butterfly. Moderate deer palatability.

Maintenance: Naturally open, loose and shrubby in form, it makes a small tree with selective pruning. If plants stretch long, cut to nubs to allow for re-sprouting and provide more sun. Propagate by seed and softwood or semi-hardwood cuttings.

Notes: Ah, the sweet smell of summer! From its flowers that is . . . its leaves exude a pungency most find mildly disagreeable. Texas kidneywood makes a superior alternative to the invasive non-native butterfly bush (*Buddleja davidii*). Wild thickets are readily simulated in a garden, and the wood makes a good dye source. Sometimes called beebrush, it's easily confused with another beebrush (*Aloysia gratissima*). Bees sequester nectar for making honey.

Fallugia paradoxa

Apache Plume

3–6 ft. tall, 2–4 ft. wide; spreading farther by rhizomes under favorable conditions
flowers white, 1–2 in. across; May–July, sporadically through December
fruits pink, feathery 2 in. heads; June–December
deciduous to semievergreen
sun, part shade | gravel, sand, loam, clay; caliche, calcareous | dry; well drained
arroyos, open woodlands, gravelly slopes, high desert, chaparral | western Texas

Wildlife: Nectar source for insects. Seeds appeal to birds. Dense foliage provides cover and nesting materials. Low deer palatability.

Maintenance: Grows faster and thicker with supplemental water during drought. If desired, cut woody stems to the ground to refresh timeworn plants. Propagate by seed, cuttings, layering, and transplanted suckers.

Notes: A thick, pink cloud of Apache plume in fruit gives an attractive option for a xeric landscape and works well for controlling erosion to boot. Fluffy seed tails range from dark to pale pink on different individuals, so select your plants "in plume" if possible. Close-up, the clean white flowers adorned with delicate stamen clusters reveal the plant's membership in the rose family (Rosaceae).

Forestiera pubescens

Elbowbush

5–10 ft. tall, 6–12 ft. wide; thicket forming

flowers yellow, not showy, dioecious; January–March

deciduous

shade, part sun, part shade, sun | sand, loam, clay; limestone based | mesic, dry

open woodlands, savannas, brushy prairies, streamsides | northern, western, and central Texas

Wildlife: Early-season nectar source for a wide range of pollinators. Small blue-black fruits on female plants provide forage for birds and mamals. Dense growth creates excellent cover. Host plant for Io moth and hairstreak caterpillars. Moderate deer palatability.

Maintenance: Distinctive branching at right angles—which inspires the common name—makes a natural-looking pruning job difficult. If necessary, cut just above nodes for light trimming, or remove branches close to the trunk or near the ground for heavier pruning. Propagate by seed, layering, and cuttings.

Notes: You might just walk past this shrub without notice unless you happen across the pollinators roiling among the flowers that offer an important early-season nectar source when little else is producing. Though not at all showy, this unsung hero is a real workhorse, functioning as an outstanding wildlife supporter, reliable understory screen, and effective physical barrier even after winter leaf drop. Flowers appear before foliage in late winter, making it a harbinger of spring, explaining the alternate name of spring herald.

Ilex decidua

Possumhaw Holly, Deciduous Yaupon

8–20 ft. tall and wide

flowers white, ¼ inch across, not showy, dioecious; March–May

fruits bright orange-red berries, ⅓ in., on female trees; November–February

deciduous

part shade, part sun, sun | sand, loam, clay; caliche, appreciates high organic content | mesic; tolerates periodic slow drainage

woodlands, bottomlands, coastal plains | eastern third of Texas

Wildlife: Mammals, including opossums, and birds dine on fruits. Flowers attract bees. Animals shelter in its dense thickets. High deer palatability.

Maintenance: Two ways to manage this fire sprouter include: selecting a few main stems, limbing up the rest to make a multitrunked specimen, and removing suckers along the trunk and at the base; or cuttting them to the ground periodically to resprout into shrubs, shearing the tops to promote dense screening or wildlife cover. More sun produces more berries. Propagate by seed, cuttings, layering, and transplanted suckers. Vegetative propagation ensures female plants.

Notes: Possumhaw holly is glorious in winter when the dearth of foliage reveals its berries. Pollination for fruit set requires males, and wild plants, including closely related species like yaupon, will do the trick. Heaviest fruiting occurs in full sun. As winter wanes, enjoy the descent of mockingbirds, robins, and flocks of cedar waxwings.

Ilex vomitoria

Yaupon Holly

12–30 ft. tall, 10–15 ft. wide; may form thickets

flowers white, ¼ inch wide not showy, dioecious; April–May

fruits red berries, ¼ in. diameter, on female trees; October–February

evergreen

part shade, sun, part sun, shade | gravel, sand, loam, clay | dry, mesic; adapted to slow drainage

low woodlands, hummocks, bottomlands | northern, central, and eastern Texas along the coast

Wildlife: See possumhaw holly. Moderate to low deer palatability.

Maintenance: See possumhaw holly.

Notes: A versatile and reliable choice for evergreen foundation plantings, windbreaks, garden backdrops, sound insulation, and screens. Dwarf forms offer drought- and disease-resistant substitutes for boxwood, but most remain fruitless. Other options include yellow-fruited, fastigiate, and weeping cultivars. Plants naturally form impenetrable thickets in eastern Texas, becoming more treelike farther west. Related to yerba mate, yaupon holly brews into a delicious caffeinated beverage that is increasingly available commercially. Native Americans blended yaupon holly with other herbs and ceremonially vomited after imbibing. This ritual informed the species name, *vomitoria*. Retching was likely self-induced or instigated by other ingredients since yaupon holly leaves are not emetogenic. Berries, however, should be avoided.

Leucaena retusa

Goldenball Leadtree

15–25 ft. tall, similarly wide

flowers orange-yellow, 1 in., globose, sweet scented; April–October following rains

deciduous

sun, part shade | rocky, sand, loam, clay; igneous and limestone based | dry; well drained

dry canyons, mountains | Edwards Plateau to the eastern Trans-Pecos

Wildlife: Flowers draw bees and small butterflies. High to moderate deer palatability.

Maintenance: Apply supplemental water to establish new plants and during unusually dry periods. Prune into a multi- or single-trunked tree as you wish. Protect its weak, brittle wood from strong winds. Propagate by seed and semi-hardwood cuttings.

Notes: Enough light filters through the airy canopy to give the gardener a good assortment of plants to grow below such as autumn sage, doctorbush, or even prickly pears that complement the long-blooming golden puffballs. Be intrigued, not alarmed, at the vertical splits in the gray bark that reveal bright orange underneath. Trees grow rapidly.

Leucophyllum frutescens

Cenizo

4–8 ft. tall and wide

flowers rose-lavender, sometimes white, pink, or violet, ¾–1 in. wide; late spring and summer, particularly after rain

evergreen

sun | rocky, gravel, sand, loam, clay; caliche, calcareous | dry; well drained

rocky hillsides, arroyos, scrub, chaparral | western, southern, and central Texas

Wildlife: Larval host for several species of moths and butterflies. Nectar attracts bees and butterflies. Very low deer palatability.

Maintenance: Too much shade produces leggy or leaning shrubs. To rehabilitate, cut back hard in winter and supply more sun. Shear into tight hedges, leave alone, or trim lightly depending on your taste. No supplemental irrigation is necessary in most areas, but some leaves may shed during extremely dry spells; shrubs rot if overwatered. Propagate by seed, softwood or semi-hardwood cuttings, and layering.

Notes: Widely cultivated for good reason! As an adaptation to intense Southwestern sun, protective hairs allow shrubs to thrive in hot, dry settings while lending a hoary glow. *Cenizo* means "ash" in Spanish, reflecting its color, which contrasts beautifully against walls or dark foliage. Perfect for hedging, as a specimen, or an accent. Several cultivars exist with variations in foliage and flower color.

Lindera benzoin

Spicebush

6–20 ft. tall, 5–12 ft. wide
flowers yellow, ⅓ in., fragrant, dioecious; March–May
fruits red, ½ in., flavorful on female plants; August–September
deciduous
part sun, part shade, shade | sand, loam, clay | mesic; well drained
low woodlands, creek banks, swamps | central and eastern Texas

Wildlife: Various wildlife eagerly dine on nectar and berries. Kelly green leaves support several species of swallowtail butterfly and silk moth caterpillars. Low to moderate deer palatability.

Maintenance: If desired, prune after flowering. Propagate by seed.

Notes: Foraging for wild foods undoubtedly connects one with the riches of the natural world. Spicebush leads the pack of delectable edibles with leaves, twigs, and berries used to season teas and sweet or savory dishes. But the best aroma and spicy flavor derive from the glossy red ripe fruits. Spicebush thrives in forest settings, but forms denser foliage and compact shape with more sun. Attractive, low-branching, multitrunked trees cuddle up comfortably with other woodland garden neighbors and display luminous yellow foliage in fall.

Mahonia trifoliolata

Agarita

3–5 ft. or taller, 3–6 ft. wide

flowers yellow, ½ in., strongly fragrant; February–April

fruits red, ⅓ in., choice edible; May–July

evergreen

part shade, full sun, part sun | rocky, clay, loam; caliche, calcareous | dry, mesic; well drained

open woodlands, rocky slopes and flats, cliffs, savannas | throughout Texas except east

Wildlife: Outstanding wildlife resource! Honey-scented flowers provide important early forage for bees, who make high-quality honey; fruits fuel birds and mammals; and everyone takes cover under its protective foliage, earning it the alternate name of babysitter bush. Low deer palatability.

Maintenance: Light tipping encourages fuller growth. If too spindly, cut back hard and provide more sunlight. Propagate by seed.

Notes: In spite of annoyingly slow growth and foliage wickedly armed enough to plant under a wayward teenager's window, flowers bring intense sweetness into the smellscape, followed by mouthwatering sweet-tart fruits. But how to collect for your fine jelly through those needle-sharp defenses? For relatively pain-free harvesting, thresh with a stick, remove the drop cloth you so cleverly placed in advance, and then winnow spiders and sticks from the berries. Shrubs appear gray-green in eastern parts, transitioning to a cool blue-gray farther west. Bright yellow wood and roots furnish a yellow dye.

Malpighia glabra

Barbados Cherry

standard form 10 ft. tall, 6 ft. wide; weeping form 3–4 ft. tall and wide

flowers pink with yellow, ½ in. across; April–October

fruits red, ½–¾ in.; May–frost

deciduous to semievergreen

part sun, part shade, sun | sand, loam, clay; calcareous | dry, mesic; well drained

thickets, brush, palm groves, prairies, plains | southern Texas

Wildlife: Mammals and birds enjoy fruits. Butterflies and bees visit flowers. Larval host for several species of skippers, hairstreaks, and other butterflies. Low deer palatability.

Maintenance: Protect from prolonged temperatures under 20°F. Tops may freeze or plants may even perish in cold winters. Trim dead tips after new growth becomes evident. Cut dwarf forms by half or to 4 in. stubs. Propagate by seed, softwood or semi-hardwood cuttings, and layering.

Notes: Ruffled flowers resembling those of crape myrtle burst into full bloom all at once, then appear scattered throughout the season. Plants carry enticing cherries and flowers simultaneously. *Malpighia glabra* and its close relative *M. emarginata* are both known as acerola, the latter being a popular superfood. Both are high in vitamin C and enjoyable in a compote or fresh. Two distinct forms give gardeners options: the standard form grows erect as a low-branching tree, however, severe cold renders it unreliable in much of the state; the weeping form has arching branches and a short stature, serving well as a decorative hedge, filler between other plants, or a specimen in a container.

Malus ioensis

Prairie Crabapple

30 ft. tall, similarly wide
flowers pink to white, 1–1½ in., fragrant; April–May
fruits greenish to yellow, 1½ in.; September–October
deciduous
sun, part shade | loam, clay; limestone | mesic; well drained
thickets, woodland edges | central Texas

Wildlife: Flowers lure a variety of pollinators. Fruits known to be eaten by twenty or more species of birds and mammals. High deer palatability.

Maintenance: Cut away suckers growing into unwanted areas, otherwise low-maintenance. Propagate by seed, cuttings, and transplanted suckers.

Notes: Prairie crabapple is squat enough to be planted under utility lines and features a broad, rounded crown, exfoliating bark, and striking tangerine to grenadine foliage in fall, chiefly when grown in sun. It also works well in the understory. Its graceful yet sturdy beauty calls for a prominent position, but heed the sharp spines. Deliciously scented blossoms are followed by small, sour and astringent, chartreuse crabs that feed wildlife and are also collected by foodies to craft jelly, cider, or vinegar.

Mimosa borealis

Fragrant Mimosa

2–6 ft. tall and broad
flowers pink, ½ in. clusters, fragrant; March–July
deciduous
sun, part shade | rocky, sand, loam, clay; caliche, limestone based | dry; well drained
rocky hills, canyons, scrub | Panhandle, western and central Texas

Wildlife: Nectar feeds butterflies and bees. Low deer palatability.

Maintenance: Nominal pruning as preferred. Propagate by seed and semi-hardwood cuttings.

Notes: A light hand with clippers can prune fragrant mimosa into an intimately sized specimen tree. Beware of the "wait-a-bit" prickles (that's what you say to your hiking companion as you untangle yourself from its clutches), which contrast with the soft pink froth of flowers. Keep larger plants from crowding it and use short groundcovers that won't interfere with its lower branches. Cenizo and prickly pears behind and snake herb, frogfruit, or woolly stemodia below would create a well-composed scene. Many native mimosas prove garden worthy, but the non-native, invasive *Albizia julibrissin*, also known as mimosa, should not be planted. Fragrant mimosa tolerates extreme heat.

Morella cerifera

Wax Myrtle

standard form 8–20 ft. tall, 6–12 ft. wide; dwarf form 6 ft. tall and wide; colonizing by stolons

flowers inconspicuous; March–April

fruits frosty blue, ⅛ in., dioecious; September–November

evergreen

part shade, part sun, sun | sand, loam, clay; neutral to acidic, moderately salt tolerant | mesic, wet; adapted to poor drainage

forests, moist grasslands, marshes, swamps, fresh to slightly brackish stream banks | eastern third of Texas

Wildlife: Birds consume fruits. Larval host for hairstreak butterflies and giant silk moths. Low to moderate deer palatability.

Maintenance: Apply extra water when grown west of its natural range. Shear for a hedge or crown shaping. Prune into a tree form by removing suckers as preferred. Propagate by seed, softwood or semi-hardwood cuttings, layering, and transplanted suckers.

Notes: Wax myrtle's dense, evergreen foliage makes for excellent screening, while its roots fix nitrogen. Best suited to hedging, the dwarf form stays fuller at the ground. Those familiar with bayberry will recognize the zesty scent of wax myrtle as a close relative; both supply wax from their berries for candle making. Dwarf wax myrtle is a good soil stabilizer, particularly in sandy areas, and some sources acknowledge it as a separate species, *Morella pusilla*.

Parkinsonia aculeata

Retama

12–15 ft. tall (occasionally 30 ft. tall), similarly wide
flowers yellow and orange, ½ in., in 5–6 in. clusters, lightly perfumed; April–August
deciduous
sun | sand, loam, clay; saline tolerant | dry, mesic; well drained
disturbed grasslands, pastures, floodplains, chaparral | southern half of Texas

Wildlife: Bees convert nectar into a fragrant honey. Small mammals and seed-eating birds relish the seeds. Thorny branches make popular nest sites. Moderate deer palatability.

Maintenance: Prune as needed, taking care around sharp spines. Cold tolerant to the low teens Fahrenheit but may die to the ground. No significant insect or disease concerns. Propagate by seed and semi-hardwood cuttings.

Notes: Lithe, low-branching or multitrunked spiny trees adorn dry gardens as accents or specimens. Fine leaves allow plenty of light to filter through, supporting Gregg's mistflower, mealy blue sage, wild poinsettia, and the like. Flowers flush heavily in spring, then subsequently after rains. It is one of several plants commonly called paloverde, which in Spanish means "green stick," referencing the bright green photosynthesizing trunk and twigs. True to the nature of early colonizing plants on disturbed sites, retama seeds out vigorously, becoming invasive in some areas worldwide.

Prunus caroliniana

Carolina Cherry-laurel

15–20 ft. tall, 8–15 ft. wide
flowers white, 1–2 in. spikes, fragrant; February–April
evergreen
sun, part shade, part sun | deep sand, loam, clay loam; moderately salt tolerant | mesic; well drained
low woodlands, coastal forests, fields, thickets | Gulf Coast to Post Oak Savanna and Blackland Prairies

Wildlife: Birds eat cherries. Flowers attract bees, butterflies, and other pollinators. High to moderate deer palatability.

Maintenance: Ensure good drainage, particularly in clay-based soils. Naturally dense and upright, prune or shear lightly to shape. Heavy pruning results in a ragged crown with blunt sticks and is generally unnecessary. Monitor for borers, mites, and scale on stressed trees. Propagate by seed and cuttings.

Notes: This thick and fast-growing evergreen functions as privacy screening and windbreaks, and provides a dark background to contrast with brighter garden plants. Lustrous leaves smell pleasantly of almonds when crushed, but leaves, twigs, and seeds contain prussic (hydrocyanic) acid, making them toxic. However, many birds happily consume the cherries, digesting the pulp and passing the seeds. Cultivars offer a selection of mature sizes.

Prunus mexicana

Mexican Plum

15–35 ft. tall, 20 ft. wide
flowers white, pink, 1 in. across, strongly fragrant; February–March
fruits orange, mauve, red; July–September
deciduous
part shade, part sun | sand, loam, clay | dry, mesic; well drained
woodlands, river bottoms, prairies | Pineywoods, Post Oak Savanna, Houston, Blackland Prairies, Edwards Plateau

Wildlife: Flowers call in a motley of pollinators! Plums feed birds and mammals. Foliage hosts cecropia moth caterpillars. High to moderate deer palatability.

Maintenance: Dropping plums make a mess in the wrong location. Occasional suckers may need to be clipped out. Propagate by seed and softwood cuttings.

Notes: Both romantically gorgeous and deliciously scented, the blossoms host raucous parties for a variety of pollinators, if only for a week or two. Single-trunked trees occasionally sucker, and sharp spines arise here and there on branches. Horizontal striations of shiny silvers and browns, and conspicuous lenticels on young bark are common in members of the genus *Prunus*. Bark peels off in chunks on older trunks. Broad leaves naturally cup, sometimes appearing wilted and scorched in the quiet violence of summer. For this reason, I prefer to plant Mexican plum under the protection of the understory. Some folks enjoy the tart edible plums fresh, but most prefer them prepared in recipes with ample sugar.

Ptelea trifoliata

Wafer Ash, Hop Tree

15–20 ft. tall, 10 ft. wide

flowers yellowish green, small, intensely scented; April

fruits bright green, papery samara, 1 in.; August–September

deciduous

part shade, part sun, sun | gravel, sand, loam, clay | mesic, dry; good drainage

alluvial thickets, rocky slopes | throughout Texas except southern tip

Wildlife: An abundant collection of pollinators arrive when trees are in bloom. A mainstay for "orangedogs," the citrus orchard pest name for the ravenous bird poop–mimicking caterpillar of the otherwise beloved giant swallowtail butterfly. Moderate to low deer palatability.

Maintenance: Prune to shape as preferred. Propagate by seed and softwood or semi-hardwood cuttings.

Notes: Feeding the anticipation and delight of humans and small pollinators alike, once a year the tree unfolds scrumptious vanilla-clove-perfumed blossoms. Its visual elegance lies in the light gray, interwoven, ascending branches, at their highest potential under skilled hands with loppers. Even at mature height, they avoid interference with power lines. Neither ash nor hop, but rather a member of the citrus family (Rutaceae), the bitter papery fruits, called samaras, substitute for hops in beer brewing. Cheers!

Rhus trilobata

Fragrant Sumac, Skunkbush

3–6 ft. tall, similarly wide; may form thickets by rhizomes

flowers inconspicuous, dioecious; March–April

fruits orange-red, ¼ in.; August–September

deciduous

part shade, sun | gravel, sand, loam, clay; caliche | dry, mesic; well drained

slopes, thickets, canyons, stream banks | western two-thirds of Texas

Wildlife: Bees enjoy nectar. Dense foliage offers cover. Berries provide winter fare for birds (particularly gallinaceous birds) and small mammals. Host for hairstreak butterfly larvae. Moderate to high deer palatability.

Maintenance: Remove unwanted suckers. Propagate by seed, softwood or semi-hardwood cuttings, layering, and transplanted suckers.

Notes: Thicket-forming and smaller than other sumacs, fragrant sumac fills gaps between larger garden residents, with lacy textured, lobed leaves providing contrast. Autumn pulls a variety of reds, purples, and oranges from the foliage. The sumac family (Anacardiaceae) includes cashews, mangoes, and poison ivy. Members of the genus *Rhus* are not toxic, and fruits soaked in water yield a refreshing beverage high in vitamin C.

Rhus lanceolata

Flameleaf Sumac, Lance-leaf Sumac

12–20 ft. or more tall; colonizing by rhizomes
flowers white, small, in pyramidal panicles 4–8 in. long, dioecious; July–August
fruits dark red, ⅛ in. wide, in clusters on female plants; September–December
deciduous
sun, part shade | sand, loam, clay; caliche, calcareous, sometimes acidic | dry, mesic; well drained
prairies, savannas, rocky hillsides | mostly central and western Texas

Wildlife: Bees feed on flowers. Fruits feed birds, especially those in the pheasant family (Phasianidae). Larval host for several hairstreak butterflies. Moderate to high deer palatability.

Maintenance: Trim out unwanted suckers and stems that occasionally die back due to fungal afflictions. Propagate by seed, semi-hardwood cuttings, and transplanted suckers.

Notes: Brilliant scarlet, maroon, and orange make flameleaf sumac one of the all-time best Texas fall foliage plants. An underplanting of plateau goldeneye and asters is sure to coax the cameras along with a parade of pollinators. According to the *Illustrated Flora of North Central Texas*, sumacs' "foliar fruit flag" color change signals to birds that lunch is ready!

Rhus virens

Evergreen Sumac

8–12 ft. tall, 10–15 ft. wide

flowers white, in 1–2 in. clusters, dioecious; July–September

fruits brick red, ¼ in., on female plants; September–November

evergreen

sun, part shade | rock, gravel, sand, loam, clay; caliche, limestone or igneous | dry; well drained

rocky hillsides, arroyos, bluffs | western, central, and southern Texas

Wildlife: Butterflies and bees sip nectar. Birds and other animals feast on fruits. Foliage offers shelter. Moderate to high deer palatability.

Maintenance: Shape as desired. Ensure perfect drainage to avoid rot. Propagate by seed.

Notes: This thick, rounded shrub typically sweeps the ground with its boughs, but may be limbed up into a low-branching tree. Pallid partners such as cenizo and big muhly stand out against the glossy, dark, evergreen foliage. Leaves drop in early spring and are quickly replaced, so technically it's not a true evergreen. Although our state has many sumacs from which "rhus juice" can be made by steeping fruits in water, some favor this one for its superior rich, tart flavor. Pulverized sumac fruits add a pleasing sourness to Middle Eastern dishes.

Sabal minor

Dwarf Palmetto

4–7 ft. tall (taller and trunk forming in standing water), 4–10 ft. wide

flowers white, tiny, on open clusters up to 6 ft. long; May–June

fruits black, ½ in.

evergreen

shade, sun, part sun, part shade | sand, loam, clay | mesic, wet, dry; adapted to slow drainage and standing water

swamps, lowlands, river terraces, floodplains | eastern, central, and into southern Texas

Wildlife: Fruits eaten by mammals and birds. Flowers visited by bees. Thick foliage offers cover and nesting sites. Low deer palatability.

Maintenance: Surprisingly drought tolerant but grows faster with ample water. Trim away brown leaves and spent flower stalks as desired. Propagate by seed.

Notes: Although reputed as the most cold tolerant of our native palms, dwarf palmetto's large fanning leaves convey a decidedly tropical flavor. Speaking of flavor, enjoy fruits raw (spit out seeds) or stewed and strained into a rich syrup. Easy to grow, this usually trunkless palm forms a thicket when planted closely, while farther spacing highlights its form.

Sambucus nigra

Elderberry

5–20 ft. tall and wide; suckering into colonies

flowers white, tiny, in 10 in. wide clusters, fragrant; May–July

fruits dark purple; June–August

deciduous

sun, part shade | gravel, sand, loam, clay; rich soils preferred | wet, mesic

riparian banks, alluvial woodlands, bogs, ditches | two subspecies cover most of Texas: *Sambucus nigra* ssp. *canadensis* to the east, *S. nigra* ssp. *cerulea* in the Big Bend region

Wildlife: Birds and mammals dine on fruits. Bees and small butterflies take nectar. Low to moderate deer palatability

Maintenance: If preferred, prune heavily or down to the ground in winter to encourage dense new growth. Control suckers as necessary. Propagate by seed, softwood cuttings, and transplanted suckers.

Notes: Lacy, saucer-sized flower clusters rival your great-aunt's best tatting project. Tiny blossoms (called elder blow) fall like summer snowflakes to blanket the garden. Cold and flu remedies are derived from the flowers, as are foods ranging from fritters to St-Germain liqueur. Please consume with caution. Cook flowers and fruits, and reject all else as toxic. Beware of poisonous look-alikes.

Senegalia berlandieri

Guajillo

9–15 ft. tall and wide

flowers white, ½ in. globes, intensely perfumed; February-May

deciduous

sun, part shade | gravel, sand, loam, clay; caliche | dry; well drained

dry hillsides, slopes, and brushlands | Rio Grande Plains, Edwards Plateau, Big Bend

Wildlife: Bees eagerly take nectar. Mammals and birds consume seeds. Host for long-tailed skipper and Reakirt's blue butterfly larvae. Moderate deer palatability.

Maintenance: Protect from prolonged temperatures below 20°F. Propagate by seed.

Notes: Copious scented and comely flowers in spring (along with their pollinator friends) and fernlike leaves that allow filtered light to sustain plants below make for a charming addition to a southern Texas landscape. A few small thorns are nothing to fret over, and occasional branches lack them altogether. The Rio Grande Valley is famous for its exceptionally tasty guajillo honey. If you, like me, learned that guajillo is in the genus *Acacia*, then let's do some updating. In 2005, the International Botanical Congress made the change to the genus *Senegalia*.

Sophora secundiflora

Texas Mountain Laurel

10–30 ft. tall, 10–20 ft. wide

flowers purple, ½–¾ in. long, in 3–7 in. drooping clusters, insanely fragrant; February–April

fruits dark brown pods, 3-4 in. long, bright red seeds poisonous; fall

evergreen

sun, part shade, part sun | sand, loam, clay; calcareous | dry, moist; well drained

dry open woodlands, brushy slopes and plains | Rio Grande Plains north to Austin and west to Trans-Pecos

Wildlife: Blossoms attract bees, red admiral butterflies, and other insect pollinators. Low deer palatability.

Maintenance: Prone to attacks by genista broom moth caterpillars (a.k.a. sophora worm). At first spotting, snip off branch tips where young larvae congregate. Once caterpillars disperse, Bt (*Bacillus thuringiensis*), a bacterium that infects lepidopterans (moths and butterflies), is a more practical option. Be judicious in applying Bt to avoid harming desirable species. Propagate by seed and softwood cuttings.

Notes: Not to be confused with the very different mountain laurels (*Kalmia* spp.) of the eastern United States, our Texas mountain laurel is an outstanding landscape tree tolerant of heat and drought, with glistening dark foliage and flowers redolent of artificial grape candy that many love but others find overwhelmingly cloying. Trees grow slowly, so you might be tempted to spring for larger plants, but smaller ones catch up in a few years. The scarlet seeds used for beads contain the highly poisonous alkaloid sophorine (consider all plant parts toxic).

Styphnolobium affine

Eve's Necklace

15–30 ft. tall, 20 ft. wide

flowers pink, white, in 4–6 in. drooping clusters, fragrant; March–May

fruits black pods, 4–6 in. long; fall

deciduous

sun, part shade, part sun | sand, loam, clay; limestone based | dry; well drained

plains, meadows, pastures, savannas, open woodlands | Edwards Plateau to north-central Texas

Wildlife: Bees and other pollinators nectar at flowers. Moderate deer palatability.

Maintenance: Prune to shape as desired. Propagate by seed.

Notes: Seeds sprouting in the woods grow like stiff-stemmed vines, using nearby trees for support until they mature to stand freely. In open, sunny areas, seedlings grow into specimens with full crowns and straight trunks. Ornamental bean pods persist on trees through winter, reminiscent of a string of beads, hence the jewelry reference in the common name. All parts of the plant, including flowers and seeds, should be thought of as poisonous.

Symphoricarpos orbiculatus

Coralberry

1–3 ft. tall; colonizing indeterminately
flowers powder pink to white, small; April–July
fruits magenta, ⅛ in., in clusters; September–February
deciduous
part shade, shade | sand, loam, clay | mesic, dry; good drainage
thickets, stream banks, open woodlands | eastern third of Texas

Wildlife: Many animals appreciate the cover and nesting sites the wiry mass provides. Foliage feeds snowberry clearwing moths. Flowers offer nectar, but fruits are typically ignored due to mild saponin toxins. Moderate deer palatability.

Maintenance: If left unchecked, rhizomes (underground spreading stems) and stolons (stems rooting into the ground) form extensive colonies. Cut plants to stumps every few years to keep them tight and fresh. Reduce powdery mildew by keeping foliage dry and well ventilated. Propagate by layering, division, cuttings, and seed.

Notes: Coralberry's deciduous nature allows for full viewing of the persistent fruits through winter. Dense masses effectively outcompete most weeds and, when planted under live oaks, will hide the oak suckers. Its thicket-forming habit gives good erosion control.

Tecoma stans

Yellow Bells, Esperanza

4–6 ft. tall, 3–5 ft. wide

flowers yellow, 2–3 in. long, in showy clusters; April–November

deciduous

sun, part shade | rocky, gravel, sand, loam; limestone based | dry, mesic; well drained

gravelly plains, slopes, arroyos, and canyons | mostly southern and western Texas

Wildlife: Nectar source for bees, butterflies, moths, and hummingbirds. Small mammals consume seeds. Caterpillar host for dogface butterflies. Moderate to low deer palatability.

Maintenance: For best flowering, mimic monsoon rain patterns by keeping plants dry between soakings. Tip branches occasionally to encourage more flowering and maintain bushiness. After winter, trim off damaged tissue or cut to 4 to 6 in. Protect roots in colder locales. Propagate by seed and softwood cuttings.

Notes: Venerated both for bold floral displays and unflappable heat and drought tolerance, yellow bells plays well with cenizo, flame acanthus, and winter underplanting such as bluebonnets. *Tecoma stans* var. *angustata*, native to the southwestern United States, is related to commonly cultivated tropical varieties, but tolerates heat, cold, and drought better and has a shorter stature and narrower foliage than its southern siblings. Intermediate forms sometimes occur. *Esperanza* means "hope" in Spanish.

Ungnadia speciosa

Mexican Buckeye

8–15 ft. tall and broad

flowers pink; March–May

deciduous

sun, part shade, part sun | rocky, sand, loam, clay; caliche, calcareous | dry, mesic; well drained

rocky canyons, arroyos, hillsides, desert grasslands, woodland edges | mostly western and central Texas

Wildlife: Bees nectar on blossoms. Small mammals feed on seeds. Hosts caterpillars of Henry's elfin butterflies. Low to moderate deer palatability.

Maintenance: Limb up malleable plants into multitrunked trees or leave low spreading. Propagate by seed.

Notes: Mexican buckeye performs reliably, offering hardy spring floral displays with leaves flushing just after blooming begins. Autumn delivers golden foliage. Similar in flower color to peaches and redbuds, and overlapping bloom seasons lead understandably to misidentification. "Buckeye" is a misnomer. This species resides in the soapberry family (Sapindaceae), whereas true buckeyes belong to the horse-chestnut family (Hippocastanaceae). Seeds are toxic.

Vachellia constricta

Whitethorn

6–15 ft. tall, slightly broader than tall
flowers golden yellow to orange, ½ in. pom-poms, sweetly perfumed; May–August
deciduous
sun | sand, loam; caliche, calcareous | dry; well drained
desert flats, dry slopes, gravelly plains, washes, mesas | mostly Trans-Pecos

Wildlife: Nectar fuels a wide range of small pollinators including bees. Beans eaten by quail and other birds. Moderate deer palatability.

Maintenance: Prune into an elegant multitrunked specimen, or leave be for a looser look. Propagate by seed.

Notes: The first time I saw whitethorn in full bloom in Big Bend State Park, I was gobsmacked! What's not to love about cute yellow balls all over the place? An equally fascinating array of pollinators evidently agree. Unsurprisingly, the common name nods to its well-armed nature, however, sometimes thornless individuals arise. To fill in around the bare stems in winter, good companions include Gregg's dalea and sacahuista.

Viburnum rufidulum

Rusty Blackhaw

12–15 ft. or more tall, 8–10 ft. wide

flowers white, small, in broad clusters 3–4 in. wide; March–April

Pretty bluish black, raisin-flavored fruits ripen in November

deciduous

part shade, part sun, sun | sand, loam, clay; limestone based | mesic, dry; well drained

thickets, open woodlands, stream banks | eastern half of Texas

Wildlife: Nectar nourishes bees and other insect pollinators, particularly red admiral butterflies. Birds and mammals consume fruits. High deer palatability.

Maintenance: If desired, shape mature plants, leaving young shrubs alone to find their own way. Propagate by seed and semi-hardwood cuttings.

Notes: It takes patience to tolerate the awkward adolescence of this slow-growing gem. Its arching stems transform from gangly to handsome upon maturity. In shady locations, or with additional pruning, plants take on a tree-like form. In sunnier spots, foliage thickens and branches tickle the ground. Lustrous dark leaves foil the glowing white constellations of flowers, converting to shades of red, pink, and orange in autumn. Reddish brown ("rusty") hairs covering twigs inspire the common name.

Viguiera stenoloba

Skeleton-leaf Goldeneye, Resinbush

2–4 ft. tall, 3–5 ft. wide
flowers golden, 1 in. wide daisies; October–November
evergreen; deciduous in colder areas
sun, part shade | rocky, sand, loam, clay; caliche, calcareous | dry; well drained
rocky deserts, hillsides, plains | western and southern Texas, mostly along the Rio Grande Valley

Wildlife: Bees, moths, butterflies, and other insect pollinators visit flowers. Birds consume seeds. Thick vegetation makes good nesting and bedding sites. Moderate deer palatability.

Maintenance: Occasional light shearing promotes bushiness. Full sun and minimal watering foster compact growth. Propagate by seed, softwood cuttings, and layering.

Notes: Extraordinarily forgiving of heat and drought, plants make an excellent high groundcover or short hedge with the late-season bonus of sunny daisies. Tuck between autumn sage and desert lantana for a photogenic scene. They perform well in planters, patio pots, and hellstrips (that angry space between a sidewalk and street).

Large and Shade-Producing Trees

As noted in the introduction of the previous chapter, determining size classes for trees is somewhat arbitrary, and there are species that overlap these chapter categories. The following woody plants normally reach 25 feet tall or more, and those with a canopy high enough to picnic under constitutes to me a "shade tree." But, along with genetics, growing conditions dictate ultimate sizes. Plentiful moisture, deep soil, and fertilizers lead to larger and faster-growing plants, albeit expending more resources in the process if not naturally occurring. Often the trade-off for pushing rapid growth is weaker wood. Generally speaking, slower-growing trees form sturdier wood and live longer. A reasonable strategy of planting both naturally fast- and slow-growing species positions the slower growers to replace the faster ones upon their decline.

Many trees mature to majestic heights, but the slow-to-develop tendencies of some challenge one's patience. To compensate, you might find it tempting to install larger specimens, but numerous studies and experience show that trees from smaller containers catch up in a mere few years. Like resilient kids whose wounds heal faster, smaller trees establish more rapidly, requiring a shorter amount of time for supplemental watering and pampering. The best time to plant a tree was twenty years ago. The second best time is now! Plant them as a gift to future generations.

According to the 2021 City of Austin's Community Tree Report, 33 million trees, valued at $12.3 billion shade more than 30 percent of the city. They offer ecosystem services such as sequestering carbon and decreasing stormwater runoff, urban heat accumulation, energy costs, and pollution. On a residential level, trees increase property values and provide physical and emotional well-being. Buildings broiling in the sun of summer yearn for the shade of tree canopies, and deciduous species allow the comforting winter rays to warm our houses.

Keep in mind that excessive shade reduces nourishing sunlight for flowers. Placing trees successfully requires strategy and forethought. Visualize a young tree at mature size and assess its future influence on the garden below. While wearing your soothsayer cape, avoid crowding trees too close to structures or each other.

Acer grandidentatum

Bigtooth Maple

20–30 ft. tall (can reach up to 45 ft. tall)
flowers minute, wind pollinated; March–April
deciduous
part shade, sun | sand, loam, clay; calcareous | mesic; well drained
moist canyons in mountains and plateaus, woodlands | Trans-Pecos, Edwards Plateau

Wildlife: Trees provide cover, nesting sites, and nest-building materials. Moderate to high deer palatability.

Maintenance: Periodic soaking during dry spells reduces summer leaf scorch. Propagate by seed.

Notes: Reds, oranges, and yellows reliably dominate a fall landscape where bigtooth maples grow. Rose-hued samaras (winged fruits) contribute additional color earlier in the season. Lost Maples State Natural Area in the Edwards Plateau is home to the easternmost population of the species (hence the descriptor "Lost"). The species name, *grandidentatum*, means large tooth, referring to the leaf shape.

Carya illinoinensis

Pecan

50–60 ft. tall, 50 ft. wide

flowers minute, wind pollinated; March–May

fruits surround brown nuts, 1–1½ in., delicious; September–October

deciduous

sun, part shade | sand, loam, clay; deep | mesic

wooded bottomlands, stream banks | throughout most of Texas, primarily in the Blackland Prairies

Wildlife: Mammals and birds eat the tasty nuts. Moderate deer palatability.

Maintenance: Nuts pose a slipping danger on pathways. Deep-rooted seedlings make removal from garden beds difficult. A variety of pests from aphids to caterpillars afflict the trees. You'll notice them, but they usually cause little damage. Deep soils make happy trees. Propagate by seed, cuttings, and grafts.

Notes: This emblem of the South, adopted in 1919 as the state tree of Texas, enriches southern delicacies such as pecan pie and pralines. Hundreds of cultivars feature improved nut production, and byproduct shells, commercially available in some areas, make a preferred mulch. Leaves emerge hesitantly in spring to avoid late frosts and create a welcomed dense shade through summer months. In spite of their fast growth, some live 300 years or more. Don't be confused by *illinoensis*, a common misspelling of the species name.

Cercis canadensis

Redbud

flowers dark to light pink to white, ¼ in. long; March–April

deciduous

sun, part shade, part sun | sand, loam, clay; limestone based | fast drainage, see details below

Wildlife: Bees and butterflies appreciate nectar. Larval host for Henry's elfin butterfly caterpillars. High deer palatability.

Maintenance: Best with minimal supplemental water, reserve irrigation for establishment and drought. Propagate by seed.

Notes: Edible flowers adorn all varieties with a pretty pink fuzz emerging directly from the branches and trunk as an odd spectacle called cauliflory (literally "stem flower"). Three varieties of *Cercis canadensis* occur in Texas and hybrids arise where ranges overlap. Select the one best suited to your region:

Eastern Redbud (*C. c.* var. *canadensis*): northeastern parts of Texas in savannas and woodlands with 35 in. or more annual rainfall; single-trunked trees reach 40 ft. Matte-textured leaves are larger than the other varieties. Cultivars feature white or double flowers, red leaves, and other qualities.

Texas Redbud (*C. c.* var. *texensis*): north-central Texas through the Edwards Plateau with 20–30 in. of rain. Trees and leaves reflect intermediate forms between the other two varieties.

Mexican Redbud (*C. c.* var. *mexicana*): Trans-Pecos on limestone soils where 12–20 in. of rain fall per year; multitrunked trees grow to 20 ft. Leaves with ruffled edges stay smaller, and appear thicker and glossier than those of the other varieties.

Cornus florida

Flowering Dogwood

15–40 ft. tall and wide

flowers minute, with 3 in. wide showy white to pink bracts; March–June

fruits ½ in., red, in clusters; September–October

deciduous

part shade, shade, part sun | sand, loams; typically acidic, but also in loose alkaline soils | mesic

thickets, stream banks, deciduous woodlands, woodland edges | throughout most of Texas

Wildlife: Numerous bird species and squirrels eat lipid-rich berries. Flowers entice small insect pollinators. Larval host for spring azure butterfly. High deer palatability.

Maintenance: Prune as needed and apply groundcovers or mulch to keep roots cool and moist. Propagate by seed, cuttings, and layering.

Notes: This spectacularly ornamental understory tree provides year-round interest with milky white and pink flower bracts gracing spring, ruby red fruits maturing in early fall, and burgundy and purple foliage developing in autumn. Winter makes apparent the delicate, horizontally tiered form. Hard, dense, shock-resistant wood is fashioned into small woodenware articles, and extractions from roots and bark yield red dye.

Diospyros virginiana

Eastern Persimmon

40–70 ft. tall, 20–60 ft. wide

flowers yellow, green, ½ in., dioecious; April–June

fruits orange, 2 in. diameter, on female plants, choice edible; October–November

deciduous

part shade, part sun | sand, loam, clay; acid or calcareous | mesic, dry

dry woodlands, old fields, clearings | eastern Texas

Wildlife: Fruits feed mammals and many bird species. Flowers offer nectar to bees. Larval host for the spectacular luna moth. Moderate deer palatability.

Maintenance: Prune to shape as needed. Propagate by seed and root cuttings.

Notes: Spreading crown, pendulous branches, bark like alligator hide, and glistening leaves all add to the interest and beauty of eastern persimmon. But the good stuff resides in the mature fruits, which satisfy straight from the tree or flavor fruit leather and other treats. Tannins make immature fruits astringent, and freezing renders mature fruits edible. Temperament of individual trees also influences ripening. Boil leaves into a tasty beverage high in vitamin C. The dense, hard, smooth, and even-textured wood is used to make strong and accurate golf clubs and other goods.

Ehretia anacua

Anacua

20–40 ft. tall and wide
flowers white, small, in 2–3 in. clusters, fragrant; April
fruits bright orange, ¼ in., edible, sweet; April–June
evergreen, but drops leaves in early spring before quickly re-leafing
sun, part shade | sand, loam, clay; alkaline | dry
thickets, open woodlands, chaparral, brush | central and southern Texas

Wildlife: Flowers attract a host of pollinators. Fruits entice mammals and birds. Exclusive host for larvae and adults of the anacua tortoise beetle. Low to moderate deer palatability.

Maintenance: Disease free. Remove the far-traveling root suckers as needed. May defoliate or die back in northern regions; provide cold protection in the teens Fahrenheit. Propagate by seed, softwood cuttings, and transplanted suckers.

Notes: Dazzling in full bloom with countless entertaining pollinators glittering in the fragrant blossoms. Sadly, cold quashes the display in north Texas most years. Multiple trunks sometimes fuse together with age, resulting in a notable corrugated and stocky appearance. The remarkably rough leaves inspire the alternate name of sandpaper tree. Another moniker is sugarberry, alluding to the sweet edible fruits. Shade under the dense crown limits vegetation underneath, but shade-tolerant horseherb offers a good option. Darkness lightens up as the canopy grows and limbs lift.

Juniperus virginiana

Eastern Red Cedar

30–50 ft. tall, 15–20 ft. wide

flowers minute, wind pollinated, dioecious; March–May

fruits berrylike cones, frosted bluish purple, 1/3 in., on female trees; September–December

evergreen

sun, part shade, part sun | sand, loam, clay; acidic or alkaline | dry, mesic

savannas, woodland edges and openings | eastern half of Texas and Panhandle

Wildlife: Cones feed small mammals and birds, including cedar waxwings (named for their affinity for juniper fruits). Trees provide nesting material and cover. Larval host for olive juniper hairstreak butterfly. Low deer palatability.

Maintenance: Look out for cedar-apple rusts (*Gymnosporangium* spp.), which can harm nearby plants in the rose family (Rosaceae). Junipers won't resprout if burned or cut to the ground. They invade in areas where fire is suppressed. Propagate by seed.

Notes: These conifers with a compact columnar form are useful for windbreaks; they create a dark and even backdrop and are simply beautiful. Aromatic leaves entertain the nose, and insect-repelling oils make the wood great for closets, chests, and decay-resistant fence posts. Some folks despise these trees, colloquially known as cedars (more accurately called junipers), because of their prolific territorial expansion and as the cause of cedar fever. But before you chop down all of yours, see if a few might be well-placed and worth keeping.

Hesperocyparis arizonica

Arizona Cypress

30–40 ft. tall, 15–25 ft. wide
flowers minute, wind pollinated; April–May
fruits reddish brown, 1–1¼ in., may persist for several years
evergreen
sun | sand, loam | dry; well drained
hot, dry canyons and stream banks from 3,000 to 7,000 ft. | Chisos Mountains (cultivated statewide)

Wildlife: Thick foliage provides nesting sites and cover. Low deer palatability.

Maintenance: Provide occasional deep soakings for the first year or two during dry weather; trees require little water once established. A few pests and diseases make trouble, including bark beetles and spider mites. Keep trees healthy and treat quickly for best outcomes. Propagate by seed and cuttings.

Notes: These drought-adapted, highly ornamental trees with striking pale leafage and conical form suggest frosted Christmas trees. In fact, many serve just this purpose. They grow dense and fast with low-hanging boughs, making them widely planted for windbreaks. Ruefully, they only live thirty to fifty years. A number of available cultivars play with a spectrum of silvers and blues. Foliage smells fresh like the mountains.

Liquidambar styraciflua

Sweetgum

50–100 ft. tall, 30–60 ft. wide

flowers minute, wind pollinated; March–May

fruits brown, spiky 1–1½ in. balls

deciduous

part shade, sun | sand, loam; acidic | mesic

low, rich, moist woodlands, coastal plains | eastern Texas

Wildlife: Squirrels and many bird species dine on seeds. Larval host for regal moth in the far eastern edge of Texas. Moderate to low deer palatability.

Maintenance: Seeds germinate aggressively in optimal (moist) conditions. Trees develop iron chlorosis in alkaline soils. Propagate by seed.

Notes: Star-shaped leaves display a fall rainbow of rich tangerine, red, and purple. Globular woody fruits resembling a medieval morning star are fetching to view, ornamenting trees through winter. And yes, they'll put a hurt on bare feet and jam lawnmowers! Long-lived and fast-growing trees have economically significant wood used for furniture and cabinetry. The gum, which is used medicinally for a slew of ailments and for chewing, derives from a resinous layer in the bark.

Maclura pomifera

Osage Orange, Bois d'Arc

65 ft. tall and wide

flowers green, wind pollinated, dioecious; April–June

fruits chartreuse, large 4–5 in. diameter aggregation, on female trees; September–October

deciduous

sun, part shade, part sun | loam, clay | mesic, dry

prairies, savannas, pastures, woodland edges, ravines | eastern half of Texas, Trans-Pecos

Wildlife: Spiny trees offer nesting and cover. Mammals nosh on fruits. Moderate deer palatability.

Maintenance: Allow for standard tree shape, or shear into an impenetrable, spiny hedge. Propagate by seed.

Notes: Deeply braided fissures swirl around the ocher trunk, providing an unexpected source of visual intrigue. Sheared into hedges with villainous spines, they made seriously effective hedgerows before the introduction of barbed wire. Female trees spawn spectacular fruits resembling brains in time for Halloween. Be aware that weighty fruits can cause damage as they drop and create a menace on the ground. *Bois d'Arc*, French for "bow wood," recognizes the useful pliability and strength of the wood. Livestock eat fruits, hence the alternate name of horse apple.

Magnolia grandiflora

Southern Magnolia

50–75 ft. tall, 30 ft. wide
flowers white, 6–9 in. wide, intensely perfumed; April–June
evergreen
part shade, sun | sand, loam, clay; rich, acidic, calcareous | mesic
lowlands, coastal woodlands | eastern Texas

Wildlife: Many species of birds eat seeds. Beetles pollinate flowers. Low deer palatability.

Maintenance: Keep plants moist. Slow to heal when dormant, so prune as needed during the growing season. Leave lower branches to cover and protect the soil. Propagate by seed and semi-hardwood cuttings.

Notes: It doesn't get more Southern than magnolia! A heady fragrance exudes from salad plate–sized blossoms, sliding us from spritely spring into the languid days of summer. Cream-colored flowers appear to hover against the dark green, glistening leaves. Glimpsing the leaf undersides, you'll find a rich russet wool. Dense shade, surface roots, and leathery leaf litter that smothers underplantings lead many gardeners to give up and simply lay mulch. Conical-shaped trees grow quickly.

Pinus taeda

Loblolly Pine

60–100 ft. tall, 25–35 ft. wide
fruits brown cones, monoecious; September–November
evergreen
part shade | gravel, sand, loam; acidic | dry, mesic
savannas, hilly woodlands | eastern Texas

Wildlife: Squirrels and birds including turkey and quail eat pine nuts. Trees provide good nesting sites. Larval host for southern pine sphinx moth and pine elfin butterfly. Low deer palatability.

Maintenance: Lower branches drop as the tree grows. Trees may suffer from pine beetles. Before purchasing or planting, examine and avoid plants with slightly swelling stems indicating a rust infection. Propagate by seed.

Notes: Picturesque and refreshingly aromatic, loblolly is the most common pine in Texas. Fast-maturing trees lead to extensive cultivation for lumber and pulp. When added to food, the bland pollen gathered from male cones of any pine species supplies protein, iron, and beta-carotene. Although less desirable than those of piñons (*Pinus remota, P. cembroides,* or *P. edulis*), loblolly pine nuts are edible for people. The noteworthy Lost Pines population in Bastrop grows 100 miles west of the east Texas pine forest and shows stouter stature and higher drought tolerance.

Prosopis glandulosa

Honey Mesquite

20–30 ft. tall and wide
flowers creamy white, 2–3 in., fragrant; March–May, sporadically through summer and fall
fruits 4–9 in. long pods; August–November
deciduous
sun | sand, loam, clay | dry; well drained
deserts, plains, stream banks, arroyos, ranches | throughout Texas except Pineywoods

Wildlife: Bees convert nectar into high-quality honey. Hosts caterpillars of blue and skipper butterflies. Very low deer palatability (except beans, which are savored).

Maintenance: Prune to enhance form. Periodic deep soaking encourages deep taproots, making trees more drought tolerant. Propagate by seed.

Notes: Often the bane of ranchers, mesquite invades pastures due to overgrazing (which reduces grasses while leaving the trees) and fire suppression. For home landscapes, its broadly spreading canopy with crookedly sculpted trunks sheds filtered light, protecting plants below from the sun's intensity while remaining bright enough to accommodate flowering plants. Beware of tire- and shoe-puncturing thorns, or opt for 'Maverick', a thornless cultivar. Remove seeds and chew the sweet mesquite pods directly from the tree or grind them into flour. Texas barbecue gains much of its fame from mesquite wood smoke.

Quercus spp.

Oaks

With over half of all oak species in the United States, Texas boasts the greatest number of native oaks in the nation with fifty species according to the USDA Plants Database. Oaks bring important shade to landscapes, as well as majesty and permanence. Their strong, durable wood has significant economic value.

Oaks, more than any other plant group, are afflicted by insect galls (a plant's response to a parasite, typically tiny wasps harmless to humans, that results in an abnormal growth on stems or leaves). Eliminating galls is virtually impossible and not necessary. Galls inflict minimal damage, and while removing affected parts and destroying them can offer control, the parasites have likely already emerged by the time you notice them. There are hundreds of different oak galls, and many display bright colors and intriguing textures and shapes, making them worthy of study themselves.

Oak wilt, however, is a serious and potentially fatal fungal disease that plagues oaks throughout Texas. When trimming any oak, treat all cuts with pruning sealer (or paint) posthaste to reduce risk of infection. White oaks show some resistance, but live oaks and members of the red oak group are the most susceptible. Here is a summary of the two groups:

White oak group: leaves with rounded lobes without bristles
- **Example:** escarpment live oak, coastal live oak, bur oak, chinquapin oak, post oak

Red oak group: leaves with pointed lobes and tiny bristles at the tip of each lobe
- **Example:** Texas red oak

To limit redundancy, all of the oaks described below share the following characteristics:

Flowers: minute, wind pollinated; March–May

Wildlife: Wild turkey, javelina, and deer seek acorns (considered true nuts) as important food sources, and even people have relied on processed flour from ground acorns for sustenance. Insects on trees provide forage for birds. Birds and small mammals find shelter and nesting locations in vegetation. Oaks host larvae of several duskywings, hairstreaks, and other butterflies.

Maintenance: Immediately treat all cuts with pruning paint to reduce oak wilt infections. Propagate by acorns.

Quercus buckleyi

Texas Red Oak, Spanish Oak

15–30 ft. tall and wide
fruits acorns, ½ in. long
deciduous
sun, part shade | loam, clay; limestone based | dry; well drained
limestone ridges, slopes, and creek bottoms | Edwards Plateau

Wildlife: Moderate deer palatability.

Notes: An excellent landscape tree, Texas red oak gives some of our most satisfying fall color, turning crimson and scarlet around Thanksgiving, then hanging on to dried leaves longer than most deciduous trees. You're better off finding another deciduous species if you want sunlight to warm your home in winter. The name Spanish oak creates some confusion, as the trees do not come from Spain (it is speculated that the trees grew around early Spanish colonies). Texas red oak hybridizes naturally with Shumard oak, so select trees with local genetics.

Quercus fusiformis

Escarpment Live Oak, Plateau Live Oak

30–40 ft. tall, 30–50 ft. wide

fruits acorns, ⅓–½ in. long

considered evergreen (see notes)

sun, part shade, part sun, shade | rocky, sand, loam, clay; calcareous | dry

savannas, rocky hills, uplands | Grand Prairie, western Cross Timbers, Edwards Plateau, Western Texas, Rio Grande Plains

Wildlife: Low deer palatability.

Maintenance: Manually cut unwanted suckers, since most herbicides travel throughout the plant.

Notes: Like no other trees, live oaks characterize Texas. Low boughs and twisting, sometimes gnarly branches add an inimitable personality to the landscape, and some of these easy-to-climb trees build strong friendships with agile youth. Not technically evergreen, live oaks are so dubbed because they hold their leaves through winter, defoliating around March only to immediately regrow new foliage. Escarpment live oak transitions to coastal live oak (*Quercus virginiana*) from west to east, so plant locally sourced trees.

Cabinet Oak (*Q. fusiformis*) at the Texas White House

Quercus macrocarpa

Bur Oak

60–80 ft. tall (can reach up to 100 ft. tall), similarly broad

fruits acorns, 1–2 in. long

deciduous

sun, part shade, part sun, shade | sand, loam, clay | dry, mesic; well drained

prairies, open woodlands, sandy ridges, stream edges | eastern half of Texas

Wildlife: Moderate to low deer paltability.

Maintenance: The large, deeply lobed leaves of the majestic bur oak rake up easily.

Notes: Trees grow with a broad, open crown. The species name, *macrocarpa*, literally means "large fruit," and refers to the acorns that fatten up to a diameter of nearly 2 in. Keep this in mind as you select a site to avoid posing a stumbling hazard for distracted pedestrians. All Texas native oaks have edible nuts when properly processed into flour. Due to their size, bur oak acorns offer some of the best foraging for the effort.

Quercus muehlenbergii

Chinquapin Oak

40–60 ft. tall, 20–40 ft. wide

fruits acorns, 1 in. long

deciduous

sun, part shade | rocky, sand, loam, clay; calcareous | mesic, dry; well drained

creek and river bottoms, canyons of western Texas mountains | Trans-Pecos, Hill Country, Blackland Prairies

Widlife: Low to moderate deer palatability.

Notes: Relatively fast growing, chinquapin oak reaches its tallest stature in deep, moist soils, staying shorter in the generally drier soils of western Texas. It gains its handsome character from luxurious, coarsely toothed, lustrous foliage that glows golden in autumn. The common name nods to its resemblance to the Allegheny chinquapin, a chestnut not an oak, although both belong in the same family (Fagaceae).

Quercus stellata

Post Oak

40–50 ft. tall, 30–40 ft. wide
fruits acorns, ½–¾ in. long
deciduous
sun, part shade | sand, loam; acidic | dry; well drained
dry sandy woodlands and savannas, upland ridges, prairie edges |
Cross Timbers, Post Oak Savanna, Llano Uplift

Wildlife: Moderate to low deer palatability.

Maintenance: Exceedingly sensitive roots resent distur-
bances from compaction, paving over, burying, and overwatering, all of which often prove fatal.

Notes: Slow growing and living several hundred years, post
oak is the most common oak in Texas. Trees form a dense
oval crown with stout, twisted, gnarly branches taking on
exceptional character with maturity.

Sapindus saponaria

Soapberry

20–50 ft. tall, 15–30 ft. wide; thicket forming by rhizomes
flowers white, small, in showy panicles 5–10 in. long, dioecious; May–June
fruits yellow, amber drupes, ½ in., on female trees; September–October
deciduous
sun, part shade, part sun | sand, loam, clay; limestone | dry, mesic; well drained
stream banks, grasslands, woodland edges, rocky hillsides | throughout Texas

Wildlife: Soapberry hairstreak butterfly caterpillars dine on foliage, and the flowers are the main nectar source for adults, but bees are the tree's primary pollinators. Low to moderate deer palatability.

Maintenance: For a single-stemmed specimen tree, periodically remove suckers. Propagate by seed, semi-hardwood cuttings, and transplanted rhizomes.

Notes: Soapberry grows into a respectable shade tree, particularly in deep soils, or forms impressive groves of clones connected by rhizomes, so a large stand may consist of only a couple of individuals. Females bear translucent honey-colored drupes (berries) containing the toxic alkaloid saponin that is used for poisoning fish and as a lathering agent in shampoo or laundry soap. Leaves range from pale yellow, golden, and pumpkin to russet in fall.

Taxodium distichum

Bald Cypress

40–100 ft. tall, 25–60 ft. wide

fruits 1 in. globose cones; October–December

deciduous

sun, part shade | sand, loam, clay; acidic or calcareous | mesic; adapted to poor drainage

swamps, stream banks, moist areas | eastern Texas through the western Edwards Plateau

Wildlife: Birds find cover and nesting sites in the branches. Cones nourish waterfowl, other birds, and small mammals. Exclusive larval host for bald cypress sphinx moth. High deer palatability.

Maintenance: Remove low branches interfering with foot or vehicle traffic. Knees damage lawn mowers and trip inattentive pedestrians. Propagate by seed.

Notes: Young conical trees eventually mature with grand, flat-topped silhouettes. Trunks flare into ridges and tree-stabilizing buttresses toward the ground, with "knees" popping up from roots, sometimes far from the trunk. Gray-green, fine-textured foliage shifts to terra cotta around Thanksgiving before dropping for winter. Most conifers remain evergreen, so its deciduous nature leads to the common name. Trees are very long-lived, some reaching 1,200 years old! Rot-resistant heartwood makes durable boats, docks, and other items.

Ulmus crassifolia

Cedar Elm

40–70 ft. tall, 30–50 ft. wide

flowers minute, wind pollinated; July–October

deciduous

sun, part shade | sand, loam, clay; alkaline | mesic, dry; tolerates seasonal slow drainage

woodlands, savannas, ravines, open slopes | southeast two-thirds of Texas

Wildlife: Small mammals and birds eat seeds. Birds glean insects from foliage. Trees provide cover and nesting habitat. Larval host for question mark and mourning cloak butterflies. Moderate deer palatability.

Maintenance: Fall-ripening seeds germinate in spring, scaring a lot of gardeners with their rampant proliferation. Fortunately, most seedlings perish over the summer, leaving only a few to pull later in the year. Small leaves left on the ground compost quickly, lessening the need for raking. Propagate by seed.

Notes: Cedar elms make excellent long-living shade trees with a moderate growth rate. Some older specimens could respectably pass as oaks. Why corky "wings" form on branches remains a mystery, but they certainly prompt conversations. Rough-textured leaves—the *crassifolia* part of the name—turn yellow in fall. Plants from southern areas of Texas tolerate drought more and stay shorter than those in the north, so plant from local sources for best results.

Vachellia farnesiana

Huisache

15–25 ft. tall and wide
flowers orange-yellow, ¼–½ in. spheres, strongly scented; February–April
deciduous
sun, part shade | sand, loam, clay; caliche | dry; well drained
ranches, scrublands, arroyos | southern half of Texas

Wildlife: All sorts of pollinators enjoy the flowers; bees make huisache honey. Thorns offer safety for nesting birds. Low deer palatability.

Maintenance: Reduce "middle-aged spread" with regular pruning. Acacia beetles may girdle branches. Remove and burn, or otherwise destroy affected branches before adults emerge in fall. Protect from extreme cold. In central Texas, many trees froze to the ground or died in the prolonged severe freeze of February 2021. Propagate by seed.

Notes: These low-branching trees with rounded, spreading crowns have been marching slowly northward with each decade as the climate warms generally, only to be taken out by unprecedented cold at the northern reaches of their range. Early blossoms sometimes get brutalized by late frost. Light blue-green feathery leaves cast soft, filtered shade; sharp thorns sprout from trunks and twigs, so wear shoes when passing underneath! If the genus name confuses you, that's because huisache was an *Acacia* until 2005, when the International Botanical Congress reclassified it into the genus *Vachellia*. Flowers yield an ingredient for perfume.

Vines

Texas summers are hot! Vines offer an excellent way to cast shade relatively quickly onto a home or patio. They occupy fences for privacy and screening, soften hardscapes, or hide unsightly features in the landscape. On a trellis or arbor, they can fit into spaces too narrow to accommodate trees or shrubs.

While more sun prompts stronger flowering and fall color on select species, vines are generally amenable to various light conditions, often beginning their lives under a protective shrub or tree that shades their roots from direct sun and excess heat. If large enough, vines can overtake their hosts, reaching the top of the canopy to enjoy full sun. This strategy also benefits vines targeted by deer. Young vines evade browsing under shelter from other plants (or with additional protections from the gardener) until they are tall enough to extend beyond reach of hungry mouths.

Most of us are glad that height doesn't deter the hungry mouths of caterpillars, even if that requires a certain amount of tolerance for shredded or disappearing foliage. From bejeweled Gulf fritillaries on passionvines to transparent clearwing moths chewing on coral honeysuckle, these creatures enhance the beauty and richness of our gardens beyond flowers and attractive foliage.

When growing vines, take note of their support strategy. Twining species must be able to wrap around their supporting structure, whereas those with tendrils can grab onto a coarsely textured surface. Others attach by adhesive discs or penetrating rootlets, which sometimes cause damage to wood or soft masonry. Most vines reach upwards, but some ramble on the ground in mounds or as groundcovers.

Bignonia capreolata

Crossvine

20–30 ft. tendriled climber (can reach up to 50 ft.)
flowers reddish orange with yellow, 2 in. long, in clusters of two to five; March–May, otherwise sporadic
evergreen woody perennial
part shade, sun, part sun, shade | sand, loam, clay; acidic or calcareous | mesic, dry; tolerates slow drainage
forested floodplains and uplands, swamps | eastern Texas

Wildlife: Hummingbirds and bees make their daily rounds on the flowers. Low deer palatability.

Maintenance: Provide sturdy support for this robust climber. Soak deeply during drought. Easily grown statewide with ample moisture and organic matter. Propagate by seed and cuttings.

Notes: Flowers usually show yellow with reddish orange throats but can be reddish orange with yellow throats. The common cultivar 'Tangerine Beauty' flaunts fully orange flowers with throats speckled or streaked with yellow. In sun, the spring flush almost completely obscures the foliage. The related deciduous trumpet creeper (*Campsis radicans*) covers a larger geographic range and fools casual observers as a dead ringer. Crossvine attaches with clawed tendrils, behaving more politely than its aggressive cousin that pushes destructive aerial rootlets into soft surfaces.

Clematis pitcheri

Purple Leatherflower

8–10 ft. tendriled climber

flowers purple to reddish purple, 1–1½ in. long; May–October

deciduous herbaceous perennial

part sun, part shade, shade | sand, loam, clay; limestone based | moist; well drained

woodlands, thickets, near seeps or streams | throughout much of Texas

Wildlife: Hummingbirds and bumblebees visit flowers. Wiry stems make good cover for nesting birds. Moderate deer palatability.

Maintenance: Brittle stems may die past a hard bend but regrow quickly. Leaf miners cosmetically mar foliage. Cut plants to ground after damaging frost. Propagate by seed and softwood cuttings.

Notes: The unusual and handsome fleshy textured petal-like sepals recurve at the mouth, resembling a small nodding tulip. Observe flowers at close range, as the dark color is easily overlooked from a distance. Just as the blooms inevitably spur conversation, so do the octopus-like seed heads typical of the genus *Clematis*. Twining leaf stems (petioles) act as tendrils to secure the plant to its substrate. The more delicate and less common congener scarlet leatherflower (*C. texensis*) also accepts cultivation.

Gelsemium sempervirens

Carolina Jessamine

12–20 ft. twining climber

flowers yellow, 1–1½ in. long, very fragrant; February–April, intermittently in fall

evergreen woody perennial

sun, part shade, part sun | sand, loam, clay; prefers well-composted soils | mesic

thickets, woodlands | Pineywoods

Wildlife: Sphinx moths, bees, and butterflies visit flowers. Low deer palatability.

Maintenance: Remove from areas where it is not invited. Soak deeply during drought. Easily grown statewide with ample moisture and organic matter. Support its massive growth with a sturdy trellis or fence. Propagate by seed and semi-hardwood cuttings.

Notes: Dark lustrous foliage on twining stems form a gorgeous opaque screen. Vines in full flower may appear solid yellow, and even just a few blossoms saturate the garden with perfume. All parts are toxic to humans and livestock if consumed, and honey from bees foraging on the flowers may contain contaminants. Some people experience contact dermatitis from the sap. Wear long sleeves and wash up after handling.

Ipomoea cordatotriloba

Purple Bindweed

8–15 ft.; twining climber or rambler

flowers pink with purple throat, 2 in. wide; May–October

deciduous herbaceous perennial

sun, part shade | sand, loam, clay | mesic, dry

disturbed soils along fencerows, fields, roadsides, rambling on shrubs and trees | throughout Texas except Panhandle

Wildlife: Flowers see butterflies, bees, and hummingbirds. Low deer palatability.

Maintenance: Cut back after frost if desired. Plant with caution and discourage it from overrunning its bounds. Propagate by seed and root division.

Notes: Those familiar with this vine may believe I've lost my mind to include it in this book. Please know that this plant is at once terrific and terrible! Its aggressive and weedy nature makes it unsuitable for many gardens, but in uncultivated areas where you want nearly continuous and copious flowering, easy purple bindweed requires little or no supplemental water once established, although you'll see more blossoms with periodic soaking. Flowers of the morning glory genus (*Ipomoea*) open early, closing by midafternoon or staying open later under cloudy skies. As the species name, *cordatotriloba*, indicates, foliage may appear heart-shaped or deeply trilobed, both shapes occurring even on the same plant.

Lonicera sempervirens

Coral Honeysuckle

12–20 ft. twining climber

flowers outside red, inside orange, red, or yellow (cultivars display various colors), trumpets 1½–2 in. long, in clusters; mostly March–June, sporadically year round

semievergreen woody perennial

part shade, part sun, sun | well-composted sand, loam, clay | mesic woodlands and thickets with ample organic matter | eastern half of Texas

Wildlife: Hummingbirds, moths, butterflies, and bees are drawn to blossoms. Birds consume fruits. Host to spring azure and snowberry clearwing caterpillars. High to moderate deer palatability.

Maintenance: Provide good air circulation. Irrigate in the morning and avoid wetting leaves to reduce powdery mildew. Thrives in full sun with more water and compost. Propagate by seed, softwood or semi-hardwood cuttings, and layering.

Notes: The lovely, twining, medium-sized coral honeysuckle serves fauna well and owes its popularity to being easy to grow and a reliable bloomer, particularly with more sun. I've even witnessed full displays on a south-facing sunny wall during a warm January! Unlike the rambunctious, invasive Hall's honeysuckle, it is not fragrant nor unruly.

Maurandella antirrhiniflora

Snapdragon Vine

6–10 ft.; twining climber or rambler

flowers purple, sometimes hot pink, ½–¾ in. long; March–October

deciduous herbaceous perennial

part shade, part sun | gravel, sand, loam, clay; caliche, limestone based, salt tolerant | mesic, dry; well drained

open woodlands, woodland edges, dunes, bluffs, weaving up shrubs and fences | south and western half of Texas

Wildlife: Flowers welcome bees, butterflies, and hummingbirds. Larval host for common buckeye butterfly. Low deer palatability.

Maintenance: Cultivate as a reseeding annual north of its natural range. Cut back after frost, trim to shape as preferred. Propagate by seed.

Notes: Looking for a dainty climber that won't overwhelm that cute little trellis you just found garage saling? Snapdragon vine fits a small frame. Set loose, it rambles unceremoniously over old wood piles or dangles casually from a bluff. This delicate yet vigorous twiner holds luminous, green, triangular-shaped leaves. It's not a true snapdragon, but a relative equally suitable for small fingers to maneuver flowers into wide-mouthed puppets.

Merremia dissecta

Alamo Vine

8–15 ft.; twining climber or rambler

flowers white with burgundy throats, 2–3 in. wide; May–November

deciduous herbaceous perennial

sun, part shade | sand, loam, clay; caliche, rocky soils | dry, mesic; well drained

stream valleys and draws, fields, disturbed sites, growing over shrubs | southern half of Texas

Wildlife: Butterflies, bees, and hummingbirds sip nectar. Moderate to low deer palatability.

Maintenance: Train or trim away stems threatening to enshroud other plants. Cut back after frost if desired. Propagate by seed.

Notes: Alamo vine sits in the morning glory family (Convolvulaceae). However, its charming Victrola-shaped flowers open midday instead of early morning like its relatives. Vigorous—some say aggressive, so locate it accordingly—twining stems hold dark green, deeply lobed palmate leaves and intricate seed pods shaped like a ballerina donning a tutu. These ornamental qualities, along with its noteworthy heat tolerance and easy cultivation, make Alamo vine a fine choice.

Parthenocissus quinquefolia

Virginia Creeper

up to 40 ft. long; adhesive climber or trailer

flowers small and easy to miss; spring

fruits bluish black, ¼ in. diameter; ripening in summer

deciduous woody perennial

part sun, sun, part shade, shade | sand, loam, clay; rocky caliche, limestone based | mesic; well drained

open woodlands, streamsides, brush country | mostly central, eastern and northern Texas

Wildlife: Birds take fruits. Larval host for several sphinx moth species. Moderate to high deer palatability.

Maintenance: Remove errant growth from trees and structures. Propagate by seed, hardwood or semi-hardwood cuttings, and layering.

Notes: An upright or draping vine, or rambling groundcover, Virginia creeper's autumn performance brings orange, crimson, and purple when grown in full sun. It also takes to dimmer situations, just not so flamboyantly colorful. Use caution when growing it on wooden structures—adhesive disclike suckers may cause surface damage (but bear no penetrating rootlets). This supportive strategy allows vines to grip firmly onto flat walls. Although a member of the grape family (Vitaceae), Virginia creeper fruits are highly toxic to humans.

Passiflora lutea

Yellow Passionflower

10–15 ft.; tendriled climber or trailer

flowers yellowish green, 1 in. across; May–October

deciduous herbaceous perennial

part sun, part shade, shade, sun | sand, loam, clay; rocky, limestone based | mesic; well drained

woodlands, thickets | eastern half of Texas

Wildlife: Nectar source for bees and butterflies. Texas native passionflowers in the genus *Passiflora* support Gulf fritillary, zebra longwing, Julia, and other butterfly caterpillars. Moderate to low deer palatability.

Maintenance: Cut back after killing frost or caterpillar defoliation to improve appearance. Note: When considering placement, keep in mind that all passionflower vines sucker from roots. Propagate by seed, root division, and cuttings.

Notes: Enjoy the novel, intricate flowers most easily observed at close range. Sturdy vines appear fragile, affixing to shrubs and trellises by tendrils. Native maypop (*P. incarnata*) displays large, lavender, eye-catching flowers, but its aggressiveness reaches the category of "noxious weed" according to some local authorities, adding irony to its USDA code of "PAIN6." Smaller species such as *P. tenulloba* or *P. affinis* behave themselves better, but are harder to find in the trade.

Vitis mustangensis

Mustang Grape

40–70 ft. tendriled climber or rambler
flowers yellow, small, fragrant, dioecious; April
fruits dark purple to black, ¾ in., in clusters; June–September
deciduous woody perennial
part shade, part sun, sun, shade | sand, loam, clay; limestone based | mesic, dry
woodlands, woodland edges, along streams, on fences, trees, and shrubs | eastern half of Texas

Wildlife: Nourishes fruit-eating birds and mammals. Flowers support bees. Tangles shelter nesting birds. Low deer palatability.

Maintenance: If left unchecked, it will devour shrubs and trees. Train and tie stems into preferred directions. Rake fallen grapes if desired. Propagate by seed.

Notes: Vigorous tendriled vines lend dense shade quickly. Falling grapes may create a nuisance, but only female plants produce fruits. Unripe fruits make a mouthwatering green grape pie, while mature grapes cook down to a flavorful inky purple syrup suitable for a slew of recipes. Try it over vanilla ice cream—it's as dazzling as it is tasty! Grape skins contain irritating oxalic acid, so wear gloves when handling. To avoid burning your mouth, process them before consuming. Or for a treat in the field, squeeze the pulp into your mouth and discard the skins. The feltlike undersurface of the leaves differentiates this species from others. Leaves range from deeply divided to unlobed, with different variations often on the same plant. Tricky!

Wisteria frutescens

American Wisteria

25–30 ft. twining climber

flowers lavender, occasionally white, 1 in., in 6 in. clusters, intensely fragrant; April–May

deciduous woody perennial

sun, part shade, part sun | sand, loam, clay; rich in organic matter, neutral to slightly acid | mesic

woodlands, river banks, upland thickets | Pineywoods

Wildlife: Nectar supports butterflies and bees. Hosts marine blue and other butterfly larvae. Low deer palatability.

Maintenance: Blossoms appear on new wood, so a light winter pruning stimulates stronger blossoming. May show chlorotic in alkaline conditions, so plant in neutral or slightly acidic soils. Apply iron (ferrous) sulfate or other treatments formulated for chlorosis. Periodically guide the direction of stem growth, and prevent them from twining on themselves and becoming constricted. Propagate by seed and softwood cuttings.

Notes: Springtime brings this garden confection into full glory with its heady scent and romantically drooping flower clusters. Twining vines bloom after leaf-break, and though robust, it's far less aggressive and a far superior choice than its better-known Asian relatives.

Bibliography

Ajilvsgi, Geyata. 1990. *Butterfly Gardening for the South*. Dallas, Texas: Taylor Press

Allen, Charles M., Dawn Allen Newman, and Harry H. Winters. 2002. *Trees, Shrubs, and Woody Vines of Louisiana*. Pitkin, Louisiana: Allen's Native Ventures

Bender, Kelly, and Noreen Damude. 1999. *Texas Wildscapes: Gardening for Wildlife*. Austin, Texas: Texas Parks and Wildlife Press

Correll, Donovan Stewart, and Marshall Conring Johnston. 1979. *Manual of the Vascular Plants of Texas*. 2nd ed. Richardson, Texas: University of Texas at Dallas

Diekelmann, John, and Robert O. Schuster. 2002. *Natural Landscaping: Designing with Native Plant Communities*. 2nd ed. Madison, Wisconsin: University of Wisconsin Press

Diggs, George M., and Barney L. Lipscomb. 2014. *The Ferns and Lycophytes of Texas*. Fort Worth, Texas: Botanical Research Institute of Texas and Austin College

Diggs, George M., Barney L. Lipscomb, and Robert J. O'Kennon. 2000. *Shinners & Mahler's Flora of North Central Texas*. 2nd ed. Fort Worth, Texas: BRIT press

Doughty, Robin W., and Matt Warnock Turner. 2019. *Unnatural Texas? The Invasive Species Dilemma*. College Station, Texas: Texas A&M University Press

Eason, Michael. 2018. *Wildflowers of Texas*. Portland, Oregon: Timber Press

Enquist, Marshall. 1987. *Wildflowers of the Texas Hill Country*. 2nd ed. Austin, Texas: Lone Star Botanical

Everitt, James H., D. Lynn Drawe, and Robert I. Lonard. 2002. *Trees, Shrubs, and Cacti of South Texas*. 3rd ed. Lubbock, Texas: Texas Tech University Press

Flores, Dan L. 2016. *American Serengeti: The Last Big Animals of the Great Plains*. Lawrence, Kansas: University Press of Kansas

Gould, Frank W. 1978. *Common Texas Grasses: An Illustrated Guide*. College Station, Texas: Texas A&M University Press

Greenlee, John. 1992. *The Encyclopedia of Ornamental Grasses: How to Grow and Use Over 250 Beautiful and Versatile Plants*. 3rd ed. New York, New York: Michael Friedman Publishing Group

Lehmann, Val W. 1969. *Forgotten Legions: Sheep in the Rio Grande Plain of Texas*. El Paso, Texas: Texas Western Press

Lynch, Daniel. 1981. *Native and Naturalized Woody Plants of Austin and the Hill Country*. Austin, Texas: Daniel Lynch

Johnson, Lady Bird, and Carlton B. Lees. 1993. *Wildflowers Across America*. New York, New York: Abbeville Publishing

Knight, Eric M., and Stacy Coplin. 2021. *Foraging Texas: Finding, Identifying, and Preparing Edible Wild Foods in Texas*. Guilford, Connecticut: Falcon Guides

Lellinger, David B. 1985. *A Field Manual of the Ferns and Fern-Allies of the United States and Canada*. Washington, D.C.: Smithsonian Institute

Loflin, Brian, and Shirley Loflin. 2006. *Grasses of the Texas Hill Country*. College Station, Texas: Texas A&M University Press

Loughmiller, Cambell, and Lynn Loughmiller. 2018. *Texas Wildflowers: A Field Guide*. 3rd ed. Austin, Texas: University of Texas Press

Mielke, Judy. 1994. *Native Plants for Southwestern Landscapes*. Austin, Texas: University of Texas Press

Morey, Roy. 2008. *Little Big Bend: Common, Uncommon, and Rare Plants of Big Bend National Park*. Lubbock, Texas: Texas Tech University Press

Nabhan, Gary Paul. 1985. *Gathering the Desert*. Tucson, Arizona: University of Arizona Press

Nokes, Jill. 2001. *How to Grow Native Plants of Texas and the Southwest*. Rev. and updated ed. Austin, Texas: University of Texas Press

Ogden, Scott. 1992. *Gardening Success with Difficult Limestone, Alkaline Clay, and Caliche*. Dallas, Texas: Taylor Publishing Company

Peace, Tom. 2000. *Sunbelt Gardening: Success in Hot-Weather Climates*. Golden, Colorado: Fulcrum Publishing

Powell, A. Michael, and James F. Weedin. 2004. *Cacti of the Trans-Pecos and Adjacent Areas*. 2nd ed. Lubbock, Texas: Texas Tech University Press

Powell, A. Michael, James F. Weedin, and Shirley A. Powell. 2008. *Cacti of Texas: A Field Guide, with Emphasis on the Trans-Pecos Species*. Lubbock, Texas: Texas Tech University Press

Powell, A. Michael, Richard D. Worthington, and Shirley A. Powell. 2018. *Flowering Plants of Trans-Pecos Texas and Adjacent Areas*. Fort Worth, Texas: BRIT press

Rainer, Thomas, and Claudia West. 2015. *Planting in a Post-Wild World: Designing Plant Communities for Resilient Landscapes*. Portland, Oregon: Timber Press

Richardson, Alfred, and Ken King. 2011. *Plants of Deep South Texas: A Field Guide to the Woody and Flowering Species*. College Station, Texas: Texas A&M University Press

Simpson, Benny J. 1988. *A Field Guide to Texas Trees*. 2nd ed. Houston, Texas: Gulf Publishing

Stern, William T. 1992. *Stern's Dictionary of Plant Names for Gardeners*. Portland, Oregon: Timber Press

Tull, Delena. 1999. *Edible and Useful Plants of Texas and the Southwest: A Practical Guide*. Austin, Texas: First University of Texas Press

Tull, Delena, and George Oxford Miller. 2003. *Wildflowers, Trees, and Shrubs of Texas*. Rev. ed. Taylor Trade Publishing, Lanham, Maryland

Turner, B. L., et al. 2003. *Atlas of the Vascular Plants of Texas, Volume 1: Dicots*. Fort Worth, Texas: BRIT press

Turner, B. L., et al. 2003. *Atlas of the Vascular Plants of Texas, Volume 2: Ferns, Gymnosperms, Monocots*. Fort Worth, Texas: BRIT press

Turner, Matt Warnock. 2009. *Remarkable Plants of Texas*. Austin, Texas: University of Texas Press

Tveten, John, and Gloria Tveten. 1996. *Butterflies of Houston and Southeast Texas*. Austin, Texas: University of Texas Press

Vines, Robert A. 1984. *Trees of Central Texas: A Field Guide*. 2nd ed. Austin, Texas: University of Texas Press

Vines, Robert A. 1977. *Trees of East Texas: A Field Guide*. Austin, Texas: University of Texas Press

Warnock, Barton H. 1977. *Wildflowers of the Davis Mountains and Marathon Basin Texas*. Alpine, Texas: Sul Ross State University

Wakowski, Sally. 1988. *Native Texas Plants: Landscaping Region by Region*. Austin, Texas: Texas Monthly Press

Weber, Jim, et al. 2018. *Native Host Plants for Texas Butterflies: A Field Guide*. College Station, Texas: Texas A&M University Press

Wrede, Jan. 2010. *Trees, Shrubs, and Vines of the Texas Hill Country: A Field Guide*. 2nd ed. College Station, Texas: Texas A&M University Press

Yarborough, Sharon C., and A. Michael Powell. 2002. *Ferns and Fern Allies of the Trans-Pecos and Adjacent Areas*. Lubbock, Texas: Texas Tech University Press

Acknowledgments

First and foremost, my deepest appreciation goes to all of the living beings of the natural world who have made immense impacts on my life by capturing my attention, pulling me into their worlds, and teaching me about their idiosyncratic and beautiful ways. I am endlessly enchanted by the magic of life.

Many pieces must fall into place for a book to be birthed, and I am deeply grateful to a slew of people for their support and assistance in making this project happen. At the very top of my list is my dearest life partner, David Mahler, for his professional and domestic support, understanding, influence, tolerance of my attempts to work forty-hour days, and holding me close through it all with a smile.

Appreciation for administrative support including image management, research and data entry, formatting, and, from time to time, chucking a chuckle or two at my humor goes to Charmaine Richardson, Julie Marcus, Lisa Cole, Sophie Lemkin, Camille Lewis, and with special gratitude, to Katie Kraemer. Pat and Byron Rathbun provided the most charming writer's retreat imaginable, and for that I appreciate their generosity. Deep gratitude goes to Lee Clippard, my boss and model human, for sanctifying much of the time I've needed to accomplish this feat.

Hearty thanks go to Anna Strong for contributing to the passage regarding species of greatest conservation need, to Dr. Sean Griffin for reviewing content addressing the issues around plant adaptations to climate change, and to Joe Marcus for delivering insights, patience with my continuous requests for assistance, and playful banter. The folks at Timber Press deserve applause for guiding me through the book creation process and for their encouragement and endurance through all of my deadlines.

Countless contributors to the Wildflower Center's Native Plants of North America database (NPONA) have made plant information available to millions of seekers, including me for use in this work. I am exceptionally indebted to the photographers of the hundreds of images included here, with special gratitude for the talented volunteer work of photographers Bruce Leander and Bill Boyd.

Past and present colleagues, friends, and notably my parents, Maria Amaya and Wayne DeLong, have encouraged and taught me to enthusiastically observe—and fall in love with—the delightful intricacies of the natural world, including native plants. It is impossible to adequately recognize the contributions of every horticulturist, botanist, ecologist, restorationist, native plant lover, and ancestral land steward, so that's a tremendous thank you to all accumulators of knowledge who have built the foundation from which this work benefits.

Photography Credits

Map on page 32, Wikimeda/Modified from: Gould, Frank W.; Hoffman, Garlyn O.; Rechenthin, Clarence A. (1960). Vegetational Areas of Texas.. Texas Agricultural Extension Service; Texas Agricultural Experiment Station. Public Domain.

OER Commons/Author: Chandler Hambridge CC BY4.0, 41

Al Braden, 6 top middle, 74 bottom middle, 97 right, 119 right

Alan Cressler, 106 left, 138 left, 198 right, 199 left, 208 bottom right, 218

Andrea DeLong-Amaya, 18, 28, 31, 44, 47, 50 bottom, 51, 83 left, 145

Andy and Sally Wasowski, 63 left, 67 right, 83 right, 86, 91 right, 102 left, 107 top, 118, 122, 130 right, 132 left, 134 right, 137, 141 right, 142 (top left, lower right), 146 left, 147 right, 150 left, 152 right, 154, 156, 157 left, 158 left, 160 top right, 165 right, 167 left, 181, 191, 194, 196 right, 200 right, 205, 210, 211, 213 right, 223 right

Beth Anderson, 159 right

Bill Carr, 135

Bill J. Boyd, 20, 22, 23 middle and bottom, 24, 25, 26, 27

Bruce Leander, 2, 5, 6 (top left, bottom row), 8, 10 bottom, 12, 16, 23 top, 33, 34, 37, 39 top, 43, 49, 54, 55, 56, 58, 60 (top middle, middle), 62 right, 64 right, 65, 68, 70 left, 74 (top left, middle left, bottom right and left), 76, 82 left, 85, 87, 92, 93, 95 right, 96, 98 left, 100, 101 left, 108 top, 109 right, 113 right, 114 left, 119 left, 120, 131, 136, 139 right, 152 left, 160 (middle center, bottom right), 167 center and right, 171, 172 (top left, middle right, bottom left and right), 176, 179 right, 180, 187, 189 left, 195, 197, 208 top left, 228 (top center, middle center, bottom left and center), 231, 232 left, 233 left, 235, 237

Campbell and Lynn Loughmiller, 227

Carl Fabre, 168 left

Carolyn Fannon, 142 middle left, 144, 157 right

Charmaine Richardson, 72 left, 79 left, 91 left

Damon E. Waitt, 160 bottom left, 168 right, 223 left

David Mahler, 39 bottom

Dennis Fagan, 11

Doug Sherman, 74 middle left, 81 left, 107 left

Eric Beckers, 6 top right, 160 (top left and center, middle left), 162, 164 right, 165 left, 206 left

Harry Cliffe, 201 right

James Garland Holmes, 142 top right, 151, 226 right

Jerry Garrett, 166

Joanna Wojtkowiak, 46

John Averett, 10 top

Joseph A. Marcus, 48, 50 top, 60 (top left, bottom left, bottom right), 62 left, 64 left, 66 right, 67 left, 71 left, 73, 74 (top middle, middle), 77, 78 left, 80 right, 81 right, 84 right, 90 bottom, 102 right, 103 right, 104, 110 left, 112 left, 114 right, 117, 121 right, 123 top, 127 left, 132 right, 138 right, 142 lower left, 146 right, 148, 149 right, 163, 169 right, 170, 172 top right, 177, 178, 182 right, 192, 193 left, 196 left, 203, 204, 228 top right, 232 right, 233 right

Julie Makin, 188, 226 left

Katie Kraemer, 141 left

Keeper Trout, 160 bottom center, 164 left

Lauren Gersn, 222

Lee Page, 30, 82 right, 84 left, 94 left, 99 right, 108 bottom, 110 right, 115, 121 left, 124 right, 126, 127 right, 128 left, 133, 134 left, 142 (top center, middle right), 149 left, 150 right, 172 (top center, middle center), 179 left, 186 left, 189 right, 190 left, 201 left, 208 top center, 216, 221, 228 middle right

Lynn Pyle, 60 top right, 63 right, top right, 80 left, 88, 94 right, 95 left, 106 right, 109 left, 112 right, 113 left, 124 left, 128 right

Melody Lytle, 35, 60 middle right, 71 right, 172 bottom center, 184, 193 right, 225 left, 228 (top left, middle left, bottom right), 234, 236

Michael Dana, 139 left

Myra B. Allison, 140 right

Norman G. Flaigg, 125

Patsy Chaney, 219 left

Paul Cox, 130 left, 208 bottom center, 217 center

Peggy Romth, 98 right, 206 right

R.W. Smith, 60 middle left, 69, 89 right, 101 right, 129, 208 (middle left, bottom left), 213 left, 214 right, 215 left

Rachel Cywinsky, 208 middle right, 214 left

Ray Mathews, 66 left, 78 right, 90 top, 111 left, 142 bottom center, 153, 185, 198 left, 202, 215 right, 217 right, 230

Stephanie Brundage, 53, 140 left, 172 middle left, 174, 175, 190 right, 207, 208 top right, 212, 224

Stephanie Brundage, 72 right, 97 left, 107 bottom right, 111 right, 142 middle center, 155, 182 left, 199 right, 217 left

Steven Schwartzman, 123 bottom

Thomas L. Muller, bottom middle, 70 right, 79 right, 183, 219 right

W.D. and Dolphia Bransford, 89 left, 105, 160 middle right, 169 left

Wynn Anderson, 103 left, 186 right, 200 left, 225 right

Index

Acacia spp., 200, 227

Acer grandidentatum, 210

Acer negundo, 36

acorns, 23, 220, 223

adapted plants, 15–17, 19

Adiantum capillus-veneris, 76

Aesculus pavia

   var. *flavescens*, 174

   var. *pavia*, 174

agarita, 189

agave, 26, 80, 161

Agave americana, 14, 162

Ageratina havanensis, 175

Ajuga, 72

Alamo vine, 234

Albizia julibrissin, 191

alkali sacaton, 158

Allium canadense, 77

   var. *canadense*, 77

Allowissadula holosericea, 78

Aloe spp., 168

Aloysia gratissima, 176, 182

Aloysia macrostachya, 176

Ambrosia trifida, 24

American beautyberry, 23, 40, 72, 159, 178

American century plant, 162

American chestnut, 17

American lotus, 111, 112

American robin, 22, 23

American wisteria, 237

anacua, 214

anacua tortoise beetle, 214

Andropogon gerardii, 144

Andropogon glomeratus, 145

animal habitat, 61

Anisacanthus quadrifidus var. *wrightii*, 177

annuals, 75–141

antelope-horns milkweed, 79, 80

Apache plume, 183

aphids, 79

Aquilegia, 78

Aquilegia canadensis, 78

Aquilegia chrysantha var. *hinckleyana*, 30

Arizona cypress, 216

Arkansas yucca, 171

Asclepias asperula, 79

Asclepias incarnata, 145

Asclepias tuberosa, 79

Asclepias viridis, 80

Ashe juniper, 17, 22

aster, 24

Astrolepis sinuata, 80

autumn sage, 103, 131, 207

available water, 39

Ayurvedic medicine, 62

baby blue-eyes, 36, 40, 103, 111, 127

Bacillus thuringiensis (Bt), 24–25, 84, 200

   var. *aizawai*, 137

   var. *kurstaki*, 137

Bacopa monnieri, 62

Baileya multiradiata, 81

bald cypress, 226

bald cypress sphinx moth, 226

Barbados cherry, 189

Barbara's buttons, 25, 109

basketgrass, 153

bats, 26

bayberry, 192

"beardtongue", 117

beargrass, 153

beebrush, 176, 182

bell pepper, 14, 85

Berlandiera betonicifolia, 81

Berlandiera lyrata, 82

Bermuda grass, 42, 45

big bluestem, 144

big-foot water clover, 67

big muhly, 55, 152

Bignonia capreolata, 230

   'Tangerine Beauty', 230

big red sage, 30

bigtooth maple, 210

bird pepper, 85

bitterweed, 137

black-chinned hummingbird, 24

black dalea, 40, 91, 94

blackfoot daisy, 35, 109

Blackland Prairies, 33

blanket flower, 37, 95

"blood of the dragon", 167

bluebonnet, 15, 30, 33, 36, 38, 39, 45, 52, 66, 107, 117, 123, 144, 169, 203

blue butterfly, 91, 110, 219

blue curls, 119

blueflag, 39

blue mistflower, 88

bluestem, 101

bobwhite quail, 17

bog garden, 62

Bois d'Arc, 217

bordered patch butterfly, 24, 97, 127, 141

botanical names, 29

Bouteloua curtipendula, 146
Bouteloua dactyloides, 62
Bouteloua eriopoda, 147
Bouteloua gracilis, 147
Bouteloua hirsuta, 147
Bouteloua rigidiseta, 147
"bow wood", 217
box elder, 36
Brazilian skipper butterfly, 84, 137
Brazos penstemon, 112, 118
brown-eyed Susan, 127
buckeye butterfly, 64, 70
Buddleja davidii, 182
Buddleja marrubiifolia, 178
buffalogourd, 90
buffalograss, 62
bumblebee, 93, 99, 106, 108, 132, 231
bunting, 23
bur oak, 220, 223
bushy bluestem, 40, 145
bushy skullcap, 66, 94, 134, 137
butterfly bush, 182
butterfly gaura, 112
butterfly milkweed, 79
buttonbush, 159, 179

cacao, 110
cacti, 26, 35, 40, 80, 161–171
caliche, 35, 36, 41
Callicarpa americana, 178
calliopsis, 89
Callirhoe involucrata, 83
Calylophus berlandieri
   ssp. *berlandieri*, 84
   ssp. *pinifolius*, 84

Calyptocarpus vialis, 63
Campsis radicans, 230
Canada wild onion, 77
Canada wild rye, 150
candelilla, 116, 165
Canna glauca, 84
canna leafrollers, 84, 137
Capsicum annuum, 14, 85
cardinal, 23
cardinal flower, 100, 106, 155
Carex blanda, 147
Carex emoryi, 148
Carex planostachys, 147
Carex spp., 147
Carex texensis, 147
Carolina buckthorn, 40
Carolina cherrylaurel, 194
Carolina jessamine, 232
Carya illinoinensis, 211
cashew, 180, 196
cassius blue butterfly, 141
catalpa, 179
cecropia moth, 195
cedar, 215
cedar-apple rust, 215
cedar elm, 48, 226
cedar sage, 53, 132, 147
cedar sedge, 147
cedar waxwing, 23, 215
cenizo, 40, 187, 191
Cephalanthus occidentalis, 179
Cercis canadensis, 212
   var. *canadensis*, 212
   var. *mexicana*, 212
   var. *texensis*, 212
chalk soils, 41

Chamaecrista fasciculata, 86
Chasmanthium latifolium, 148
checkerspot butterfly, 97, 117
cherry sage, 131
chestnut blight, 17
chickadee, 23
chile pequin, 23, 40, 72, 78, 85
chile petin, 85
Chilopsis linearis, 179
Chinese tallow tree, 15
chinquapin oak, 220, 223
chisme, 169
chives, 77
Chloris cucullata, 149
Chloris verticillata, 149
chocolate daisy, 82
Chrysactinia mexicana, 87
Cladium mariscus ssp. *jamaicense*, 149
clammyweed, 45, 117, 121, 125
claret cup, 164
clay, 41
Clematis pitcheri, 231
Clematis spp., 231
Clematis texensis, 231
coastal live oak, 220, 222
coastal water-hyssop, 62
columbine, 49
columbine duskywing butterfly, 78
common buckeye butterfly, 64, 128, 233
common dogface butterfly, 66
common sunflower, 97
compost, 36, 41
conifers, 23
Conoclinium coelestinum, 88
Conoclinium greggii, 88
container gardens, 49

Cooperia drummondii, 89
Cooperia pedunculata, 89
Cope's treefrog, 23
coralbean, 182
coralberry, 202
coral honeysuckle, 229, 233
coral yucca, 166
Cordia boissieri, 180
Coreopsis basalis, 89
Coreopsis tinctoria, 89
Cornus florida, 213
Cortaderia selloana, 15
Cotinus obovatus, 180
cottontail rabbit, 23
cow tongue, 169
creek sedge, 38, 147
crescent butterfly, 128
crevice garden, 35
Cross Timbers, 33
crossvine, 230
Croton, 23
Cucurbita foetidissima, 90
cultigens, 14
cultivars, 14
cutleaf penstemon, 116
Cynodon dactylon, 45
Cyperus esculentus, 45
cypress, 31

dainty sulphur butterfly, 97
daisy, 24, 207
Dalea frutescens, 91
Dalea greggii, 91
damianita, 26, 35, 87
Dasylirion texanum, 163
Dasylirion wheeleri, 163
datura, 92
Datura, 21
Datura wrightii, 92

deadheading, 75, 93
deciduous trees, 173
deer, 26–27, 220
Delaware skipper butterfly, 154
desert garden, 135
desert lantana, 103, 135, 207
desert marigold, 81, 103
desert willow, 179
design, 61
devil's claw, 14, 45, 123, 125
devil's shoestring, 153
Dichondra argentea, 64
    'Silver Falls', 64
Digitalis spp., 117
Diospyros texana, 181
Diospyros virginiana, 213
disease, 21
doctorbush, 103, 121
dogface butterfly, 182, 203
dollarweed, 65
dove, 23
dragonflies, 122, 137, 150
Drummond phlox, 45, 119
Drummond wood-sorrel, 114, 151
duck, 129, 149, 179
duck-potato, 129
dwarf palmetto, 23, 198
dwarf wax myrtle, 192
Dyschoriste linearis, 64

eastern gamagrass, 159
eastern persimmon, 213
eastern redbud, 212
eastern red cedar, 215
eastern tailed-blue butterfly, 107
echinacea, 24, 146
Echinacea angustifolia, 93
Echinacea purpurea, 93
Echinacea spp., 94

Echinocactus texensis, 164
Echinocereus coccineus, 164
Echinocereus reichenbachii, 165
Echinocereus spp., 164
ecological succession, 36–38
ecoregions, 31–35
Edwards Plateau/Hill Country, 34
Ehretia anacua, 214
elbowbush, 184
elderberry, 199
elder blow, 199
Elymus canadensis, 150
Elymus virginicus, 150
emory sedge, 148
Engelmann daisy, 23, 94, 130
Engelmannia peristenia, 94
Equisetum hyemale, 150
Equisetum spp., 165
Erigeron modestus, 94
Erythrina herbacea, 182
escarpment live oak, 220, 222
esperanza, 203
Eumorpha fasciatus, 106
euphorbia, 165
Euphorbia antisyphilitica, 165
Euphorbia cyathophora, 95
evergreens, 173
evergreen sumac, 198
Eve's necklace, 201
Eysenhardtia texana, 182

fall aster, 136
fallen leaf mulch, 46
Fallugia paradoxa, 183
false aloe, 168
false day-flower, 138
false dragonhead, 120
false foxglove, 114, 117, 149
false gromwell, 114

false yucca, 166

feathergrass, 152

ferns, 39, 76, 80, 138

fertilizer, 19, 20–21, 25, 26, 38, 209

finch, 23, 113, 140

fire sprouters, 173

firewheel, 95

flame acanthus, 110, 177

flame-leaf sumac, 197

flea beetles, 113

flowering dogwood, 213

fluttermill, 113

Forestiera pubescens, 184

Formal Home Inspiration Garden, 50

four-nerve daisy, 35, 94, 134, 137

foxglove, 117

fragrant mimosa, 191

fragrant sumac, 95, 196

frogfruit, 47, 70, 191

frostweed, 140, 141

Gaillardia pulchella, 95

gayfeather, 53, 104, 134, 149

Gelsemium sempervirens, 232

genista broom moth, 107

giant coneflower, 53, 128, 145

giant ragweed, 24

giant silk moth, 192

giant spiderwort, 38, 92, 139

giant swallowtail butterfly, 196

Glandularia bipinnatifida, 96

globemallow, 135

goldenball leadtree, 186

golden-cheeked warblers, 22

golden groundsel, 36, 40, 69, 147

goldenrod, 134

goldenwave, 89

goldfinch, 87

gorgone checkerspot butterfly, 127

"gossip", 169

grackle, 22

grama, 147

granite, 41

grape, 234, 236

grasses/grasslike plants, 37, 43, 45, 54, 143–159

grasshoppers, 84

gray hairstreak butterfly, 66, 83, 107, 181

greasegrass, 158

green milkweed, 80

green skipper butterfly, 62

"green stick", 193

Gregg's dalea, 46, 91, 205

Gregg's mistflower, 53, 61, 88, 121, 193

grosbeak, 23

groundcovers, 61–73

guajillo, 200

Gulf cordgrass, 157

Gulf fritillary, 229, 235

Gulf muhly, 54, 112, 151

Gulf penstemon, 118

Gulf prairie, 31

Gymnosporangium spp., 215

habitat, 22–27, 35–36, 55, 57, 69

hairstreak butterfly, 110, 184, 189, 192, 196, 197

hairy grama, 147

hairy water clover, 67

Halberdleaf hibiscus, 98

Hall's honeysuckle, 23, 233

heartleaf hibiscus, 99

heart-leaf skullcap, 133

heartwood, 226

heavenly bamboo, 15, 19

Helenium amarum, 97

Helenium spp., 97

Helianthus annuus, 97

Helianthus argophyllus, 97

Helianthus maximiliani, 98

Helianthus spp., 23

hellstrip, 83, 104, 109, 124, 207

henbit, 15

Henry's elfin butterfly, 204, 212

herbicide, 45

herbs, 75

Hesperaloe parviflora, 166

Hesperocyparis arizonica, 216

Heyder's pincushion cactus, 168

Hibiscus laevis, 98

Hibiscus martianus, 99

Hibiscus spp., 98

High Plains, 35

Hinkley's columbine, 30

honey mesquite, 38, 219

hooded windmillgrass, 149

hops, 196

hop tree, 196

horse-chestnut, 204

horse crippler, 164

horseherb, 47, 63

horsemint, 24, 26, 110

horsetail, 49, 150

huisache, 17, 227

hummingbird, 24, 25, 72, 78, 79, 93, 96, 97, 98, 101, 102, 103, 106, 108, 110, 115, 116, 117, 118, 120, 130, 131, 132, 133, 139, 162, 164, 166, 168, 174, 175, 177, 179, 180, 182, 203, 230, 231, 232, 233, 234

hummingbird bush, 177

Hydrocotyle spp., 65

Hydrocotyle umbellata, 65

Hymenocallis liriosme, 100

Ilex decidua, 185

Ilex vomitoria, 186

Indigofera miniata, 66

indigo sawfly, 78
inland sea oats, 53, 54, 114, 118, 133, 138, 148
invasive plants, 15–17, 19
Ipomoea cordatotriloba, 232
Ipomoea spp., 232
Ipomopsis aggregata, 101
Ipomopsis rubra, 101
iris, 40, 101, 155
Iris pseudacorus, 101
Iris virginica, 101
irrigation, 39, 47, 55

jalapeno pepper, 14, 85
Jamaica sawgrass, 98, 149
janais patch butterfly, 177
Jatropha dioica, 167
javelina, 220
jay, 23
Jimsonweed, 61, 92
Johnsongrass, 42, 45
Julia butterfly, 235
junco, 23
juniper, 23, 215
Juniperus ashei, 17
Juniperus spp., 23
Juniperus virginiana, 215

Kalmia spp., 200
Katie's dwarf petunia, 128
kin, 24
Kosteletzkya pentacarpos, 102
Kosteletzkya virginica, 102
kudzu, 17

lace cactus, 49, 165
Lamium amplexicaule, 15

lance-leaf sumac, 197
lantana, 15, 54
Lantana achyranthifolia, 103
Lantana camara 'New Gold', 15
Lantana montevidensis, 103
Lantana urticoides, 103
large buttercup, 123, 125, 141, 169
large trees, 209–227
lawn, 61
leafcutter ants, 21
leaf miners, 78
leatherstem, 167
legume, 36
lemon beebalm, 110
Leucaena retusa, 186
Leucanthemum vulgare, 45
Leucophyllum frutescens, 187
liatris, 104
Liatris punctata, 104
Liatris pycnostachya, 104
light, 40
lily, 153, 163
limestone-based soils, 41
Lindera benzoin, 188
Lindheimera texana, 105
Lindheimer daisy, 105
Lindheimer globemallow, 135
Lindheimer muhly, 54, 95, 98, 121, 152
Lindheimer shield fern, 138
Liquidambar styraciflua, 217
Liriope muscari, 21
little bluestem, 15, 54, 156
live oak, 202
livestock, 17, 38
living/green mulch, 46–47
lizard-tail, 102, 132
Lobelia cardinalis, 106
loblolly pine, 219
long-tailed skipper butterfly, 200
Lonicera japonica, 23

Lonicera sempervirens, 233
Ludwigia octovalvis, 106
Ludwigia spp., 29, 106
luna moth, 213
Lupinus spp., 107
Lupinus texensis, 107
lyre-leaf sage, 72, 114

Maclura pomifera, 217
Magnolia grandiflora, 218
Mahonia trifoliolata, 189
maidenhair fern, 39, 76
maintenance, 52–55, 75
malachite butterfly, 128
mallow, 78, 102, 110, 115
Malpighia emarginata, 189
Malpighia glabra, 189
Malus ioensis, 190
Malvaviscus arboreus var. *drummondii*, 108
Mammillaria heyderi, 168
manfreda giant-skipper butterfly, 168
Manfreda maculosa, 168
mango, 180, 196
marbleseed, 114
marine blue butterfly, 237
marsh, 31
Marshallia caespitosa, 109
Marsilea macropoda, 67
Marsilea vestita, 67
Maurandella antirrhiniflora, 233
Maximilian sunflower, 98
maypop, 235
meadow sedge, 38
mealy blue sage, 24, 25, 94, 101, 130, 193
Melampodium leucanthum, 109
Melochia tomentosa, 110
Mentha spp., 124
Merremia dissecta, 234

mesquite, 17, 38, 219

metalmark butterfly, 141

Mexican buckeye, 204

Mexican hat, 126

Mexican long-nosed bat, 26

Mexican marjoram, 103

Mexican olive, 14, 17, 180

Mexican petunia, 128

Mexican plum, 195

Mexican redbud, 212

milkweed, 24, 79

mimosa, 191

Mimosa borealis, 191

Mimosa roemeriana, 68

mineral mulch, 46–47

mint, 124, 130

Missouri primrose, 113

mistflower, 24

mistletoe, 21

mockingbird, 23, 85

monarch butterfly, 79, 80, 114, 140

monarda, 110

Monarda citriodora, 110

monkeygrass, 21

Morella cerifera, 192

Morella pusilla, 192

morning glory, 64, 232

mountain laurel, 200

mourning cloak butterfly, 226

Muhlenbergia capillaris, 151

Muhlenbergia lindheimeri, 152

muhly, 46, 54

mulch, 20–21, 46–47, 61

mustang grape, 236

Nandina spp., 23

Nandina domestica, 15

narrow-leaf waterprimrose, 98, 106, 122

Nassella tenuissima, 152

native plants

  adapted plants, 15–17, 19

  available water, 39–40

  climate change, 17

  cultivating, 21–22, 39–55, 57

  definition, 13–14

  disease, 21

  ecological succession, 36–38

  ecoregions, 31–35

  establishing, 2

  garden design, 48–52

  geography, 14

  habitat, 22–27, 35–36, 55, 57, 69

  invasive plant prevention, 21

  invasive plants, 15–17, 19

  irrigation, 47, 55

  light, 40

  maintenance, 52–55, 75

  mulch, 20–21, 46–47, 61

  naturalized plants, 15–17, 19

  pest resistance, 21

  planting, 45–46

  regional identity, 21

  seasonal succession, 38–39

  shade, 40

  soil, 25–36, 40–41, 61

  water conservation, 20

  watering, 55

  wildlife habitat, 22–27, 69

native shredded hardwood mulch, 46

Naturalistic Home Inspiration

    Garden, 51

naturalized plants, 15–17, 19

Nelumbo lutea, 111

Nemophila phacelioides, 111

Neoptilia tora, 78

nettle, 24

nitrogen, 21, 36, 86, 192

Nolina lindheimeriana, 153

Nolina texana, 153

nuthatch, 23

nutsedge, 45

Nymphaea mexicana, 112

Nymphaea odorata, 112

oak, 220–224

oak leaf roller, 24

obedient plant, 100, 120

Oenothera lindheimeri, 112

Oenothera macrocarpa, 113

  ssp. *incana*, 113

Oenothera speciosa, 113

Oenothera spp., 23, 29, 112

olive juniper hairstreak butterfly, 215

onion, 77

Onosmodium bejariense, 114

opossum, 185

Opuntia ellisiana, 169

Opuntia engelmannii var.

    linguiformis, 169

Opuntia spp., 169

"orangedogs", 196

orange sulphur butterfly, 86

organic mulch, 46–47

Osage orange, 217

Oxalis drummondii, 114

ox-eye daisy, 45

Packera obovata, 69

paintbrush, 45

painted bunting, 94

painted lady butterfly, 97

pale-leaf yucca, 171

palm, 198

palm-leaf mistflower, 88

paloverde, 193

pampas grass, 15, 152

Panicum virgatum, 154

paperflower, 116, 124

Parkinsonia aculeata, 193

parrot, 85

Parthenocissus quinquefolia, 234

partridge pea, 25, 38, 45, 86, 101

Passiflora affinis, 235

Passiflora lutea, 235

Passiflora tenuiloba, 235

Pavonia lasiopetala, 115

pea, 36

peacock butterfly, 128

pecan, 36, 39, 211

pecan shell mulch, 46

penstemon, 146

Penstemon baccharifolius, 116

Penstemon cobaea, 117

perennials, 75–141

persimmon, 23

pesticides, 23, 38

pest resistance, 21

pests, 24–25

petunia, 128

Phacelia congesta, 119

Phaon crescentspot butterfly, 70

pheasant, 197

Phlox drummondii, 119

   ssp. *mcallisteri*, 119

Phoradendron spp., 21

Photinia ´fraseri, 19

Phyla nodiflora, 70

Physostegia angustifolia, 120

Physostegia intermedia, 120

Physostegia pulchella, 120

Physostegia spp., 120

Physostegia virginiana, 120

pickerelweed, 102, 106, 122

pigeonberry, 111, 127, 147

pill bugs, 62

pine, 23

pine elfin butterfly, 219

pineywoods, 31

pink autumn sage, 151

pink evening primrose, 39, 103, 113, 144

pink skullcap, 15

Pinus spp., 23

Pinus taeda, 219

Piper auritum, 132

plains coreopsis, 89

plains yucca, 171

planting, 45–46

plant profiles, 59

plateau goldeneye, 138, 141

plateau live oak, 222

Plumbago scandens, 121

Poa arachnifera, 154

poison ivy, 180, 196

Polanisia dodecandra, 121

pollination, 25–26

pollinator syndrome, 25

Pontederia cordata, 122

Portulaca pilosa, 169

possumhaw, 23, 72, 185, 186

post oak, 220, 224

post oak savanna, 31–33

powdery mildew, 36

powdery thalia, 137

prairie beardtongue, 117

prairie coneflower, 126

prairie crabapple, 190

prairie fleabane, 49, 94, 134, 137

prairie goldenrod, 53, 134, 147

prairies, 62

prairie verbena, 94, 96, 113

prickly pear, 16, 17, 23, 25, 38, 55, 95, 169, 191

primrose, 29

Primula spp., 29

Proboscidea louisianica, 123

Prosopis glandulosa, 219

   'Maverick', 219

prostrate lawn-flower, 63

Prunus caroliniana, 194

Prunus mexicana, 195

Prunus spp., 195

Psilostrophe tagetina, 124

Ptelea trifoliata, 196

Pueraria spp., 17

purple bindweed, 232

purple coneflower, 53, 55, 93, 121, 127, 130

purple leatherflower, 231

purpletop, 158

purple trailing lantana, 103

purslane, 169

Pycnanthemum albescens, 124

Pyracantha spp, 23

pyramid bush, 110

quail, 205

queen butterfly, 79, 80, 88

Quercus buckleyi, 221

Quercus fusiformis, 222

Quercus macrocarpa, 223

Quercus muehlenbergii, 223

Quercus spp., 220

Quercus stellata, 224

Quercus virginiana, 222

question mark butterfly, 226

rabbits, 83, 91, 138

rain garden, 62, 128, 148, 154, 159, 179

rainlily, 89

Ranunculus macranthus, 125

Ranunculus spp., 125

rare plants, 30

Ratibida columnifera, 126

Rawson's metalmark butterfly, 88

Reakirt's blue butterfly, 66, 91, 200

recycled glass mulch, 46

red admiral butterfly, 24, 200, 206

red buckeye, 174

red columbine, 78

red death, 41

red oak, 220

red tip photinia, 19, 21

red yucca, 166

regal moth, 217

regional identity, 21

resinbush, 207

retama, 17, 36, 193

Rhus lanceolata, 197

Rhus spp., 196

Rhus trilobata, 196

Rhus virens, 198

Rhynchospora colorata, 155

ringtail cats, 23

river fern, 49, 54, 138

Rivina humilis, 127

robin, 23

rock garden, 35, 84, 87, 135, 165

rock penstemon, 113, 116, 147

rock rose pavonia, 26, 115

Rolling Plains, 34–35

rootbeer plant, 132

rose, 183

rouge plant, 127

Rubus trivialis, 71

Rudbeckia hirta, 127

Rudbeckia maxima, 128

Ruellia brittoniana 'Katie', 128

Ruellia nudiflora, 128

Ruellia simplex, 128

Ruellia spp., 128

rusty blackhaw, 206

Sabal minor, 198

sacahuista, 153, 205

sage, 15

Sagittaria latifolia, 129

Sagittaria spp., 129

saltmarsh mallow, 102, 106, 122

salvia, 24, 133, 146

Salvia coccinea, 130

Salvia farinacea, 130

Salvia greggii, 131

Salvia longispicata ´ *farinacea* 'Indigo
     Spires', 15

Salvia lyrata, 72

Salvia pentstemonoides, 30

Salvia roemeriana, 132

samaras, 196

Sambucus nigra, 199

sand, 41

Sandia hairstreak butterfly, 153

sandpaper tree, 214

sandy loam, 41

sangre de drago, 167

Sapindus saponaria, 225

Sapium sebiferum, 15

satyr butterfly, 145, 149, 150

Saururus cernuus, 132

scarlet gilia, 101

scarlet leatherflower, 231

scarlet pea, 66, 94

scarlet sage, 118, 130, 139

Schizachyrium scoparium, 156

Scutellaria ovata, 133

Scutellaria suffrutescens, 15

Scutellaria wrightii, 134

seasonal succession, 38–39, 75

sedge, 147, 155

Sedum spp., 21

Senegalia berlandieri, 200

Senegalia spp., 200

sensitive briar, 68

serrano pepper, 14, 85

sesame, 123

shade, 40, 54

shade-producing trees, 209–227

shrubby boneset, 40, 54, 78, 141, 175

shrubs, 173–207

sideoats grama, 146

silk moth, 188

silverleaf sunflower, 97

silver ponyfoot, 64, 73

skeleton-leaf goldeneye, 207

skipper butterfly, 78, 84, 110, 111, 114, 144,
     145, 146, 147, 149, 150, 156, 157, 158,
     159, 170, 189, 219

skullcap, 24

skunkbush, 196

sleepy orange butterfly, 86

small trees, 173–207

smoketree, 180

snakeherb, 64, 191

snapdragon vine, 233

sneezeweed, 94, 97, 134

snowberry clearwing moth, 202, 233

soapberry, 204, 225

soapberry hairstreak butterfly, 225

soil, 35–36, 40–41, 61

soil amendments, 20–21, 41, 45

Solidago altissima, 134

Solidago canadensis, 134

Solidago nemoralis, 134

Sophora secundiflora, 200

Sorghastrum nutans, 157

Sorghum halepense, 45

sotol, 26, 161

southern dewberry, 71

southern magnolia, 14, 218

southern pine sphinx moth, 219

South Texas Plains, 33

Spanish dagger, 171

Spanish red oak, 222

Spartina spartinae, 157

species of greatest conservation need
     (SGCN), 30

Sphaeralcea angustifolia, 135

Sphaeralcea lindheimeri, 135

Sphaeralcea spp., 135

sphinx moth, 21, 25, 78, 92, 100, 106, 113, 232, 234

spicebush, 188

spice lily, 49, 168

spiderlily, 100

spiderwort, 38, 139

spineless prickly pear, 169

Sporobolus airoides, 158

spring azure butterfly, 213, 233

squarebud primrose, 84, 86

squirrel, 17, 138

standing cypress, 101

star sedge, 155

Stemodia lanata, 73

Styphnolobium affine, 201

succulents, 161–171

sugarberry, 214

sulphur butterfly, 91

sumac, 23, 196, 197, 198

summer hibiscus, 78

sunflower, 23, 24, 45

swale garden, 128

swallowtail butterfly, 104, 188

swamp milkweed, 145

sweetgum, 217

switchgrass, 54, 98, 101, 154

Symphoricarpos orbiculatus, 202

Symphyotrichum drummondii var. *texanum*, 136

Symphyotrichum oblongifolium, 136

syrphid flies, 114

tall goldenrod, 134

Taxodium distichum, 226

Tecoma stans, 203

    var. *angustata*, 203

Tetraneuris scaposa, 137

Texan crescent butterfly, 177

Texas aster, 136

Texas bluegrass, 154

Texas greeneyes, 81

Texas horned lizards, 17

Texas kidneywood, 182

Texas lantana, 39, 40, 54, 103, 110, 113, 130

Texas Mixed Border Home Inspiration Garden, 50

Texas mountain laurel, 200

Texas persimmon, 181

Texas redbud, 212

Texas red oak, 220, 221

Texas sedge, 147

Texas sotol, 163

Texas yellowstar, 66, 105, 169

Thalia dealbata, 137

Thelypteris kunthii, 138

Thelypteris ovata var. *lindheimeri*, 138

thistle, 24

Thompson yucca, 171

tickseed, 89

timesharing, 38, 75, 97, 108, 127, 139

Tinantia anomala, 138

Torrey yucca, 171

Tradescantia gigantea, 139

Tradescantia occidentalis, 139

Tradescantia ohiensis, 139

Trans-Pecos, 35

Tridens flavus, 158

Tripsacum dactyloides, 159

tropical sage, 45, 54, 130

trumpet creeper, 230

tulipán del monte, 99

"tulip of the mountain", 99

turf, 61–73

turkey, 23, 77, 138, 220

turkeyfoot, 144

Turk's cap, 38, 40, 53, 54, 108, 133, 139

twist-leaf yucca, 132, 171

Ulmus crassifolia, 226

Ungnadia speciosa, 204

Vachellia constricta, 205

Vachellia farnesiana, 227

Vachellia spp., 227

velvet mallow, 40, 78, 103

Verbesina virginica, 140

Viburnum rufidulum, 206

Viguiera dentata, 141

Viguiera stenoloba, 207

vines, 229–237

Virginia blueflag, 100, 101

Virginia creeper, 234

Virginia wild rye, 150

Vitis mustangensis, 236

wafer ash, 196

water, 39

water canna, 84, 100

water clover, 67

water conservation, 20

water garden, 49

watering, 46, 55

waterlily, 39, 112

water-pennywort, 65

wavy-leaf cloakfern, 80

wax mallow, 108

wax myrtle, 192

webworm, 24

Wedelia acapulcensis var. *hispida*, 141

weeds, 36, 42, 43, 45, 47, 52–53, 61

wet garden, 148

wetland horsetail, 165

Wheeler sotol, 163

whitebrush, 176

whiteleaf mountain mint, 124

white-lined sphinx moth, 112, 113

white mistflower, 175

white oak, 220

white peacock butterfly, 62, 70

white plumbago, 121

white-tailed deer, 27

whitethorn, 205

white topped sedge, 155

white waterlily, 112

white-winged dove, 167

wildflower meadow, 36–37, 42–43, 45, 47

wildlife habitat, 22–27, 57, 69

wild onion, 9, 92

wild petunia, 66, 128

wild poinsettia, 45, 95, 193

willow, 179

windmillgrass, 116, 149

winecup, 38, 53, 83, 86, 94, 113

Wisteria frutescens, 237

wood fern, 111, 138

wood nymph butterfly, 158

woodpecker, 23

"woody lilies", 26

wooly beebrush, 176

wooly butterfly-bush, 178

wooly stemodia, 40, 73, 191

xeric garden, 87, 158, 183

xerophytic fern, 80

yaupon holly, 23, 185, 186

yellowbell, 110, 203

yellow buckeye, 174

yellow Indian grass, 157

yellow iris, 101

yellow passionflower, 235

yellow rose, 169

yellow waterlily, 112

yellow water lotus, 40

yucca, 26, 161, 170–171

Yucca arkansana, 171

Yucca glauca, 171

yucca moth, 170

Yucca pallida, 171

Yucca rupicola, 171

Yucca spp., 170–171

Yucca thompsoniana, 171

Yucca torreyi, 171

Yucca treculeana, 171

zebra longwing butterfly, 235

zexmenia, 23, 46, 53, 61, 141

zigzag iris, 39

© Philip Hawkins

© Bruce Leander

Andrea DeLong-Amaya is the director of horticulture at the Lady Bird Johnson Wildflower Center, overseeing the gardens and nursery programs with a passion for sharing the value of native plants in planned landscapes. She's been a staff member since 1998 and has over thirty years of experience with native plants in horticulture, ecology, and garden design. She has appeared countless times on *Central Texas Gardener*, PBS's long-running television program, and was a two-time guest on WNYC's *Science Friday*. Jennifer Jewell featured her work in her 2020 book, *The Earth in Her Hands: 75 Extraordinary Women Working in the World of Plants*. DeLong-Amaya teaches classes in native plant horticulture and has contributed numerous articles to publications such as Taunton's *Fine Gardening*, *Horticulture Magazine*, *Rodale's Organic Gardening*, American Public Gardens Association's *Public Garden*, *Texas Gardener*, and *Wildflower* (the Center's member magazine).

The Lady Bird Johnson Wildflower Center at the University of Texas at Austin uses native plants to restore and create sustainable, beautiful landscapes. We carry out our mission of inspiring the conservation of native plants through our gardens, research, education, and outreach programs. In doing so, we improve water quality, provide habitat for wildlife, and enhance human health and happiness. In 2017, we were officially designated the Botanic Garden and Arboretum of Texas.

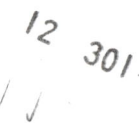